WHITE LIES

WHITE LIES

Melville's Narratives of Facts

By JOHN SAMSON

Cornell University Press

ITHACA AND LONDON

Copyright © 1989 by Cornell University

First published 1989 by Cornell University Press.

International Standard Book Number 0-8014-2280-9
Library of Congress Catalog Card Number 88-43324

Printed in the United States of America

*Librarians: Library of Congress cataloging information
appears on the last page of the book.*

*The paper in this book is acid-free and meets the guidelines for
permanence and durability of the Committee on Production Guidelines
for Book Longevity of the Council on Library Resources.*

To
Richard F. Berryman
and
Bridget M. Berryman

Contents

Acknowledgments

A ND what are you, reader," Ishmael questions rhetorically,
"but a Loose-Fish and a Fast-Fish, too?" In my interpretations here I am a Loose-Fish, and any weaknesses in the readings are my own; at the same time, I am bound fast to those
without whose help I could not have formed these readings.
Michael Colacurcio and Robert Elias read early versions of this
work; their patience, understanding, and knowledge were and
continue to be exceptional and inspirational. James Duban and
Milton Stern read the entire manuscript, which has benefited
considerably from their thoroughness and prescience. The people at Cornell University Press—Bernhard Kendler, Barbara
Salazar, and Marilyn Sale—have been universally helpful, efficient, and knowledgeable. Earlier forms of the *Typee* and *Omoo*
chapters appeared in *American Quarterly* 36 (1984) and *American
Literature* 56 (1984), respectively, and I am grateful for their
editors' permission to use the material here. I am also indebted
to the many Melville scholars whose work has preceded mine
and particularly to those involved in producing the Northwestern-Newberry edition; my footnotes acknowledge my debt,
but here I wish to express my sincere appreciation to those who
have made my study of Melville a pleasure and a challenge.

My teachers at both Cornell and Bemidji State universities

gave generously of their time and care; I could not have developed and channeled my love of literature if not for Michael Field, Heinz Puppe, Philip Sauer, Reeve Parker, Dorothy Mermin, and others. My friends at Cornell provided support, suggestions, and an atmosphere of intellectual inquiry, and John Bethune and Cheryl Spector continue to lend a sympathetic ear to my musings on Melville. Gail Coffler, herself an accomplished Melvillean, has given me much enthusiastic encouragement and sound advice; Daniel Williams has been an exemplary friend, colleague, and Americanist; and both continue to demonstrate what is best in this profession. My students—at Cornell, Heidelberg, and Texas Tech—have listened to, questioned, challenged, and inspired my ideas.

At Texas Tech my senior colleagues David Leon Higdon, Ernest Sullivan, and Donald Rude have been models of thorough scholarship, insightful criticism, and scintillating collegiality. Jeffrey Smitten, Joel Weinsheimer, and Norwood Andrews have also been helpful guides. My greatest appreciation goes to those friends and colleagues who have made my Lubbock years happy and productive ones: Donna and Bruce Clarke, Donneva and Doug Crowell, Lynne and William Rossi, Laurie Finke and Robert Markley, Michael Schoenecke, Michael Walsh, and Laurie Churchill; Bruce has been my theoretical adviser, Doug my creative adviser, Bob my professional adviser, and Donna and Donneva my advisers in sound common sense.

Above all, I am grateful to Dick and Bridie Berryman, to whom this book is dedicated and from whom I have learned what is genuinely important.

JOHN SAMSON

Lubbock, Texas

WHITE LIES

"Alle Wahrheit ist einfach."—Ist das
nicht zweifach eine Lüge?—
FRIEDRICH NIETZSCHE, *Götzen-Dämmerung*

1

Introduction

Genre, Ideology, and Melville's Narratives

EXPLAINING to his publisher John Murray his reasons for straying in *Mardi* from the generic path he had successfully followed in *Typee* and *Omoo*, Melville writes: "Well: proceeding in my narrative of *facts* I began to feel an incurable distaste for the same; & a longing to plume my pinions for a flight, & felt irked, cramped & fettered by plodding along with dull common places,—So suddenly standing [abandoning?] the thing alltogether, I went to work heart & soul at a romance which is now in fair progress, since I had worked at it under an earnest ardor."[1] Melville repeats such disparagements of his "narratives of facts"—not only *Typee* and *Omoo*, but also *Redburn*, *White-Jacket*, and *Israel Potter*—in other letters, but never, I believe, without irony. For Melville himself admits that "an author can never—under no conceivable circumstances—be at all frank with his readers" and claims, for example, that *Moby-Dick* is literal truth.[2] Moreover, when Melville dismisses the literary value of these books, particularly to Murray, he increases their market value in a literary genre that demanded an

---

[1] *The Letters of Herman Melville*, ed. Merrell Davis and William Gilman (New Haven, 1960), 70. In quoting from Melville's writings I use the standard editions available as this book goes to press.
[2] Ibid., 96 and 139–40.

unartistic, even amateurish relation of experiences. The literary prowess apparent in *Typee* had in fact led Melville's publishers to suspect him of being a romancer.

Like Melville's suspicious publishers, many critics seem uneasy about evaluating and classifying these books: they have been labeled travel books, anatomies, autobiographies, propaganda tracts, picaresque tales. Charles R. Anderson and other careful scholars following him have increasingly identified Melville's "borrowings" and "inventions" and thus have proved conclusively that these books are not simply autobiographical. Similarly, the criticism of these works has been moving away from the "disparagement" Melville voices and toward a fuller appreciation of their artistry. They are serious and accomplished fiction—novels—and yet they are, as Melville insists, narratives of facts—an apparent ambiguity that can be clarified by a close examination of both the evidence of Melville's generic understanding and the recently published work of such critics as M. M. Bakhtin, Michel Foucault, and Hayden White.

I

Melville's insistent generic classification is neither casual nor naive, for much of what we know to be his early (and continuing) reading was in the genre then commonly called narratives of facts. Melville wrote to Hawthorne that "until I was twenty-five, I had no development at all. From my twenty-fifth year I date my life. Three weeks have scarcely passed, at any time between then and now, that I have not unfolded within myself."[3] At that age Melville was on board the *United States*, likely reading extensively from the ship's library, which was composed primarily of those factual narratives. Ishmael's statement that "a whale-ship was my Yale College and my Harvard" applies as well to Melville; his curriculum, according to Jay

[3]Ibid., 130.

Leyda's catalogue of the ship's library, included Prescott, Darwin, and the Harper's Family Library, seventy-two volumes of histories, travel narratives, and memoirs.[4] Anderson, attempting to ascertain the factuality of Melville's South Seas books, adds to this list many of the sources Melville used when working on them. The works Melville mentions or echoes in these books and in *Israel Potter*—a considerable body of literature, for in *Typee* alone Melville cites over fifty volumes—and those that scholarship can determine he likely read provide a clear view of the parameters of the genre in which Melville conceived his own narratives and against which he could gauge the significance of his own personal experiences. Here I am adopting Ralph Cohen's insistence that "Classifications are empirical, not logical. They are historical assumptions constructed by authors, audiences, and critics in order to serve communicative and aesthetic purposes. . . . [G]enres provide expectations for interpretations, and, a variant of this, genres provide conventions for interpretations."[5]

The collective body of narratives of facts that Melville read constitutes a virtually complete survey of what might be called, loosely following Evelyn Page, the literature of exploration.[6] From the time of Columbus, whose four letters to the Spanish Court were widely translated and reprinted, sailors, missionaries, and traders—all explorers in their own way—going into

[4]*The Melville Log*, ed. Jay Leyda (1951; rpt. New York, 1969), 1:180; for a list of what the Harper's Family Library contains, see the back of any volume in the series. Charles R. Anderson's *Melville in the South Seas* (New York, 1939) is the pioneer study of Melville's sources; more recent examples are: Howard P. Vincent, *The Tailoring of Melville's "White-Jacket"* (Evanston, Ill., 1970); Mary K. Bercaw, *Melville's Sources* (Evanston, Ill., 1987); and Merton M. Sealts, Jr., *Melville's Reading*, rev. ed. (Columbia, S.C., 1988).

[5]Ralph Cohen, "History and Genre," *New Literary History* 17 (1986): 210.

[6]Evelyn Page, *American Genesis: Pre-Colonial Writing in the North* (Boston, 1973). See also William Spengemann, *The Adventurous Muse: The Poetics of American Fiction, 1789–1900* (New Haven, 1977); Howard Mumford Jones, *O Strange New World: American Culture: The Formative Years* (1952; rpt. New York, 1964); Edmundo O'Gorman, *The Invention of America* (Bloomington, Ind., 1961); John Seelye, *Prophetic Waters: The River in Early American Life and Literature* (New York, 1977); and Percy G. Adams, *Travel Literature and the Evolution of the Novel* (Lexington, Ky., 1983).

the New Worlds kept and published records of their experiences. The literature of exploration encompasses not only original descriptions of the Americas, Africa, Asia, and the Pacific, but also eighteenth-century Americans' revolt against, and nineteenth-century Americans' exploration of, their Old Home. The narratives, with little or no organization and controlled sense of voice or tone, include geographical data and descriptions, descriptions of the people and customs encountered, histories of the places visited, tribal myths, legends about previous explorers, crackpot ideas, pseudoscientific philosophizing—along with narrative of personal experience. A literary goulash, with one essential, if indistinct, ingredient: factuality. In fact and by convention, every narrator insists that his is a true account, a narrative of *facts*. From Columbus on, the explorers confronted a world radically alien to what they and their societies had been accustomed—alien not only geographically but naturally and culturally. To convince their readers of the legitimacy of their experiences, the explorer-narrators had always to stress the factuality of their reports—or, like Columbus, risk being ridiculed as insane. Yet as Lennard J. Davis has shown, a variety of forces—religious, legal, technological, and social—tended to involve authors and readers with a definition of "factuality" that included much "fictionality" as well; "it does seem," he says, "that a major problem for the Early Modern reader and writer was how to create a narrative that would be clearly and unambiguously either factual or fictional. . . . [T]he need for a veracious narrative discourse is there, but so too is the inability of language to fulfill the need."[7]

To many critics, the "inability" Davis describes is primarily a result of the vital and necessary connections between genre and ideology, between the forms of literary expression and the system of belief shared by the culture in which that expression is generated and received. Cohen succinctly states, "My assumption is that an author in making a generic choice involves

[7]Davis, *Factual Fictions: The Origins of the English Novel* (New York, 1983), 153; see more generally 43–153.

himself in an ideological choice,"[8] an assumption no less applicable to historical narratives than to plays or novels. The work of Hayden White in particular has been a concerted attempt to decode the tropological forms and ideological premises of historical writing and "to consider historical narratives as what they manifestly are: verbal fictions, the contents of which are as much *invented as found* and the forms of which have more in common with their counterparts in literature than they have with those in the sciences."[9] In further explaining these "fictions of factual representation," White touches on the role of both narrator and reader:

> The historian shares with his audience *general notions* of the *forms* that significant human situations *must* take by virtue of his participation in the specific processes of sense-making which identify him as a member of one cultural endowment rather than another. In the process of studying a given complex of events, he begins to perceive the *possible* story form that such events *may* figure. In his narrative account of how this set of events took on the shape which he perceives to inhere within it, he emplots his account as a story of a particular kind. The reader, in the process of following the historian's account of those events, gradually comes to realize that the story he is reading is of one kind rather than another. . . . And when he has perceived the class or type to which the story he is reading belongs, he experiences the effect of having the events in the story explained to him. He has at this point not only successfully *followed* the story; he has grasped the point of it, *understood* it, as well. The original strangeness, mystery, or exoticism of the events is dispelled, and they take on a familiar aspect, not in their details, but in their functions as elements of a familiar kind of configuration. . . . They are familiarized, not only because the reader now has more *information* about the events, but also

[8]Cohen, "History and Genre," 214. Many recent critics, from a wide variety of perspectives, have reiterated this point; see, for example, Davis, *Factual Fictions* and *Resisting Novels: Ideology and Fiction* (New York, 1987); Lester H. Cohen, *The Revolutionary Histories: Contemporary Narratives of the American Revolution* (Ithaca, N.Y., 1980); and Jacques Derrida, "The Law of Genre," in *On Narrative*, ed. W. J. T. Mitchell (Chicago, 1981), 51–77.

[9]Hayden White, *The Tropics of Discourse: Essays in Cultural Criticism* (Baltimore, 1978), 82.

because he has been shown how the data conform to an *icon* of a comprehensible finished process, a plot structure with which he is familiar as a part of his cultural endowment.[10]

The "story form" or "plot structure" White discusses involves both form and content; Melville's sources (and the readers of those narratives of facts) perceive and represent their experiences according to the structural paradigms of the genre and to the ideological assumptions of their white culture.

That is to say, these narrators of facts, exclusively white Europeans and Americans, are biased in their perception from the moment their exploration begins. From the first they, like Columbus, had four central goals: scientific, to discover and analyze the geographical and cultural conditions of unknown areas and peoples; religious, to Christianize and civilize those peoples; commercial, to develop trade with them; and millennial, to find the Earthly Paradise.[11] Their experience in these areas, whitened by their own system of values, led to the establishment of four conclusions, four ideological "facts" that they narrate: that other races are more primitive than the white race, farther back on a line of cultural development; that the Christians form a religious elite because of their closer connection with God; that capitalistic economics promote cultural development; and that America signals the End Times of human history. Accordingly, these ideological positions influence their perception and presentation of the events they experience in the exploration itself. Columbus's conception of the natives as primitive savages allowed him to describe them in fantastic, inhuman terms, thus opening the way for exploitation; his belief in commerce furthered the exploitation by permitting slavery as long as it brought profits; his Christianity justified this slavery by invoking the curse of labor, which beset all men since the fall from Eden; and his millennialism convinced him that the Orinoco River led to the Earthly Paradise. From this time to Melville's, sailors tried forcibly to introduce elements of European civilization into native societies, often destroying them

[10]Ibid., 86.
[11]Spengemann, *Adventurous Muse*, 15, discusses Columbus in this light.

in the process; missionaries tried to Christianize the natives, and ridiculed and banned their mythologies and rites; traders tried to open new markets, even if it meant depleting the natives' resources and disrupting their lives; and virtually everyone saw, in radically different ways, the New Worlds as the gateway to the paradise to be regained.

The more general foundation of each of these doctrines is the idea of history as progress, what M. H. Abrams calls the Christian pattern of history. He characterizes it as follows: "it is finite; it has a clearly defined plot; it is providential; it is right-angled; and it is symmetrical."[12] That is to say, man's history begins in paradise, from which he has an abrupt fall, proceeds along a finite line ordained by God and filled with cataclysmic turns, and ends in the apocalyptic regaining of paradise. It is easy to see how the ideology of exploration is subsumed by the idea of progress; exploration itself is a microcosm of progressive history, a symmetrical voyage out and back focused upon cataclysmic events. But it is equally easy to see how this ideology served the whites at the expense of those races with different, though not necessarily less complex and developed, civilizations. It served as well a personal function, providing not only a standard of reference but also a sense of intellectual security as the explorers encountered a world of situations, ideas, and values highly alien to them. As White's analysis implies, this security is also shared by the narratives' readers, who find in the literature of exploration further confirmation of their own cultural values.

Like White, Melville is not a typical or naive reader, is neither satisfied nor comfortable with the adequacy of "familiarized" accounts to express experiences like those he personally had in the Typee valley or Liverpool. The literature of exploration, immensely popular in the 1840s and 1850s, did initially provide a framework into which Melville could fit (and publish) his own observations, his experiences, and most important, his ideas. His narratives of facts follow the process he

---

[12]M. H. Abrams, *Natural Supernaturalism: Tradition and Revolution in Romantic Literature* (New York, 1971), 35.

outlines in *Redburn*: "For material, they use odds and ends of old rigging called '*junk*,' the yarns of which are picked to pieces, and then twisted into new combinations, something as most books are manufactured."[13] Melville's books are vital rewritings of his junky "sources": he reads the narratives in comparison to his experiences, picks out the yarns (or tales, in nautical slang) most expressive of their generic and ideological context, twists or tropes them to his purposes, then re-presents them closely following the prescriptions of the narrative genre. Thus his books contain much seemingly innocuous geographical, cultural, and nautical description, but Melville does not merely adopt uncritically the formal and intellectual characteristics evident in his sources; he reacts to them in his re-presentation. He sees the ideological "facts" of these narratives as less than true and in his own narratives controverts them. In short, Melville uses the narratives of facts not just as a source or as a genre to follow but as a subject of his own writing. In each, Melville presents his narrator as typifying an attitude held by the narrators of the literature of exploration, much of which he claims to have read. Melville heightens and extends his narrator's tendencies, exposes the contradictions and biases within his ideology, and ends with the narrator's evasion or denial of experiences in conflict with his ideology. These books do have a narrative unity, but one based more on ideology than conventional voice.

In *Typee*, Tommo, who has been reading narratives of encounters between whites and natives, forms an anticipatory image of the natives that guides his perceptions throughout his stay in Typee. He considers the natives, paradoxically, both noble and ignoble savages, stereotypical images that remain in conflict in his mind; both images, though, relegate the natives to a more "primitive" status than the progressed whites. Tommo's attitude is condescending and racist; it allows him to dominate the Typees but precludes his experiencing their culture. His conflicting preconceptions eventually force him to choose

---

[13]*Redburn: His First Voyage . . .* , ed. Harrison Hayford, Hershel Parker, and G. Thomas Tanselle (Evanston and Chicago, 1969), 114–15.

either a culturally relative point of view or his own progressive racism, and he decides upon the latter and must flee.

Paul and Long Ghost, Melville's protagonists in *Omoo*, follow the path mapped out by the missionary narratives they have been reading. At best a parodic missionary, Melville's narrator nevertheless wishes to reap the benefits available to the religious elite and to escape from the highly politicized world around him, the tyrannous shipboard society and the legalistic missionary-ruled society on Tahiti. Melville structures the book around a series of comic quests for the sacred, each attempting but failing to move beyond the political world. In these ways Melville dismantles and satirizes the self-interested attitudes and devastating effects of the missionaries to the South Seas.

In *Redburn*, Melville's narrator has again been reading misleading narratives. Redburn dreams of following the footsteps of genteel travelers to Europe, where he hopes to find money, maturity, and heritage. His romantic dreams of becoming a gentleman are subverted, however, by the reality of a laissez-faire economic system that recognizes no superiority but financial. In Liverpool, where he sees this economic system at its most pernicious, Redburn transforms his dreams of gentility into a vision of the American millennium and becomes a typical messianic nationalist. But this conviction is no less romantic than his original, and Melville again undercuts it with the economic reality of the emigrants and the emigrant Harry Bolton. When Redburn must finally choose between his American and Christian duty and the economic desire for status and security, he chooses the latter and casts off Harry to his eventual death.

White-Jacket, amplifying the millennial theme of the previous book, is narrated by a sailor typical of the naval narrators Melville used as sources. From the perspective of millennial necessity, White-Jacket urges reform of the hierarchical system on board, which oppresses "the people." Paradoxically, though, his reformism becomes an increasing elitism, which leads him to perceive "the people" as depraved and which negates the reformist stance he has so strenuously promoted. This ambivalence is easily recognizable: in his narrator's attitudes Melville is criticizing both sailor-narratives and the ideology supporting them, Whiggism, the dominant political ideology in the late 1840s. A typical millennial Whig, White-Jacket becomes increasingly idealistic, concerned not with rectifying the affairs of this world but with awaiting, in his elitist main-top, the advent of the next.

The third-person narrative structure of *Israel Potter* is slightly more complex than that of the earlier books, yet Melville's revisionism is as strong and vital. In re-presenting the life and remarkable adventures of Israel Potter, Melville's narrator invokes the ideology of American Revolutionary heroism evident in the narratives of Franklin, Jones, and Allen, but it is an ideology rife with internal contradictions and markedly inapplicable to Israel's own story. The writings of the Revolution promote the causes of egalitarianism, democracy, and improved conditions for all Americans, yet they actually lead to the enshrinement of a self-serving political elite that does little to meliorate the poverty of the common American like Israel. Melville heightens and exposes these anomalies and indicates their foundations in Franklinian pragmatism, in filiopietism, and in the typological imagination—a philosophical matrix that dominates the American mind from the Revolution to Melville's 1850s. From this "cultural endowment" Israel's—and Melville's narrator's and America's—expectations are formed; but in Melville's natural world they are defeated.

In each of these books, the exploration ends not by the protagonist's coming to a mature perception of the world and his relation to it but by his becoming more deeply entrenched in his biased and self-contradictory ideology. Thus Melville ironically indicates that a belief in progress on the historical level precludes progress on the individual. His narrators and protagonists undergo little or no development, suffer no cataclysmic changes, follow no plot, reach no paradisiacal end. Each becomes less integrated with his society, becomes more of an isolato. Each, however, attempts to counteract this isolation by narration, hoping through it to reaffirm and strengthen his connection with his audience and with his own past, lost experiences.

Distinguishing the authorial perspective from the perspec-

tive of the first-person narrator is always problematic, I recognize, since the basis for making the distinction is provided by
the discourse of the narrator himself. Yet, just as the disparity
between a narrator's statements and his actions opens a space
in which authorial irony can unveil itself, the juxtaposition
(and Melville frequently works by juxtaposition) of a reading of
Melville's sources with the incomplete understanding and application of those sources evidenced by Melville's narrators reveals the presence and distance of Melville the author. For
instance, Redburn's silly dismissal of Adam Smith, the economic ignorance he so amply demonstrates, and the thoroughness
with which the novel is infused with Smithian concepts indicate
incisively Melville's superior knowledge. Of course, on occasion
the narrators do clearly speak for Melville—as in some passages that Melville removed from the American Revised Edition of *Typee*, for example—but to grant more distance between Melville and his narrators is also to recognize a greater
coherence in these works, a coherence that I believe is Melville's intention and not merely my misprision. It is as well to
grant Melville more narrative control than some readers may
feel is warranted; however, the opposing tendency, to undervalue his achievement, has stained Melville's reputation during
his lifetime and after and has been revealed as increasingly
untenable as these novels have received more concerted critical
attention. If I sin in my effort to give Melville his full due, it is
"to strike the uneven balance." As Melville said of Hawthorne
(or himself), "He is immeasurably deeper than the plummet of
his critics."[14]

Thus what I hope emerges from this concerted study of
Melville's narratives of facts is first a picture of him as a power-
fully ironic critic of culture whose understanding is every bit as
deep and wide-ranging in these books as in what are usually
called his "major novels." Even from *Typee* on, Melville's criticism of "civilization" or white culture is *radical* in two key
senses of the word: he is highly skeptical of the traditions,

---

[14]"Hawthorne and His Mosses," reprinted in *Moby-Dick*, ed. Harrison Hayford and Hershel Parker (New York, 1967), 541.

institutions, and values of his culture; and his skepticism reaches *to the roots*, the ideological bases of the culture. His narratives of facts thus examine ideology as does a Marxistic critique of "a system of illusory beliefs—false ideas or false consciousness"—opposed by true(r) ideas or consciousness.[15] Melville's opposition to the dominant ideology of his culture redefines that ideology as "white lies," in that it is the less-than-true system of belief upon which the white civilization grounds its experiences, and in that it operates by a convenient acceptance of untruth, a sweeping under the ideological carpet of actions and ideas not logically or readily assimilable.[16] In his narratives of facts Melville (to continue the metaphor) pulls out the carpet from under the white culture to expose the clutter beneath, to expose its white lies. He is in essence examining and rejecting his culture's myths, an ambivalent word indicating both a system of belief and something untrue.

The astonishing modernity of Melville, which critics such as Charles Feidelson acclaim, thus stems not only from his openness to ambiguity and his symbolic depth, but also from his awareness of the dynamics of cultural forces.[17] Yet in his application of this awareness Melville is modern novelistically as well, for in his narratives of facts he puts into use a conception of the novel that has only recently been fully articulated. In their combining fictional and actual events—historical and personal—Melville's narratives are perfect examples of Davis's definition: "novels are framed works (even if they seem apparently unframed) whose attitude toward fact and fiction is constitutively ambivalent. . . . In this sense, the novel is about reality and at the same time is not about reality; the novel is a

---

[15]Davis, *Factual Fictions*, 215.

[16]The relation of my title and subtitle is thus one of contrast and might best be glossed by Michel Foucault's knowledge/power distinction, which stresses that an examination of "subjugated knowledges" (like the narratives of facts genre) can expose the mechanisms of power and repression in a culture's discourses; see particularly "Two Lectures," in *Power/Knowledge: Selected Interviews and Other Writings, 1972–1977*, ed. Colin Gordon, trans. Colin Gordon, Leo Marshall, John Mepham, and Kate Soper (New York, 1980), 78–108.

[17]Charles Feidelson, Jr., *Symbolism and American Literature* (Chicago, 1953), 162–219; and James Baird, *Ishmael* (Baltimore, 1956).

factual fiction which is both factual and factitious. It is a report on the world and an invention that parodies that report."[18] Davis's last point is crucial for understanding Melville's attitude toward his "sources," for much of the abundant humor, black or otherwise, of these novels arises from Melville's parodic representation of both specific passages and general tendencies in the originals. *Typee*'s pop-gun war, for example, may seem like so much dull filler—albeit in high-fiber prose—unless seen as a takeoff on actual events and ideological convictions in the narratives of William Ellis and David Porter.

Of considerable relevance to the conception of Melville's narratives as novels is the recently published work of M. M. Bakhtin, who even more fully than Davis argues for the vital interplay in the novel of genre and ideology, fact and fiction. Bakhtin, too, recognizes that "the novel parodies other genres (precisely in their role as genres); it exposes the conventionality of their forms and their language; it squeezes out some genres and incorporates others into its own peculiar structure, reformulating and re-accentuating them."[19] To Bakhtin, this generic engagement is vitally inherent in all discourses, for "each word tastes of the context and contexts in which it has lived its socially charged life; all words are populated by intention."[20] As he repeatedly stresses, the novel in particular is marked by this living presence of contexts—intentions, genres, ideologies—in dialogue within the text. Labeling this phenomenon "heteroglossia," the novel as a mixture of discourses, Bakhtin argues that "diversity of voices and heteroglossia enter the novel and organize themselves within it into a structural system. This constitutes the distinguishing feature of the novel as genre." The novelist, that is, "welcomes the heteroglossia and language diversity of the literary and extraliterary lan-

---

[18]Davis, *Factual Fictions*, 212; Davis, following Foucault, grounds this definition in a study of cultural forces (see 7–24).

[19]M. M. Bakhtin, *The Dialogic Imagination: Four Essays*, ed. Michael Holquist, trans. Caryl Emerson and Michael Holquist (Austin, 1981), 5; see also Bakhtin, *Speech Genres and Other Late Essays*, ed. Emerson and Holquist, trans. Vern W. McGee, (Austin, 1986), 5.

[20]Bakhtin, *Dialogic Imagination*, 293.

guage into his own work not only weakening but even intensifying them."[21]

To examine how Melville's sources operate in his novels, then, is to recognize that those sources appear in the text as a "dialogism" of discourses, whose interrelationships more than merely indicate Melville's thematic and stylistic intentions, they *are* his thematic and stylistic intentions. For example, in *Redburn* one finds the languages (or rather the images of the languages) of not only traditional literary genres (the Bible, Shakespeare) but of the nonfictional sea narrative (Dana), the semifictional sea novel (Briggs), the travel guidebook (*The Picture of Liverpool*), the economic text (Smith), the political analysis (*The Democratic Review*), along with extraliterary languages (Melville's family)—some heightened, some weakened, all vitally ideological. In the dialogue among them Melville's themes and purposes are clearly evident. In comic novels such as Melville's narratives, "the incorporated languages and socio-ideological belief systems, while of course utilized to refract the author's intentions, are unmasked and destroyed as something false, hypocritical, greedy, limited, narrowly rationalistic, inadequate to reality."[22] Melville's narratives express his intentions in a comic re- and un-writing (or deconstruction?) of the source-discourses.

Melville's analysis in each of these novels thus involves three areas: genre, ideology, and narrative. Accordingly, I move in each of my chapters from how Melville adopted and adapted specific passages and general tendencies of the particular subgenre to how his adaptation forms a comment on the ideology of his sources to how this ironic, skeptical attitude involves the narrative representation as well. This critical turn emphasizes the abstract dimension of Melville's engagement with his sources, but it is also meant to echo Melville's countermove against the process that generates white lies. The white culture's generic-ideological security—the self-assured sense that the historical tale has been told and understood—can be main-

---

[21]Ibid., 300, 298.
[22]Ibid., 311–12.

tained only if its narratives accept unquestioningly the generic claim to factuality; to move beyond that point and examine the ideological assumptions—as Melville does—is to break down that claim, to perceive history in the subversive manner of Michel Foucault.[23] Ever aware that these assumptions—of the historical factuality, the ideological neutrality, and the narrative transparency of the dominant culture's discourses—engender elitism and oppression, Melville calls attention to the unstated generic, ideological, and narratological premises and thus writes a deflationary but corrective antihistory.

The movement from *Typee* to *Israel Potter* (and eventually *Billy Budd, Sailor*), by which Melville develops this antihistory, is neither merely chronological nor simply developmental. The critics who see Melville growing toward the artistry of *Moby-Dick* then falling from that achievement are, ironically, themselves duplicating the ideology of progress Melville disdains. Yet from the generic perspective, change, if not development, is evident. From *Typee* onward Melville becomes less overt in the use of his sources, for he seems to foreground the sources more prominently in the earlier novels. Thus while *Typee* and *Omoo* seem very obviously about the narratives and the ideas they promote, *White-Jacket*'s appropriation of nautical narratives seems only a background concern. Along with this movement away from the surface, Melville becomes less concerned with the factual reporting of events and more concerned with the deeper, less obvious ideas guiding the events, so that while Tommo and Paul experience one predicament after another, White-Jacket is often an inactive observer whose philosophy seems curiously removed from his experience, and Israel Potter a virtual nonentity in a rather bare narrative that repeatedly emphasizes the themes of poverty and disenfranchisement.

These movements, generally toward the subtle problematization of the fact/fiction dichotomy, thus parallel the course of the novel as a genre, which as Davis shows has its origins in various nonfictional genres each expressing the ideology of the

[23]See White's analysis of Foucault as antihistorian in "Foucault Decoded," *Tropics*, 230–70.

culture. In reaction to both types of "factuality," Bakhtin says, "the novel begins by presuming a verbal and semantic decentering of the ideological world, a certain linguistic homelessness of literary consciousness."[24] Such a decentering, like Melville's own disenfranchisement from his society, results from an awareness of other discourses outside the cultural center: for the novel to be generated, a given national language

> must have the sense that it is surrounded by an ocean of heteroglossia. . . . [S]uch external multi-languagedness strengthens and deepens the internal contradictoriness of literary language itself; it undermines the authority of custom and of whatever traditions still fetter linguistic consciousness; it erodes that system of national myth that is organically fused with language. . . . A deeply involved participation in alien cultures and languages (one is impossible without the other) inevitably leads to an awareness of the disassociation between language and intentions, language and thought, language and expression.[25]

That is to say, the exploration that produced the narratives of facts and expressed the white culture's ideology also produced conditions necessary for the origin of the novel, which undermines both narrative factuality and white ideology. Similarly, Melville's own voyage upon that "ocean of heteroglossia" and his contact with alien cultures allowed him to develop his own highly decentering, antiauthoritarian prose fiction.

As Melville's novels thus become increasingly "novelized," they become more directly American in both setting and theme. From the generally Western concerns of *Typee* and *Omoo*, to the English and American of *Redburn*, to the more exclusively American of *White-Jacket*, to the crucially American of *Israel Potter*, Melville is moving increasingly homeward, toward an exploration of his more immediate cultural contexts.[26]

---

[24]Bakhtin, *Dialogic Imagination*, 367.

[25]Ibid., 368–69.

[26]Bakhtin, *Dialogic Imagination*, 370, indicates that the novel develops only when the national myth is questioned and when the culture begins to be aware of its ideological borders—as in the America of Melville's 1840s and 1850s. See also *Speech Genres*, 7.

And appropriately so, for the literature of exploration is, as Page and others have recognized, the first truly American literature, containing generic traits that pass from Poe to Kerouac, themes that pass from Royall Tyler to Thomas Pynchon. Melville's response is also typically American: revisionary, pluralistic, critical, satiric. D. H. Lawrence's description of the obligations of the American writer and critic is thus singularly appropriate to Melville's narratives of facts: "You *must* look through the surface of American art, and see the inner diabolism of the symbolic meaning. Otherwise, it is all mere childishness. . . . The American has got to destroy. It is his destiny. It is his destiny to destroy the whole corpus of the white psyche, the white consciousness. And he's got to do it secretly."[27]

II

To spell out what has thus far been only implicit: my own critical position relative to Melville, my "local hermeneutics," might best be called "contextualism" or "new historicism" (though I recognize that those terms mean different things to different critics).[28] Bakhtin's (and others') point that words are contextual seems irrefutable; a novel can be understood only in its contexts—textual, historical, biographical, theoretical, critical. As Hershel Parker has argued, the textual context, including both the establishment of an authoritative text and the implications for interpretation of the author's process of

[27]D. H. Lawrence, *Studies in Classic American Literature* (1923; rpt. New York, 1964), 83–84. For a more scholarly discussion of this position see David De-Leon, *The American as Anarchist: Reflections on Indigenous Radicalism* (Baltimore, 1978).

[28]"Local hermeneutics" is E. D. Hirsch's term and distinguishes between "rules of thumb rather than rules," the latter of which he calls "general hermeneutics" and notes that it "lays claim to principles that hold true all of the time" (*The Aims of Interpretation* [Chicago, 1976], 18). For a further development of this sort of theory, see Stanley Fish, "Consequences," in *Against Theory: Literary Studies and the New Pragmatism*, ed. W. J. T. Mitchell (Chicago, 1985), 106–31.

creating that text, must take priority.[29] For the student of Melville, the Northwestern-Newberry edition and the Hayford-Sealts *Billy Budd, Sailor* are thus invaluable as established texts; and I will use (however sparingly) the textual history to support my argument about *Typee* and *Billy Budd, Sailor*, even as I recognize that such applications, however significant, must always be considered partial and indeterminate. More important to my study are, obviously, the literary-historical contexts. My historicism is of the "new" sort in stressing the inseparability of ideology from the contextual discourses and in insisting that the contexts be brought to bear upon the interpretation of the texts. Let us finally put to rest the tired and insipid position that Melville merely "borrowed" from his "sources," "improving" their style, to "fill out his volumes" or "to lend realism" to his observations and inventions.

I am less reliant, particularly in studying these Melville novels, on the biographical contexts, since their languages are not as immediately present in the texts, are not as strongly cued as, say, Melville's footnoting Ellis in *Typee* or placing *The Wealth of Nations* in Redburn's sea-bag. As Bakhtin cautions, "we must never confuse—as has been done up to now and as is still often done—the *represented* world with the world outside the text (naive realism); nor must we confuse the author-creator of a work with the author as a human being (naive biographism)."[30] One cannot, of course, simply dismiss biographically based (or psychoanalytical) readings; however, the history of the criticism of these Melville novels shows an increasing awareness of the unreliability of attempts to connect Melville's biography with the events described in the novels.[31]

[29]Parker's most incisive development of this issue is in *Flawed Texts and Verbal Icons: Literary Authority in American Fiction* (Evanston, Ill., 1984). Although I agree with Parker's insistence on reliable texts, I am uncomfortable with the extent of his appeals to and claims of "authority," in so far as this concept can be used for purposes more political than textual. Melville cautions against this sort of practice in his Captain Vere, whose claims to an authoritative reading of Billy is little more than an arrogant exercise of his own conservative power.

[30]Bakhtin, *Dialogic Imagination*, 253.

[31]Exceptions are Edwin H. Miller, *Melville* (New York, 1975); and Michael Paul Rogin, *Subversive Genealogy: The Politics and Art of Herman Melville*

The theoretical context—the application of recent critical theory to the study of Melville's narratives—is not tangential or ahistorical insofar as the theorist identifies general characteristics (literary, linguistic, psychological, historical, religious) that are evident diachronically. For my purposes here, theory first provides a useful conceptual framework for recognizing the genealogy of Melville's ideas: I suggest that Melville's view of language resembles Derrida's deconstruction, his criticism of religion Eliade's comparatism, his analysis of society Veblen's, his historiography White's or Foucault's. In so doing, I hope to provide the theoretically informed student of Melville a widened context for understanding the implications of some of Melville's more specific perceptions and practices and to indicate to all readers of Melville the depth and prescience of his understanding and the incisiveness of his presentation. Bakhtin's scholarly, historically sound description of the novel, for example, provides a corrective to the perception of Melville's narratives of facts as unsuccessful, simple, marginal, or insignificant. Moreover, theoretical analogues to Melville's positions highlight the picture of Melville's own theoretical bent, for—unlike his friend Hawthorne, whose historical understanding is more concertedly specifying—Melville's is a generalizing mind, little concerned with the precise accuracy or consistency of historical details but always aware of the larger, more abstract dimension of his representations.[32]

My own theoretical convictions have no doubt influenced this picture of Melville, for each scholar will inevitably perceive and present his or her own "Melville" in the light shed by his or

---

(Berkeley and Los Angeles, 1985). Miller's analysis tends toward the vulgar-Freudian and the thesis-ridden, problems Rogin's more accomplished and contextual analysis avoids.

[32]On this trait in Hawthorne see Michael J. Colacurcio, *The Province of Piety: Moral History in Hawthorne's Early Tales* (Cambridge, Mass., 1984). Melville's historicism more nearly resembles that of his narrator in *Pierre* (somewhat of a self-parody), who discusses "the various conflicting modes of writing history" but concludes, "I elect neither of these; I am careless of either; both are well enough in their own way; I write precisely as I please" (*Pierre; or The Ambiguities*, ed. Harrison Hayford, Hershel Parker, and G. Thomas Tanselle [Evanston and Chicago, 1971], 244).

her own personal and intellectual assumptions. One hopes to avoid thesis-ridden subjectivity, which would deny that "truth is ever incoherent";[33] but one must not hope to achieve complete objectivity, which would deny much that contemporary theory has convincingly established. A writer as deep, complex, and powerful as Melville will especially and again inevitably elicit strong, personal, and divergent responses from his readers. I therefore have no doubt as well that the Melville I have studied—with his inveterate theorizing, his skepticism, his relativism, his openness to ambiguity and paradox, his relentless individualism—has influenced even more strongly my own convictions. The insistence upon ideological examination, the resistence to authority, the skeptical deconstruction of tradition and traditional structures, and the pluralistic acceptance of divergent, even conflicting, schools of thought—in a word, the anarchism—evident in this book are thus dimensions of my own ideology, but they are intertwined inextricably with what I sincerely believe is Melville's ideology.

To make use of the insights of divergent schools of thought and yet to avoid sub-scribing to any one is not to slight the importance of the critical context of the works I am studying, however, for no student of Melville should undervalue the considerable achievements of those scholar-critics who have gone before.[34] Like the explorer who reads the accounts of previous voyagers before entering a region, the critic can more easily chart his own course (and avoid crashing upon dangerous misapprehensions) by comparing his observations to others'. Here again, no one account can be determinate or complete, and my footnotes show my debt (adequately, I hope) to all the scholar-critics who, from a wide variety of perspectives, have each plotted out accurately a sector or two of terra Melville. A judicious, pluralistic consideration of Melville criticism—and of Melville's contexts more generally—can produce *proximate* knowledge: examining the con-texts of a work

---

[33]*Letters*, 143.
[34]The finest introduction to Melville criticism is John Bryant, ed., *A Companion to Melville Studies* (Westport, Conn., 1986).

brings one nearer the proximity of authoritative interpretation, brings one nearer "the image of the author."[35] My survey
here accepts the charts of previous critical explorers as comple-
mentary and often intersecting attempts to sail toward Melville's intentions. The critic of Melville, like Ahab, may well
keep on course by pondering over "the charts of all four
oceans . . . [and] threading a maze of currents and eddies" in
the existing scholarship, but even better if he or she avoids
Ahab's "view to the more certain accomplishment of that
monomaniac thought of his soul."[36]

[35]Bakhtin, *Dialogic Imagination*, 257, discusses the use and value of biographical and historical material to form an "image of the author," which if "deep
and truthful . . . can help the listener or reader more correctly and profoundly
to understand the work of the given author."

[36]*Moby-Dick*, 171.

2

Typee

Perception and Preconception
in Polynesia

A FTER he submitted the manuscript of his first novel to the British publisher of factual narratives John Murray, Melville was forced to "parry the incredulity of those who may be disposed to regard the work as an ingenious fiction."[1] Since this time critical debate has continued to focus upon the novel's status as fiction or as history. While demonstrating what Melville culled from other sources, critics since Charles R. Anderson began to realize the extent to which Melville departed from autobiography and structured the novel's events from his imagination.[2] Compounding this generic question, many critics

---

[1]Leon Howard, "Historical Note" to Herman Melville, *Typee: A Peep at Polynesian Life*, ed. Harrison Hayford, Hershel Parker, and G. Thomas Tanselle (Evanston and Chicago, 1968), 280. All references to the text of *Typee* are cited parenthetically.

[2]Providing biographical and historical contexts for the novel are: Charles R. Anderson, *South Seas*; Howard, "Historical Note," *Typee*, 277–302; Hayford, Parker, and Tanselle, "Note on the Text" to *Typee*, 303–25; Hershel Parker, "Evidences for 'Late Insertions' in Melville's Works," *Studies in the Novel* 7 (1975): 407–24; William Spengemann, *Adventurous Muse*, 178–88; T. Walter Herbert, Jr., "The Force of Prejudice: Melville's Attack on the Missions in *Typee*," *Border States* (1973): 5–18; Lee Clark Mitchell, *Witness to a Vanishing America: The Nineteenth-Century Response* (Princeton, N.J., 1981), 189–212; and Larzer Ziff, *Literary Democracy: The Declaration of Cultural Independence in America* (New York, 1981), 1–12. Michael Clark, "Melville's *Typee*: Fact, Fiction, and

have argued, is the central problem within the book of a lack of consistency in the narrative voice, which seems to waver between a naive, nonauthorial point of view and one more obviously Melvillean.[3] To put the issue more pointedly: to ask when and to what extent Tommo is Melville is again to ask how much of the book is fiction and how much autobiography.

Like the dichotomy that characterizes American literary studies more generally, criticism of *Typee* has tended to echo rather than resolve this problem. Criticism of the book, that is, tends to be either primarily scholarship or primarily interpretation, but rarely a concerted effort to integrate scholarship with convincing interpretation.[4] Two recent critics, T. Walter Herbert, Jr., and Mitchell Breitwieser, illustrate this critical polarization: both present among the soundest readings of the novel, yet each tends toward one pole at the expense of the other.[5] Herbert reads the historical source material more thoroughly than did previous scholars, yet his reading of *Typee* itself resolves few of the narrative problems and must resort to the cliché of calling Melville "romantic." Breitwieser, on the other hand, shows great sensitivity to Melville's development of the narrator but does little to identify Tommo's psychology

Esthetics," *Arizona Quarterly* 34 (1978): 350–70, raises the crucial problems in the novel, but his overly schematic aesthetic categorization does little to help solve them.

[3]Readings focusing upon Melville's narrator include: Milton R. Stern, *The Fine Hammered Steel of Herman Melville* (Urbana, Ill., 1957), 29–65; Edgar A. Dryden, *Melville's Thematics of Form: The Great Art of Telling the Truth* (Baltimore, 1968), 36–46; John Seelye, *Melville: The Ironic Diagram* (Evanston, Ill., 1970), 11–28; William B. Dillingham, *An Artist in the Rigging: The Early Work of Herman Melville* (Athens, Ga., 1972), 9–30; Thomas P. Joswick, "*Typee*: The Quest for Origin," *Criticism* 17 (1975): 335–54; and Faith Pullin, "Melville's *Typee*: The Failure of Eden," in *New Perspectives on Melville* (Kent, Ohio, 1978), 1–28.

[4]Hershel Parker, "The 'New Scholarship': Textual Evidence and Its Implications for Criticism, Literary Theory, and Aesthetics," *Studies in American Fiction* 9 (1981): 181–97, calls for a "New Scholarship" that takes into account the contexts—bibliographical, textual, biographical, and historical—in the study of American literature. His article in *Studies in the Novel*, 409–13 (cited in n. 2 above), presents the full textual context of *Typee*, though he does not apply it to a reading of the novel.

[5]T. Walter Herbert, Jr., *Marquesan Encounters: Melville and the Meaning of Civilization* (Cambridge, Mass., 1980); and Mitchell Breitwieser, "False Sympathy in Melville's *Typee*," *American Quarterly* 34 (1982): 396–417.

within the context Melville supplies.[6] To combine these methods—to examine the dynamics between context and narration, between historical fact and Melville's fiction—will, I believe, demonstrate greater coherence in a work often faulted for its generic and narrative disunity. It will also demonstrate that between the facts in Typee and the narrative of *Typee*, Melville interposes the distancing process of perception and preconception.

I

As Tommo first hears of his destination, he imagines a rather confused picture: "The Marquesas! What strange visions of outlandish things does the very name spirit up! Naked houris—cannibal banquets—groves of cocoa-nut—coral reefs—tatooed chiefs—and bamboo temples; sunny valleys planted with bread-fruit-trees—carved canoes dancing on the flashing blue waters—savage woodlands guarded by horrible idols—*heathenish rites and human sacrifices*" (5). These are indeed "strangely jumbled anticipations," as Tommo immediately labels them, and strangely contradictory, too: the conflicting images here foreshadow Tommo's dilemma when he actually encounters the natives. "Typee or Happar?" he asks then, wondering whether they are horrible, cannibalistic savages or alluring, peaceful natives. It is a problem Tommo never resolves in the course of the novel, just as the critics have never resolved this wavering. Most differentiate Tommo's experiences from his narration of them, while others blame the inconsistency on Melville's inexperience as a writer, on last-minute additions, or on the editing of Gansevoort Melville and John Murray.

In the fact that Tommo never resolves this problem is nev-

[6]Herbert, by attempting to define "civilization" according to the anthropological model of Clifford Geertz, departs from a precise historical consideration of Melville's use of his sources; these sources become for Herbert counterpoints to Melville's "beachcomber" perspective, not materials and ideas that Melville is consciously using and critiquing in constructing his fiction. Breitwieser, on the other hand, does not apply the sources Melville explicitly mentions, but refers instead to Franklin and other American figures.

ertheless an indication of the consistency in his narrative wavering. Tommo himself redefines his anticipations as "an irresistible curiosity to see those islands which the other voyagers had
so glowingly described" and adds that he had read of these
voyagers in the narratives of Charles S. Stewart, David Porter,
William Ellis, and others (5–6). Thus Melville indicates that his
narrator's perception of the natives is historically based, thereby suggesting that the contradictions in his narrator must be
understood in the context he mentions.[7]

The reports of these voyagers whom Melville footnotes divide, with virtually no exceptions, into two clear viewpoints on
Polynesia and the Polynesians.[8] From the time of Louis de
Bougainville, who landed on Tahiti and thought he had been
"transported in to the garden of Eden," sailors conceived of
Polynesia as an unspoiled paradise and of the natives as appropriate inhabitants of it. James Cook, for example, lauds the
natives' beauty, their natural morality, their kindness and
openness.[9] Missionaries such as Stewart and Ellis, though rec-

[7]Charles S. Stewart, *Journal of a Residence in the Sandwich Islands* (1830; rpt.
Honolulu, 1970); Stewart, *A Visit to the South Seas* . . . (New York, 1831); David
Porter, *Journal of a Cruise Made to the Pacific Ocean*, 2d ed. (New York, 1822);
and William Ellis, *Polynesian Researches* (New York, 1833). These are the primary sources Melville uses in *Typee*.

[8]Using only those sources Melville cites in the novel and those that criticism
has determined he knew at the time of writing, one can trace a clear and
thorough outline of the whites' perception of Polynesia and the Polynesians.
For a representative view see the following: Louis de Bougainville, *A Voyage
Round the World* (1772; rpt. Amsterdam and New York, 1967), 220–74; John
Ledyard, *A Journal of Captain Cook's Last Voyage* (1783; rpt. Chicago, 1963), 45–
64 and 101–65; George Vancouver, *A Voyage of Discovery to the North Pacific
Ocean* (1798; rpt. Amsterdam and New York, 1967), 98–190; George von
Langsdorff, *Voyages and Travels in Various Parts of the World* (1813; rpt. Amster-
dam and New York, 1968), 1:86–188; Otto von Kotzebue, *A New Voyage Round
the World in the Years 1823–1826* (1830; rpt. Amsterdam and New York, 1967),
1:153–265, and 2:121–223; Edmund Fanning, *Voyages Round the World* . . .
(New York, 1833), 125–214; and *An Historical Account of the Circumnavigation of
the Globe* . . . (Edinburgh, 1836). Secondary summaries of this subject include:
W. Patrick Strauss, *Americans in Polynesia, 1783–1842* (East Lansing, Mich.,
1963); Louis B. Wright and Mary Isabel Fry, *Puritans in the South Seas* (New
York, 1936); and Niel Gunson, *Messengers of Grace: Evangelical Missions in the
South Seas, 1797–1860* (Oxford, 1978). Anderson, *Melville in the South Seas*,
117–78, gives a full summary of Melville's sources.

[9]Bougainville, *Voyage*, 228; *Historical Account*, 376.

ognizing the beauty of the islands, condemn the natives, who
have refused to see the providence of God as the source for
that beauty. Polynesia is thus but an uncivilized "wilderness"
and the Polynesians shameless, sinful cannibals; to Ellis, "no
portion of the human race was ever perhaps sunk lower in
brutal licentiousness."[10]

This contrast is most pronounced in the two groups' description of the Marquesans. The islands were the most beautiful
and fertile the sailors had seen; moreover, "a more honest, or
friendly and better disposed people does not exist under the
sun," Porter states, and "they rank high in the scale of human
beings, whether we consider them morally, or physically."[11] On
the other hand, Stewart finds them "more barbarous" than the
Hawaiians, while Ellis has "the belief that their morals are most
debased, that their licentiousness is of the most shameless kind,
that their propensity to theft is universal, and that they are
quarrelsome and murderous."[12]

This perceptual conflict itself became a subject of the narratives, each group deriding the other's perceptions and defend-
ing its own, and even became a source of literal conflict between the sailors and missionaries.[13] The dispute, however,
was essentially philosophic. The sailors, following Locke and
Rousseau, deduced from the idea of man's innate moral sense
that man unencumbered by civilization could most easily em-
body natural values—simplicity, sentiment, humanity. In opposition, the map the missionaries read was drawn by Calvin
and Hobbes: natives unredeemed by any civilizing and Chris-
tianizing light must exist in a fundamentally fallen state of
nature—in a life that is nasty, brutish, and short.[14]

[10]Ellis, *Polynesian Researches*, 1:87.
[11]Porter, *Journal*, 2:58.
[12]Ellis, *Polynesian Researches*, 3:235.
[13]Ibid., 1:240; Stewart, *Visit*, 2:56, 149; Kotzebue, *New Voyage*, 1:168. For a
summary of the 1825 riots in Lahaina see Ernest Dodge, "Early American
Contacts in Polynesia and Fiji," *Proceedings of the American Philosophical Society*
107 (1963): 106.
[14]Contrasting Rousseau and Calvin in *Typee* is Herbie Butterfield, "'New
World All Over': Melville's *Typee*," in *Herman Melville: Reassessments*, ed. A.
Robert Lee (London, 1984), 14–27.

Influenced by a naive reading of such ideologically opposed accounts, Tommo asks, "Typee or Happar?" but the question could as easily be "Calvin or Rousseau?" or "Missionary or Sailor?" It is little wonder Tommo is confused: it is as if he has stumbled into Cooper's forest unable to tell a Mingo from a Mohican. Throughout *Typee* Tommo wavers between the two opposing perceptions of the natives; he remains so completely reliant upon the categories in the narratives he has read that he becomes himself both an explorer and a missionary, getting the first "Peep at Polynesian Life" and consequently bringing the first peep at ambivalent white culture to the natives.

While Tommo journeys toward the Typee valley with Toby, however, he generally voices the missionaries' position and Toby generally the sailors'. When they discuss the recurrent question, "Toby insisted that it was the abode of the Happars, and I that it was tenanted by their enemies the ferocious Typees" (50). Like a missionary, too, Tommo speaks with pious, Christian diction, describing, for example, their food as a "sacred package" (54). Toby, described in terms suggesting the stereotypical Byronic sailor (32), expects the natives to be "good fellows" (56) and tends to use nautical rather than religious metaphors. In dispatching Toby early in the novel, though, Melville can heighten this dichotomy and remain truer to his original portrait of Tommo, whose "strangely jumbled anticipations" typify the initial response in the white mind to the idea of the native.

When Tommo finally reaches Typee, he therefore faces situations about which he has only vague and conflicting preconceptions and must then categorize his responses to the events even more strictly according to the stereotypes his reading has provided.[15] For instance, when one midnight Tommo awakes "apprehensive of some evil," he sees flames in the grove and figures moving around before them (93). Immediately he perceives the situation as Stewart would: the natives, "dancing and

[15]Edward S. Grejda, *The Common Continent of Men* (Port Washington, N.Y., 1974), 13–27, discusses stereotyping in *Typee*. Breitwieser, "False Sympathy," 401, more convincingly describes Tommo's indecisiveness as "a register of a social contradiction within the meaning of *America*."

capering about, looked like so many demons." Tommo, who understands as little of the natives' culture as Stewart or Ellis did, must therefore transform his fear of an unknown ritual into a fear he can recognize and control—he calls it evil, demonic "capering," terms that not only place the natives' actions into the Christian framework but also account for their apparently random behavior. Melville, seeming to support Tommo's perceptions, builds the suspense of the scene carefully through Kory-Kory's marvelously ambiguous explanation, "'Tommo, Toby, ki ki!' (eat)" (94). To the missionaries, the devil's disciples would not, of course, hesitate to eat and thereby martyr the Christians; to the sailors, the terms Melville quotes here were of equal importance, though of less certain signification. Porter, trying to dismiss what seems to be evidence of cannibalism, explains:

> One word has oftentimes many significations. . . . *Kie-kie* signifies *to eat*, it also signifies *a troublesome fellow*; may it also have many other significations, with which we are unacquainted? it may simply signify, *to cut up, to divide, to sacrifice, to keep as trophies*; whether it has these significations I am unable to say . . . but many circumstances induce me to believe that they meant no more, when they informed me that they sometimes ate their enemies.[16]

Ironically, Melville does indicate that the word means "to eat," but does not here show the natives to be cannibals. Melville's satiric perspective becomes clearer when Tommo and Toby receive their dinner and Toby exclaims, "A baked baby." In this allusion to Swift's "A Modest Proposal," Melville acknowledges that to a reader of Stewart and Ellis a response evoking all the "devilish" horrors of cannibalism and infanticide (the other horrible sin the natives reputedly commit) is superficially reasonable; but such a response does no more justice to the Typees than Swift's narrator does to the Irish. Thus reversing the stereotype of the fickle savage, Melville shows Tommo to be the fickle civilized.

[16]Porter, *Journal*, 2:41–42 and 45–46. Cf. Ledyard, *Journal*, 74.

Furthering his attempt to classify the natives' practices in patterns he can comprehend, Tommo often absurdly preserves in his actions and words his own culture amid wildly inappropriate contexts. He romanticizes life in the valley, for example, as a residence in a Polynesian "Paradise of Bachelors" complete with a "spa," a "trusty valet," "gentlemen of leisure" at "the club," and "fair damsels." Melville's satiric barbs point here in two directions: he deflates the highly "snivelized" society of America and Europe, and he more pointedly criticizes the missionaries and sailors, both of whom wanted to perceive Polynesia in civilized terms. Ellis praises "the incipient effects of civilization" in the idyllic villages into which the missionaries forced the natives (and which fostered the spread of European diseases), while Porter lauds the "pure republican policies" of the Typees' government (and claims their land for America).[17] Like the earlier explorers, Tommo, in preserving the terms of his own culture, can perceive only confusedly and partially the natives' culture. Thus the central cultural structure of Typee society, the taboo, is "thrice mysterious" to him; when he consults Cook, Carteret, Kotzebue, and others about it, though, he learns nothing. He therefore must describe the natives in familiar but absurd terms, as "a parcel of 'Freemasons' making secret signs to each other" (177).[18]

More significant is Tommo's tendency, revealed in two key ways, to describe the Typees as "Indians." First, even before he goes into Typee, "fresh in [his] remembrance" is the story of the master of the *Katherine*, who was seized by the natives and saved only by the intervention of a young native girl (25). Yet as Melville's source, Francis Olmsted, reveals, the Pocahontas-figure is Tommo's inventive addition, for he wants to see, even

---

[17]Ellis, *Polynesian Researches*, 1:29; and Porter, *Journal*, 2:79.

[18]The savage was thus always erroneously defined in relation to the civilized. On Melville's culturally relativistic criticism of savagism see Mitchell, *Witness*, 191–212; Pullin, "Melville's *Typee*," 21; and Herbert, *Marqueson Encounters*, 20. Later, 162–63, Herbert adds, "The account of [Tommo's] residence among the Typees turns, in fact, on situations in which overwhelmingly powerful interpretive responses are successively revealed to have been mistaken." James Duban, *Melville's Major Fiction: Politics, Theology, and Imagination* (De Kalb, Ill., 1983), 9, notes that this cultural chauvinism is Tommo's, not Melville's.

in Polynesia, the more familiar figure of the *belle sauvage*.[19] Second, Tommo tends to perceive his stay with the Typees as an Indian captivity, a perception that paradoxically gives him reassurance. Immediately after "I first truly experienced I was indeed a captive in the valley" (119), he begins to recover from his leg dis-ease and enjoy his stay (123). That is to say, when Tommo can fit his experience into a recognizable pattern, he can be comfortable.[20] It is as well a pattern that allows him to consider the natives not as a different but equally legitimate culture, but as inferior "savages," like most of the "red men" in American literature and history.

To see Melville's position on this issue, we need only compare Tommo's terminology with the natives' term for him. His life among the Typees begins appropriately with an initiation ceremony, the exchange of names that brilliantly illuminates the attitudes of both Tommo and the natives (72).[21] Since the name "Tom" gives is a misrepresentation, a lie, his "praiseworthy intentions" sound a note of condescension. His demand that they correctly pronounce his name once more reflects his attitude that naming eliminates apprehension, that naming is control. But it is a control Melville denies his narrator, for the name that the natives propose, "Tommo," has a meaning: it is a Marquesan verb signifying "to enter into, to adapt well to."[22] The name indicates, as does the natives' subsequent conduct,

[19]Francis Allyn Olmsted, *Incidents of a Whaling Voyage* (1841; rpt. Rutland, Vt., 1969), 197–99.

[20]Marheyo's "abo, abo" also means "to capture" in Hawaiian. Richard Slotkin, *Regeneration through Violence: The Mythology of the American Frontier, 1600–1860* (Middletown, Conn., 1973), 446–48, mentions in passing Melville's use of the captivity narrative in *Israel Potter*.

[21]Joswick, "*Typee*," 342–44, describes the naming scene as an initiation ritual; David Williams, "Peeping Tommo: *Typee* as Satire," *Canadian Review of American Studies* 6 (1975): 36–49, exposes Melville's sexual pun in his narrator's name, a joke that also indicates Tommo's role in relation to the natives; and Robert Abrams, "*Typee* and *Omoo*: Herman Melville and the Ungraspable Phantom of Identity," *Arizona Quarterly* 31 (1975): 36–37, and Paul Witherington, "The Art of Melville's *Typee*," *Arizona Quarterly* 26 (1970): 144, point out the lie in Tommo's name.

[22]Boniface Mosblech, *Vocabulaire océanien-français et français-océanien* (Paris, 1843), 102. On Melville and the Polynesian languages see Richard M. Fletcher, "Melville's Use of Marquesan," *American Speech* 39 (1964): 135–38.

that they wish him to enter into their society, but ironically Tommo not only fails to understand his newly given name, he never adapts.[23] Quite the opposite: he persists in using his own terminology for their actions, persists in applying the ideas he has read in the narratives of the missionaries and sailors.

The natives also persist in attempting to make Tommo "tomo." "Resolved to make a convert" of him (220), they approach him about tattooing—an ironic reversal of missionary proselytizing—but have as little success converting him as the missionaries did the natives.[24] They gave the natives such names as Matteo, Markee, and Lukee, led them through a cursory catechism as incomprehensible to them as the taboo is to Tommo, and assumed they had become civilized Christians. "Tommo," who like the historical natives has converted in name only, begins to feel the same nervous dis-ease he felt when he entered the valley and flees from their attempts to make him a tattooed, irrevocably verifiable member of their society. Although the Typees have been as kind and friendly toward him as Queequeg is to Ishmael, Tommo refuses to adapt to their customs—to "do to my fellow man what I would have my fellow man do to me"—and thus can never gain the bosom friendship that Ishmael shares with Queequeg.[25]

In the scene following this one, Melville amplifies Tommo's fear of integration by facing him with direct evidence confirming his suspicions of the natives' cannibalism (chap. 32), an issue crucial to both missionaries and sailors. To the mission-

[23]For another statement that Tommo never becomes uncivilized see Richard Ruland, "Melville and the Fortunate Fall: Typee as Eden," *Nineteenth-Century Fiction* 23 (1968): 312–23. Stern, *Steel*, 25, voices an opposing view.

[24]For more information on the failure of the missions, particularly those to the Marquesas, see Wright and Fry, *Puritans*, 148 and 237, and Gunson, *Messengers*, 266 and 335.

[25]*Moby-Dick*, 54. On the subject of Tommo's leg see: Joswick, *"Typee,"* 348–50; Breitwieser, "False Sympathy," 416–17; Miller, *Melville*, 122–23 and 126–27; and James Babin, "Melville and the Deformation of Being: From *Typee* to Leviathan," *Southern Review* 7 (1971): 100. John Wenke, "Melville's *Typee*: A Tale of Two Worlds," in *Critical Essays on Herman Melville's "Typee,"* ed. Milton R. Stern (Boston, 1982), 250–58, discusses the novel as Tommo's attempt to reconcile freedom and necessity as he stands between the civilized world and that of the Typees.

aries cannibalism proved conclusively the depravity of the natives and the distance between the white culture and the native.
In a situation similar to Tommo's, Rev. Pascoe Crook, missionary (briefly) to the Marquesans, adopted the native dress and
partially acquiesced in their attempts to assimilate him; but
evidences of cannibalism "had kept his mind in a continued
state of uneasiness for weeks" until he could escape.[26] The
sailors, on the other hand, must go to great lengths to explain
away the seriousness of cannibalism to preserve their noble
savage ideal. Porter, Melville's second source for chapter 32,
came upon a group of Typees suspiciously concealing the
bodies of slain enemies in the bushes. When the natives ex-
plained that the bodies were merely sacrifices, Porter con-
cluded that the misconception arose from errors in transla-
tion.[27] Lacking all but the most direct evidence, then, Porter
can remain convinced of the natives' nobility and continue to
apply his own white, European cultural categories to them.

Melville's reworking of his sources leaves Tommo no such
possibility, for the Typees are indeed cannibals, but Tommo
has to fear not so much being eaten as being assimilated into a
cultural system so radically alien to his own. The natives have
shown no malicious intents toward him, other than to restrict
his movements, for their "Tomo" childishly wants his own way
in their society; moreover, they would not wish to tattoo him, to
make him visibly a member of their society, if they were about
to eat him, and vice versa. His fear at this point, then, must
stem from a realization, perhaps subconscious, that his preconceived notions of noble savages/ignoble savages is hopelessly
muddled, that none of the ideas he has gleaned from the
narratives he has read obtain in the real world of the Typees,
who are at once innocently benevolent and fiercely cannibalistic.[28]

[26]Fanning, *Voyages*, 131–35.

[27]Porter, *Journal*, 2:41–42 and 45–46.

[28]Breitwieser says that Tommo's wavering stems from his resentment of his
white society, which "presents him with two mutually exclusive modes of self-
hood" (401). Herbert, *Marquesan Encounters*, explains it as an "ambivalent balancing" of the narrative voice due to Melville's dual status as "gentleman-
beachcomber." Neither account seems satisfactory, though Herbert is closer to
the right track when he later remarks, "Melville's fictionalizing might be taken,

II

Thus neither the missionaries' nor the sailors' account of the natives proves to be an adequate guidebook for Tommo's experience. He is as lost in Typee as Redburn is in Liverpool when following his father's old guidebook. Unlike Redburn, though, Tommo cannot abandon the prescribed ideas, conflicting and inadequate as they are, and perceive the natives in a culturally relative way. Most important, he, like the missionaries and sailors, cannot abandon these stereotypes primarily because supporting both the noble savage and the ignoble savage stereotype is a more basic preconception, the idea of progress. It encompasses the attitudes of Tommo and the missionaries and the sailors; it is a theory of history—and the place of whites and natives in it—that gives rise to all of Tommo's highly fictionalized "anticipations."

Tommo's jumbled anticipations of Polynesia, that is, coalesce out of a more general desire for progress and regeneration, a desire Tommo also adopts from previous explorers, of whom he has heard in the narratives. "In the watery path of Mendanna, cruising in quest of some region of gold," Tommo recalls, "these isles had sprung up like a scene of enchantment, and for a moment the Spaniard believed his bright dream was realized" (5). But only "for a moment." Like other explorers (and Melville's Taji), Mendanna continued westward, continually seeking greener lands, progressing onward toward his point of origin. This origin, both the geographical completion of the circumnavigation and the metaphysical return to the origin of the species, remained for European civilization ever a moment in the westering progress.[29]

For the 1840s America of Tommo and Melville one focal point of this progress was Polynesia. The American navy, un-

---

indeed, as a conscious extension of the process we have seen at work in Porter and Stewart, according to which the impulse to validate a conviction about the nature of the savage throws information into thematic patterns and sometimes leads to misapprehension of fact" (159–60). Gorman Beauchamp, "Montaigne, Melville, and the Cannibals," *Arizona Quarterly* 37 (1981): 292–309, demonstrates similarities between Melville and Montaigne on the issue of cannibalism.

[29]On Mendanna at the Marquesas see *Historical Account of the Circumnavigation*, 91.

der the aegis of the U.S. Exploring Expedition commanded by
Charles Wilkes, demonstrated in 1838–42 the popular and
governmental interest in Polynesia.[30] The missionaries, too,
were most active during this period, when a Great Awakening
was occurring among the Hawaiians, an occurrence which the
Missionary Herald reported voluminously to the mission's sup-
porters back home.[31] Nor were these two branches of the
American presence unconnected, for America—like Melville
and Tommo (12)—watched with interest the incursion of
French imperialism and Catholicism. Whether the Americans
in Polynesia wore naval uniforms or frock coats, their motives
were ultimately the same: Polynesia was to them that fertile
land (of fruit or of souls), that paradise to be regained, which
westering civilization had been actively seeking since Columbus
sailed literally and metaphorically beyond the medieval world,
but which Plato long before had apocalyptically imagined in
the Atlantis of his *Timaeus*.[32]

In the sailors' narratives Melville read, this Eden was a geographical and chronological condition: west of civilization lay
the blissful garden of man's origin, where he could still live in a
Rousseauvian state of harmony and innocence. As soon as the
explorers discovered a new Eden, however, it became civilized;
paradise retreated constantly westward, futilely pursued by the
explorers, for whom hope then came not through finding a
new unspoiled Eden but through perfecting civilization according to the values these newly discovered civilizations presented.[33] The missionaries, on the other hand, recognized

[30]See Strauss, *Americans*, 107–47.

[31]Ibid., 74–82; on Melville's use of Wilkes in *Moby-Dick* see David Jaffé, "The
Captain Who Sat for the Portrait of Ahab," *Boston University Studies in English* 4
(1960): 1–22.

[32]Melville explains the significance of Polynesia as "a sort of Elysium" to "our
visionaries" in his 1859 lecture "The South Seas," printed in Merton M. Sealts,
Jr., *Melville as Lecturer* (Cambridge, Mass., 1957), 155–80. Spengemann, *Adventurous Muse*, 14–25, discusses the ideological implications of Columbus's voyages. I am also indebted to my colleague Bruce Clarke for his discussion of the
metaphorical significance of Atlantis in Plato.

[33]Vancouver, *Voyage*, 1:v; Kotzebue, *New Voyage*, 1:167–69; and Langsdorff,
Voyages, 2:161. Melville need not have gotten his ideas of progress from the
narratives alone, for he could have read the theory in Bancroft, Motley, or
Parker, or heard of it in relation to the Millerites, Owenites, etc.

Eden as an exclusively chronological condition: the time and characteristics of man before the Fall, to be regained only through the Christianization of the New Worlds. Polynesia was to them no paradise but a wilderness of souls to be Christianized in hope of bringing on the millennium. Ellis, for example, shows a typical missionary urge to begin and end his narrative with grand millennial, apocalyptic expectations, such as the "anticipati[on of] the arrival of a period when a transformation equally decisive and lovely shall change the moral deserts of the earth into regions of order and beauty, and the wilderness shall become as a Garden of the Lord."[34]

Common to both these divergent views is nevertheless the concept of history as a teleological, finite, Janus-faced continuum, as a line progressing from Eden lost to Eden regained.[35] As much as progress is a theory of history, it is the *attitude* of those who hold this theory: the belief in man's "prospect" and "retrospect" that Walt Whitman expressed in seeking a "Passage to India," both the India of "myths and fables of eld" and the "more than India" of the transcendental spiritual ideal.[36] Like Whitman at the end of his poem, the mariners whom Melville read set sail to aid "the progress of discovery." For instance, George Vancouver typically conceived of his voyage as both increasing knowledge and spreading civilization to "the less enlightened part of our species."[37] Most of the explorers and all of the missionaries believed that Providence directs this progress of history and increase in man's God-given dominion over the earth. To the missionaries "Christianization" is the central factor in the "progress of civilization," for both are terms for the same advance toward the end of the historical line in the new Eden.[38]

Tommo, like the sailors and missionaries, narrates a Whitmanesque "progress" (58, 59, 61, 62, 70, etc.) toward a place of "universal verdure" that is "like the enchanted gardens in a

[34]Ellis, *Polynesian Researches*, 1:11 and 3:300.
[35]See A. O. Lovejoy's definition in his introduction to Lois Whitney, *Primitivism and the Idea of Progress* (Baltimore, 1934), xvii.
[36]Walt Whitman, "Passage to India," ll. 20, 224.
[37]Vancouver, *Voyage*, 1:i–iv.
[38]Ellis, *Polynesian Researches*, 4:107.

fairy tale" (49). To Melville, that is, this progress toward Eden
has a distinct element of fantasy in it; more than a religious or
sociological quest, it is a romantic dream, a fiction.[39] So it was
for many of the sailors and missionaries; the former conceived
of Polynesia as a naked heaven of bread-fruit, cocoa-nuts, and
native women, the latter as a pacific haven for pastoral piety.
But not Melville, for Tommo's ascent up the ridge of the island
takes Toby and him to a position supremely condescending,
where they "looked down upon the islanders from [their] lofty
elevation [and] experienced a sense of security" (39). Typical of
the white attitude, Tommo's feeling of superiority is consequent to his aspirations, and his security comes at the expense
of the natives', as below they are seen "hurrying to and fro,
seemingly under the influence of some hidden alarm" (39).
Again and again Tommo's journey across Nukuheva carries
him up to craggy and barren summits of Byronic and Shel-
leyan mountains in a parodic anticipation of Ahab's or Pierre's
striving; however, Tommo must always return to earth, literally and metaphorically, to eat and sleep. Idealistic dreams,
Melville is indicating, expose the unnatural attempt to put
oneself above one's fellow man. Melville thereby demonstrates
the consequences of the missionaries' and sailors' attitudes:
their most basic beliefs tend to alienate them from Polynesia
and the Polynesians.

Melville's critique, both ironic and parodic, of progress toward Eden comes to a point as Tommo and Toby enter
Typee.[40] At the moment they literally "fall" *into* Typee-Eden
(64), they unconsciously echo the words of Milton's Adam and
Eve *leaving* paradise: "The valley was now before us," Tommo
says, looking not forward to a life of toil and sweat but backward to the "labors" that brought them to Typee. Again per-

[39]On Melville's skepticism about progressive ideals see Mitchell, *Witness*,
200–203. Seelye, *Melville*, describes *Typee* as a romantic quest; Ruland, "Fortunate Fall," discusses the dream of paradise in the novel; and Breitwieser, "False
Sympathy," says, "*Typee* is a romance because Tommo attempts to use the
culture of the South Seas as a situation that will permit him to realize what is
only an 'abstract, moral person[hood]' at home" (402).

[40]Cf. Ruland, "Fortunate Fall," 319–21; Williams, "Peeping," 43–45; Witherington, "Art," 143–44; and Stern, *Steel*, 43.

verting the Miltonic epic, Tommo and Toby immediately devour the fruit of a tree Melville calls "annuee"—Hawaiian for
"sacred"[41]—but the fruit is already "much decayed" (67). If
Typee is the Eden they have been seeking, they make an un-
usual primal pair; in fact, they more resemble Satan as they
crawl on their quest "much in the fashion of a couple of ser-
pents" (39). The two natives they immediately encounter—like
God discovering Adam and Eve hiding in the bushes just after
the Fall—at first seem more like the stereotypically innocent
couple one would expect to find in Eden; however, Toby "recoil[s] as if stung by an adder" upon seeing the "wily" pair.
Thus everyone in the scene is at once Adamic and Satanic and
God-like, at once prelapsarian and fallen. This confusion is
precisely Melville's point: his parodic recasting of Milton's and
America's Eden myth reduces the grand, epic expectations of
progressive man to a purely human scale; anything else is a
product of Tommo's romantic imagination.

To Tommo and to the historical missionaries and sailors the
natives' very presence, that is, posed an acute problem to their
theory of progress. When the Europeans discovered that the
New Worlds were inhabited, they were forced to abandon the
idea of uniform progress to account for the apparently un-
progressed natives, whom they first suspected might even be
half-human Calibans. The Europeans kept the *model* of progress, though, and denominated the natives "primitives," people
in their first state, somewhere back of "civilized" people on the
line of history. The concept of primitivism—that primitive humans are good, wise, and benevolent—would seem at first
glance to be at odds with the idea of progress; yet central to
both is the same dual attitude and historical orientation.[42]
Primitivists not only look backward to the original state, but in
their desire to recapture it they look forward as well. The Calvinist missionaries were the strictest of chronological primitivists: they conceived of only two good primitives, prelapsarian
Adam and Eve, and of only two good primitive states, paradise

---

[41]Mosblech, *Vocabulaire*, 8.
[42]Whitney, *Primitivism*, 7.

lost and paradise regained. The sailors, however, followed a
primitivism, chronological and cultural, that read the biblical
text metaphorically.[43] Eden to them was the point at the beginning of human development, Rousseau's state of nature. For
Rousseau, the Fall occurred when this basic unity with nature
and this natural goodness were obscured by civilized accre-
tions. The sailors' contact with the natives therefore provided
an opportunity to observe humanity in the original state at
firsthand, to relearn thereby the values civilization had obscured, and finally to ensure its progress.[44] The primitivism
Tommo exhibits in Typee thus is nothing more than a further
rationalization of his progressive ideals, nothing more than an
aspect of the civilized attitude he never abandons.

   Although these attitudes both confuse Tommo and prohibit
him from adapting to the Typee culture, their effect upon the
Typees is much more insidious. The whites' perception of the
natives' culture as primitive and their imposition of their own
progressive values upon it is cultural supplantation, a despotic
basis for the supersession of the natives' land. Perception becomes possession (both stem from the Latin *percipio*): Tommo's
gentlemanly perception of Kory-Kory as his "valet" may seem
playful, but as a result Tommo is literally as guilty of racial
slavery as both the missionary's wife (chap. 26) and Crusoe
(44).[45] Like Tommo, both missionaries and sailors denominate
the natives "savages"; whether noble or ignoble, they are considered more primitive, "fickle," "capricious," and therefore
susceptible to ideological and actual appropriation by the civilized whites. Like Porter, whose path into the Typee valley
Tommo follows, Tommo descends to conquer. Although Melville makes his narrator guilty of this typical white practice, he
himself rails against it, using his own voice in often-cited pas-

   [43]See Lovejoy's introduction to Whitney, *Primitivism*, for a more complete
definition; see also Lovejoy, George Boas, et al., eds., *A Documentary History of
Primitivism and Related Ideas*, vol. 1 (Baltimore, 1935).
   [44]Jean-Jacques Rousseau, *The Social Contract and Discourses*, trans. G. D. H.
Cole (New York, 1950), 196–212. Melville mentions Rousseau in *Typee*, 127.
   [45]On Melville and slavery see Carolyn Karcher, *Shadow over the Promised
Land: Slavery, Race, and Violence in Melville's America* (Baton Rouge, 1980); and
Rogin, *Subversive Genealogy*.

sages he removed from the American Revised Edition.[46] Not only in the results upon the natives of Tommo's attitudes, therefore, but also in Melville's own statements condemning savagism, can we see Melville's ironic distance from his narrator and those whom he typifies.

By comparing Melville's sources to Tommo's narrative we can see with even more clarity this subtle authorial distance. For instance, the full range and depth of Melville's outraged and outrageous parody of the whites' practices comes to light in the seemingly innocuous pop-gun war (chap. 19). Virtually every narrative about the South Seas stresses the evils of putting guns into the hands of the natives, since the narrators suppose that universal warfare will immediately ensue among the "capricious savages," as it does among the Typees. Melville's use of "you" in the scene is significant, for in the whites' eyes the primary danger was to themselves and to their white supremacy. Both the sailors and the missionaries, like Tommo, were nevertheless guilty of arming the natives to achieve their own ends.

The incident, in addition, parodies the whites' system of industrialization. "For three or four hours I was engaged in manufacturing pop-guns," Tommo says, "but at last made over my good-will and interest in the concern to a lad of remarkable quick parts, whom I soon initiated into the art and mystery" (145). This was the usual proceedure of the whites: they set up the operation, allowed the natives to do most of the work, and rationalized their "interest" as "good-will." "Art and mystery"

[46]It is obviously true that, as the editors of the Northwestern-Newberry edition argue (309–11 and 315–18), such passages were removed from the American Revised Edition largely under pressure and that their content clearly expresses Melville's intentions, yet the removal of these passages (e.g., 124–26 and 195–99) results in a more carefully controlled narrative voice that allows the same sentiments to be expressed more subtly. In the letter to John Murray in which Melville complains of having to make the changes, he also admits, "The revision will only extend to the exclusion of those parts not naturally connected with the narrative, and some slight purifications of style. I am persuaded that the interest of the book almost wholly consists in the *intrinsick merit of the narrative alone* . . . & the removal of [these passages] imparts a unity to the book which it wanted before" (*Letters*, 39).

are important words, too, for the natives' idea that anything mechanical was magical provided the bait to lure them to work. Ellis's printing operation was such an attraction that the king himself got the privilege of pressing the first sheet; after the ceremony, commoners were "instructed to perform the most laborious parts" of the operation.[47] Tommo's enterprise lasts but a short time: "Like everything else, however, the excitement gradually wore away." Through industrialization the missionaries attempted to drive the natives from "indolence" and its resulting sins, and the sailors to reap profits for themselves—and both to divert the natives from any uprisings that might endanger white supremacy—but the printing and spinning cotton and processing cane sugar all failed once the novelty wore off and the natives realized the drudgery involved.[48] To ensure the progress of the primitive natives, then, the whites go to absurd and insidious lengths, but in doing so they not incidentally both gratify their own venal desires and further coalesce their idea of progress and primitivism. The results of their actions, however, Melville shows to be futile, for they are based upon an ideology inapplicable to the situation.

To Melville this progressive primitivism is not only dangerous in practice but simplistic in concept. According to Rousseau, a primitive man needed only food, a woman, and sleep; according to the Bible, Adam needed only certain selected fruits, Eve, and sleep; according to the white narrators, the Polynesians had little more than bread-fruit, sex, and sleep.[49] But to the seriously anthropological vision of Melville such a formulation ignores the very real responsibilities of family and kinship ties that bind society and are integral to human existence. Yet Tommo, like many of the "isolatoes" white culture spawns and Melville's fiction records, never "enters into" even society's most basic unit: he flees the family of the ship—the captain his "father," the ship *Dolly* his "old lady," and the crew

---

[47]Ellis, *Polynesian Researches*, 2:169.
[48]Ibid., 2:15 and 167–71. Herbert, *Marquesan Encounters*, 175, connects the doctrine of the Fall to forced labor.
[49]Rousseau, *Social Contract*, 210.

his brothers—in order to launch his Rousseauvian natural independence but finds in Typee another family—Marheyo his father, Tinor his mother, and Fayaway his potential wife.[50] In fact, the whole Typee society is a family under the patriarchal rule of Mehevi, a "naturally commanding figure" (185–86, 204). Melville thus indicates, in opposition to Rousseau, that the family ever remains the natural unit of society, and though free from restraints the individual naturally subjects himself to it, just as Ishmael submits to his relationship with Queequeg.[51] Tommo can superficially accept the family system, but when the Typees wish him to become a member of their family in full by being tattooed, he refuses. He has described Kory-Kory's tattoos as a prison (83) and now fears the loss of his own freedom from societal constraints.

As a foil to Tommo's intransigent individualism, Melville presents in Marnoo a complete cultural relativist, a man able to coexist in harmony with any culture. He is neither savage nor progressed, for his upbringing has encompassed both white and native cultures (140). He can transcend cultural categorizations, Melville reveals, because he has "ratified friendly relations with some individual" in the other culture; thus friendship, which Tommo in all his superiority never demonstrates, is the basis for Melville's cultural relativism here as in *Moby-Dick*. A natural basis as well: Marnoo's tattoo, the artu tree, combines organic nature, art, and god ("artua") and gives the lie to Tommo's insistence that tattooing would disfigure him. Marnoo, in short, demonstrates that Tommo's qualms about adapting to the Typee culture are more ideological than practical.

Deepening Melville's argument against the simplistic white ideology is the crucial issue of sexuality. An important part of Tommo's desire for progress and paradise, Melville indicates, is a desire for sexual regeneration, a logical part of the progres-

---

[50]Ibid., 4–6. See also Rogin, *Subversive Genealogy*, 43–49; Miller, *Melville*, 122–31; and Wai-Chee Dimock, "*Typee*: Melville's Critique of Community," *ESQ: A Journal of the American Renaissance*, 30 (1984): 27–39.

[51]Rousseau, *Social Contract*, 6.

sive concept of history: the perfection of the beginning included a freedom from the cares and responsibilities that cloud
fallen or civilized life, so that man could innocently enjoy all
the components of his nature. Thus we might expect that
Tommo's unnatural avoidance of familial and social relationships, based primarily upon a desire for independence, might
include the irresponsible sexuality seen in many of the sailors'
narratives. The sailors, convinced that they had found a sexual
Eden in Polynesia, often entered into liaisons with the native
women, who, in Porter's words, "attached no shame to a proceeding which they not only considered as natural, but innocent and harmless amusement."[52] The innocence and natural-
ness attracted the sailors so much that most ships stopped every
six months for "refreshments," a term that quickly became a
sexual euphemism.[53] The missionaries conceived of *Eden* similarly but stressed that the Fall had brought guilt and clothing
into the world; therefore, when the missionaries saw the Polynesians openly pursuing their favorite pastime, they were ap-
palled. In short, the missionaries did not see innocence as a
possible part of the human character.

Like the sailors particularly, Tommo seeks an Eden that has
highly sexual elements, as the images at the opening of the
novel indicate. Tommo describes the cock Pedro: in his soli-
tude, "his attenuated body will be laid out upon the captain's
table next Sunday, and long before night will be buried with all
the usual ceremonies beneath that worthy individual's vest" (4).
Tommo also reveals the fear that he himself could become like
the crew of the *Perseverance* (a travesty of Calvinism's Perseverance of the Saints?), who forever sail "somewhere off Bug-
gerry Island, or the Devil's Tail Peak" (23). A mention of the
Marquesas dismisses such homosexual fears and coalesces his
dreams of "naked houris," who indeed turn out to be a sailor's
dream come true (14–15). Such fantasies notwithstanding,
Tommo is more like a missionary, for his drive to freedom is

[52]Porter, *Journal*, 2:59.
[53]Strauss, *Americans*, 3.

coordinate with an obvious sexual repression that many critics have noticed.[54]

To contrast his narrator sharply and to counter the ideological and personal control Tommo craves, Melville shows a sly delight in sexuality through the frequent sexual innuendoes, metaphors, and situations. In an anticipation of the sexual geography Melville will use in *Omoo, Mardi*, and especially "The Tartarus of Maids," Tommo and Toby begin their journey by encountering a thicket of canes, then "coaxing and bending them to make some progress" (38). "The perspiration starting from our bodies in floods," they throw themselves repeatedly upon the canes until Tommo becomes "fatigued with my long-continued efforts, and pant[s] for breath." Then "I sunk down for a moment with a sort of dogged apathy, from which I was aroused by Toby. . . . He was laying about him lustily with his sheath-knife" (38). Melville here illustrates humorously the sexual level beneath the desire for progress and more seriously the rape of the natural order, like Tommo's later violation of the taboo (222). As Tommo and Toby "penetrate" a further valley, Tommo is "almost unmanned" by what he imagines is a serpent. A metaphorical sex-scar, his leg swells, brings feverish sensations and makes walking difficult.[55] Melville's ribald phallic joke shows that Tommo's dreams of Edenic sexuality, like all his anticipations, are snakebitten by reality.

Tommo's sexual problems increase as he and Toby enter the valley of the Typees, who are all too sexual for the repressed and injured Tommo. With marvelously sly ambiguity Melville says that the name Typee means "a lover of human flesh," and the natives do live up to their name. Sex, according to the

[54]On the issue of sex in *Typee* see: Williams, "Peeping," 38–42; Babin, "Deformation," 97–99; Miller, *Melville*, 118–31; Ziff, *Literary Democracy*, 6 and 9; Helen B. Petrullo, "The Neurotic Hero of *Typee*," *American Imago* 12 (1955): 317–23; and Gerard Sweeney, "Melville's Smoky Humor: Fire-lighting in *Typee*," *Arizona Quarterly* 34 (1978): 371–76. David Ketterer, "Censorship and Symbolism in *Typee* Revisited: The New Manuscript Evidence," *Melville Society Extracts*, no. 69 (1987), 6–8, shows that the manuscript leaves of the first draft in the New York Public Library's Gansevoort-Lansing Collection expose the sexuality even more explicitly than in the published novel.

[55]Cf. Williams, "Peeping"; Babin, "Deformation."

metaphor of Kory-Kory's making fire, is their only difficult work (111)—a wicked perversion of the curse of paradise lost and a fascinating adaptation of the Prometheus myth. Tommo prefers to avoid such orgasmic experiences as fire-making or swimming with the native girls; instead he turns to a daily row on the lake with Fayaway (131–33), whose sexuality he always treats with typically Victorian discretion and distance. He even goes so far as to make her a calico dress, which was the missionaries' first step in their attempt to cover and repress the natives' sexuality.

Thus, in Tommo, Melville captures the conflict in the psychology of progressive white society: although its desire for Eden is at least partly a sexual desire, it is a desire for sexuality without restrictions, consequences, or direct expression. Melville, like Freud, exposes the adolescent and stagnating aspects of this attitude: from the first chapter, in which both missionaries and sailors are routed by the natives' overt sexuality, Melville derides the whites' sexual attitudes. Just as they of ideological necessity cover their own and the natives' sexuality under their calico and their circumlocutions, so Melville in his revolt against this sort of prescriptive subjugation puts his sexual descriptions under the cloak of metaphor, which paradoxically illuminates the issue to those who can read by the light shed by Kory-Kory's fire.

In some respects Melville thus anticipates Michel Foucault, who shows sexual "repression" to be a complex but secondary tool in the exercise of power, the locus of which is to him, as to Melville, the family.[56] For Tommo and the whites to accept the real sexuality of the Typee society would not merely offend civilized sensibilities; it would destroy their concept of cultural primitivism, their ideological superiority. Melville, anticipating twentieth-century ethnographers, shows that tattooing represents in the taboo not primitive simplicity but a complex system virtually beyond the understanding of both whites and natives (220–24). Certainly, to enter into this society through sexual

[56]Michel Foucault, *The History of Sexuality: Volume 1: An Introduction*, trans. Robert Hurley (New York, 1980).

and familial relations is to recognize that the native culture is not more "primitive" than white culture is. Nor does Melville support the idea of chronological primitivism. If a complex society results from familial relationships between sexual humans, then society was never less complex; that is, if men and women have always been sexual, they have always engaged in familial relations, and the species has no original, primitive social state. Here Melville turns Rousseau's idea of the primitive's desire for the female against itself: rather than a condition of the original state, sexuality is an indication that there can be no original state.[57] To retain its ideas of history, then, the progressive society must repress or deflect sexuality while at the same time harboring the fiction of a primitive sexuality without consequences. The brief glimpse of Typee history that Melville presents reiterates this position and suggests a theory of history opposing the progressive. The Typee Stonehenge that Tommo stumbles upon (154–55) indicates that the present Typee culture was preceded by a "more civilized" culture, which must have been preceded by a "more primitive" culture, et cetera ad infinitum. The history of the Typees is open-ended and nonprogressive.

It is a history, however, from which Tommo feels he must escape. Like the voyagers who sailed into the Polynesian women's lives and then quickly out, leaving the native women pregnant and crying on shore, Tommo in the end escapes from "Home" and family. Ironically, though, Tommo escapes back to the conditions he so desperately wanted to leave at the beginning, and again the ship is a woman, the *Julia*. Tommo will never escape the presence of sexuality; to the end he is a "froward child" (247) rebelling against parental and societal authority, to the end a westering white man trying to "progress" (248, 249). In the nostalgic desire for paradise that he shares with progressive culture, Tommo reveals a wish for the

---

[57]See Jacques Derrida, particularly his *Of Grammatology*, trans. Gayatri C. Spivak (Baltimore, 1976); his formulation of the process of deconstruction seems to me a viable gloss on the process Melville is using to expose and attack the ideas of the white culture.

time of preadolescence, for the time before civilization can impose its chief discontent, guilt, upon the libido. In *Typee*, that is to say, Melville conflates personal development and historical development to explode progress and primitivism. The historical problem posed for the white by the native is closely related to the psychological problem posed by the woman (the native woman holds a central position in the white mythology). Her sexuality, something radically alien to the adolescent, leads him to fear any real contact with her even as he is irresistably drawn to her by his developing sexuality. That is, the fascination and the horror with which the civilized world contemplated the natives is perhaps the psychological essence of those "jumbled anticipations" with which Melville began the novel. The adolescent unable to overcome his fears and substitute reality for fantasy becomes neurotically repressed, undeveloped. White society, Melville is saying, faces a similar dilemma: it must learn to perceive the native realistically and thus abandon its fantasies of Eden, or it can stagnate in its repression and racism.

III

Tommo cannot attain Eden through his experiences in Typee, but he makes one more attempt in *Typee*. Tommo's desire to represent his experiences in his narrative is etymologically and actually the desire to make them present again, to transcend the present moment and linguistically relive a past moment. Tommo's narrative, then, is another expression of the quest for Eden that has been guiding him throughout the novel. He reveals his nostalgia for the Typee paradise perhaps most explicitly in his memories of the bread-fruit trees: "Even now, amidst all the bustle and stir of the proud and busy city in which I am dwelling, the image of those three trees seems to come as vividly before my eyes as if they were actually present, and I still feel the soothing quiet pleasure which I then had in watching hour after hour their topmost boughs waving gracefully in the breeze" (244). The trees are a particularly appropriate symbol of the Polynesian paradise Tommo longs to regain:

the bread-fruit tree is the one object most typical of Polynesia and most essential to the existence of the natives; and the trinity of trees waving in the correspondent breeze is a highly spiritual symbol. Melville's echo of the typical Wordsworthian motif here is significant: Tommo's intimations of immortality can at this point come only through recollection of his "childhood" in Typee. Indeed, most Western observers described Polynesian life as a childhood, a recognition that the native, like the Wordsworthian child, was nearer to paradise, "glorious in the might / Of heaven-born freedom on [his] being's height."[58]

Tommo's romantic evocation of nature, recollected in "bustle and stir" rather than tranquillity, is undercut by the fact that most of his actions have revealed an idealistic attempt to escape nature. As Melville presents it, nature generally is an all-encompassing symbiotic system and Typee specifically is a place where man is close to nature. Tommo discovers the interpenetrating presence of nature his first night on the island, and he tries in vain to shield himself from it (46). The Typees, in contrast, happily and harmoniously blend into the natural system, which provides them all their necessities and luxuries (the seemingly irrelevant chapters on taro, bread-fruit, etc. demonstrate this point). When the natives age and die, they return completely into nature, as do the old men turning as green as the foliage around them (92–93), or like the god carved in the likeness of a man, who "had literally attained a green old age" (178). Such a nature is a sort of cannibalism, the universal, natural cannibalism Melville refers to in *Moby-Dick*'s "The Whale as a Dish" chapter. This natural cycle is composed of an eternal food chain, in which each element gives sustenance to another, which itself gives sustenance to another, et cetera ad infinitum. If man is a part of nature, then even literal cannibalism is merely one part of nature blending into another—a natural, everyday occurrence.

[58]Wordsworth, "Ode: Intimations of Immortality from Recollections of Early Childhood," ll. 121–22. Dillingham, *Artist*, titles his chapter "Adversity Recollected in Tranquility" and describes, 17–24, Tommo's "retrospective comment" on life in Typee.

This concept of nature serves as Melville's most basic argument against the progressive idea of history to which Tommo escapes. If man is but a part of nature, then any ideas of a separate transcendence of the natural process are mere dreams and any hopes for a grand destiny for man mere egoism. Out of the Renaissance humanism that brought forth progress and primitivism comes a subjective idealism that similarly reflects a desire for the continuation of the self. In *Typee* Melville demonstrates that regeneration can come only through the self-less commingling with nature, which lives through the death of the individual. Thus the pursuit of an original state must also be fruitless. The Stonehenge ruins give Tommo "no inscriptions, no sculpture, no clue, by which to conjecture its history: nothing but the dumb stones" (155). Likewise the Typee women are tattooed with three dots on the lips—a mathematical sign of a series reaching to infinity—for they, representing sexuality and generation, are as timeless as the processes they encompass (86).

Against the force of Melville's nature, Tommo in his narrative tries and fails to reassert his linear, progressive ideals. Although he wishes to chronicle the progress of his life in Typee, his narrative has little chronological fidelity, wavering uncertainly back and forth within Tommo's stay in the valley, as well as between the time of the experience and the time of writing. Melville's condensation of ideas and scenes from South Seas narratives written over a wide time range into the moment of Tommo's narrative serves both to fragment chronology further and to focus it exclusively upon the present historical moment. Certainly, the uniformity of natural life, with its infinite past and future, makes the present the most sensible temporal focus, so for the Typees, "the history of a day is the history of a life" (149). This natural historicism is for Melville the most tenable theory of history, a process not a progress.

The paradise that Tommo's narrative seeks to evoke, however, is closely related to his idea of progress. While still in Typee Tommo connects the events he experiences to the future Eden—that is, he perceives the events Providentially—gives the events transcendent, spiritual meaning, and makes his own experience a part of the progressive pattern of history. Tommo's narration has a similar effect: narration itself involves Tommo's giving a teleology to individual events. He must of necessity select from the totality of his experience certain events to include and certain ones to omit; any selection, if not random, implies a purpose, a perception and implementation of a pattern akin to fiction. In short, to narrate one's experiences is to put them into a meaningful context and thus to raise the ontological status of those events.

Perhaps the clearest example of this typological (or Typeeological) reading is Tommo's description of the effigy of the dead chief he comes upon while walking in a sacred place (171–73). Admitting that the image haunts him even as he writes years later. Tommo describes the chief as "leaning forward and inclining his head, as if eager to hurry on his voyage. Glaring at him for ever, and face to face, was a polished human skull, which crowned the prow of the canoe. The spectral figure-head, reversed in its position, glancing backwards, seemed to mock the impatient attitude of the warrior" (172). Kory-Kory explains to Tommo that the chief is heading for heaven, an Edenic place with plenty of bread-fruit, ornaments, and women. Tommo interpets this "strange superstition" as "another evidence of the fact, that however ignorant man may be, he still feels within him his immortal spirit yearning after the unknown future" (173). This "fact" of longing, too, allows Tommo to focus upon the chief and imagine him like himself an idealist progressing single-mindedly toward the Eden ahead, as Milton Stern has so perceptively demonstrated.[59] But for Melville, ahead of the chief is only the fact of death, mockingly smiling back at the naive dreamer. Tommo, lost in his grand contemplations of the heaven beyond, attempts to progress as the stationary chief does, but Kory-Kory, for whom heaven is "not much pleasanter, he thought, than Typee," can remained contented.

The world of the Typees further frustrates Tommo's teleological quest in that the context of Typee precludes absolute

[59]Stern, *Steel*, 54–57.

meanings of the sort Tommo desires. In the valley, all meaning relates ultimately to the taboo, which is "all encompassing," that is to say, which is the system of nature itself. And therefore this system "always appeared inexplicable" (221), since as nature it is an infinite system. When a word is defined in relation to what it is not (its context), in an infinite system the meaning is infinitely deferred, and the attempt at absolute definition must fail. Thus the search for linguistic meaning attains an infinite regress similar to the search for historical origin. In Typee, Tommo reminds both Toby and Melville's readers, "it was impossible for either of us to know anything with certainty" (51).

Consequently, Tommo must rely all the more heavily upon arbitrary terms such as "Typee," "savage," "civilized," "progress," and so on. Emblematic of this linguistic process is the Moa Artua incident (174–76). When this natural god says nothing to the priest, he must "interpret" it; that is, make something up. Whether native or narrator, man interprets the ambiguity, complexity, and incomprehensibility of nature by the arbitrary act of naming. It is little matter if the priests of language believe what they say to have a transcendental origin or if they are guilty of a "vile humbug"; ultimate truths remain beyond the grasp of anyone.[60] Any claims for transcendental truths, Melville is saying, are eroded by nature.

Eroded, too, is the narrative structure that tries to re-present the natural world. If linguistic meaning is open to arbitrary interpretation, then more largely, form is also subject to a lack of closure. In *Typee*, Melville heightens the seeming arbitrariness of much of the structure to reflect the dissemination of meaning seen in individual terms and, most important, to undermine Tommo's attempts to give meaning to his experiences. Like the natural world, the novel itself is open-ended, constantly deferring meaning from one context to another. Here *Typee* also prefigures *Moby-Dick*, a more direct statement on the impossibility of finding linear structure, original meaning, or transcendental truth. Ahab's pursuit of the whale is,

[60]Ibid., 7; see also Thomas Lucas, "Herman Melville: The Purpose of the Novel," *Texas Studies in Language and Literature* 13 (1972): 660.

among other things, just such a search, and the novel itself just
such an all-encompassing structure. The blank yet infinitely
lined forehead of the whale is the symbol of the trace of linguistic meaning, for it encompasses everything and nothing.
For Melville truth, like the whale and the doubloon, is therefore different things to different men, and the quest for *the*
meaning leads to death or madness or both. Melville's attitude
toward the questor is ambivalent, though: there is always something admirable about his Ahab or Bulkington or Pierre. Although their quest into the heart of linguistic darkness is futile,
they dive deeply into the bottomless universe, while Tommo
cowers safely on the lee shore of his ideology.

As the whale's hieroglyphic forehead frustrates Ahab's ma-
nia to understand, so the natives' language forms a destructive
contrast to Tommo's desires. To Tommo, Marquesan is all
gibberish, incomprehensible, ineffectual; but to Melville it is an
appropriate medium for his comments on language in general,
for, as Porter points out, a prominent feature of Marquesan is
its multiple significations.[61] Thus in itself Marquesan is appropriately representative of the linguistic confusion Tommo
feels. Melville's orthography serves further to confuse and
compound this ambiguity, although in the Preface he playfully
says that it "*might be supposed* most easily to convey their [Mar-
quesan words'] sound to a stranger" (my emphasis). And deliberately so, for the extant portions of the first draft show Melville entirely familiar with the most common Polynesian
orthography.[62] Melville also mixes Marquesan with Tahitian
and Hawaiian, and introduces his own "Polynesian" words,
sometimes for convenience, sometimes for comedy, sometimes
for no apparent reason at all. Melville's title is a good example:
"Typee" signifies the valley on Nukuheva, a native who lives in
the valley, the culture of the natives, the reputation—"bad

[61]Porter, *Journal*, 2:1–2.

[62]The manuscript leaves in the addition to the Gansevoort-Lansing Collection reveal such spellings as "Kori Kori," "Hapaa," "Tipii," and "Faaua" (for
Fayaway); see John Bryant, "Melville, 'Little Henry,' and the Process of Composition: A Peep at the *Typee* Fragment," *Melville Society Extracts*, no. 67 (1986),
1–4.

name"—of the natives in the eyes of the whites (it is significant that Melville uses Porter's spelling rather than the more widely accepted "Taipii"), and in *Omoo* a name of the narrator. Melville's use and abuse of Marquesan helps to illustrate the dissemination of linguistic meaning, and by contrast, to expose Tommo's overly strict adherence to the questionable terminology of the narratives.

For Tommo and for the white narrators he typifies, language is one of the vehicles for the search for meaning. The narratives of facts are a re-presentation and a re-creation of the voyages of discovery, but their prescribed linguistic forms undermine the reality of the discovery. Rather than reflecting the adventure of the experience, Tommo's narrative alienates him further from the natives and Typee life and brings him closer to the civilized society that is its antithesis. In the Preface Tommo explains that he has often received psychological comfort—the succor of the port that Bulkington spurns—from telling his story: "Yet, notwithstanding the familiarity of sailors with all sorts of curious adventure, the incidents recorded in the following pages have often served, when 'spun as a yarn,' not only to relieve the weariness of many a night-watch at sea, but to excite the warmest sympathies of the author's shipmates" (xiii). By placing his narrative in the tradition of the narratives he cites, moreover, Tommo achieves a similar end: entering into the narrative tradition gives Tommo a sense of belonging to the company of sailors once again, a sense of community that his ideology precluded in Typee.

Melville's use of the narratives is quite another matter, for he represents the forms and ideas of the narratives, not to place himself in their tradition (except to sell the book to John Murray), but to subvert that tradition. Melville therefore parodies not only the content but also the style and structure of the narratives.[63] Both missionaries and sailors evince a preoccupation with novelty, so Tommo must describe the cultivation of bread-fruit and the making of tappa. "But, as I believe that no

---

[63]See Janet Giltrow, "Structure in Herman Melville's Early Narratives," *American Literature* 52 (1980): 18–32.

description of its [tappa's] manufacture has ever been given," Tommo begins—but of course everyone has given a description of it. Chapter 31 in miniature and *Typee* as a whole mock the jumbled, disorganized structure the narrators seem "to string together, without any attempt at order, a few odds and ends of things not hitherto mentioned" (226). Melville's insertion of this chapter directly amid the most suspenseful part of Tommo's narrative parodies as well the tendency clumsily to insert inane discursive passages to milk the melodrama. Ellis— describing a journey between islands when he got caught in a small canoe during a storm, fearing that this is the end, piously preparing to meet his maker—interrupts the narrative to give a brief history of the sighting of waterspouts.[64]

In general, Melville re-presents through Tommo the narratives of white encounters with natives in a way that exposes their absurdity, their contradictions, their lack of meaning. He begins with the word "savage," juxtaposes it with its opposite, "civilized," and shows that they are basically the same. Then he shows that both are meaningless and that this self-contradictory meaninglessness extends to "progress," "primitive," and even "truth" itself. Meanwhile all claims to factuality of the narratives have been effaced. Melville's subversive rewriting thus does far more than merely borrow from his sources; I do not believe that it is inaccurate or ahistorical to say that *Typee*, both in specific passages and as a whole, deconstructs Melville's sources.

A brief example of this process in miniature. Stewart describes his arrival at Nukuheva and his first encounter with the natives there:

> While yet under way, two or three canoes were seen paddling towards us from the fishing grounds, near the sea, and others from the centre of the bay: and we had scarce let go our anchor, before scores of both sexes came swimming in all directions from the shore, soon surrounding the ship, sporting and blowing like so many porpoises. They were all received on board; and we quickly had noise and confusion in abundance. Many of

[64]Ellis, *Polynesian Researches*, 2:227–34.

them, both men and women, were entirely naked, though most
of the latter brought with them a *pau* or *kihei* (petticoat or mantle) tied up in leaves or native cloth, and elevated on a short
stick, which they held above their heads with one hand, while
they swam with the other. Till they gained the deck, however,
and had time to make their toilette there, they all stood à la
Venus de Medici—an attitude which many, from an entire defi-
ciency in their wardrobe on this aquatic excursion, were obliged
to retain. I should think the number thus on board amounted to
at least one hundred and fifty, or two hundred.[65]

Melville's re-creation of this scene through Tommo's narrative
(14–15) concentrates upon the words and phrases most indicative of Stewart's biases, expands them, and exposes the conceptual problems in the text. Melville's rewriting shows, first, Stewart's preoccupation with the native women: although he says
that the natives were of both sexes, he describes exclusively the
women. In Melville, the narrator mentions only the women,
with whom he becomes increasingly captivated, until the scene
ends in "riot and debauchery," far different, though truer to
the white's inner feeling, than the original's distanced last line.
Melville, in short, exposes a veiled lust in Stewart's repetitious
mention of the naked native women. Stewart also veils his recognition of the women's sexuality behind the image of Venus,
as if nudity could only be a quality of objects of art, not the
flesh and blood of living women. Melville's narrator takes this
further: Tommo "fancies" the women "nymphs," "mermaids,"
and "sylphs"—extending the description beyond art to fairy
tale or myth.

Stewart's perception of the natives moves simultaneously in
the opposite direction, as he first sees the natives "sporting and
blowing like so many porpoises." Melville, exaggerating this
tendency as well, shows Tommo making not a simile but an
error in perception: "at first I imagined it to be produced by a
shoal of fish sporting on the surface." Even when told that it is
really a "shoal of 'whihenies,'" Tommo continues to refer to

[65]Stewart, *Visit*, 1:226–27. The parallel was first noticed by Russell Thomas,
"Yarn for Melville's *Typee*," *Philological Quarterly* 15 (1936): 16–29.

them as "creatures" or as "mermaids," half-human and half-animal. Thus Melville recognizes Stewart's tendency to "fancy" or "imagine" the natives in inhuman, unrealistic, and conflicting terms, as both animal and myth. Melville heightens these racist preconceptions, exposing their absurdity, and indicates that Stewart's misperception of the natives is based upon sexual repression—if the native women are porpoises or statues, one does not have to consider their sexuality. By re-presenting Stewart's narrative deconstructively, Melville shakes the ideological foundations of his source's language.

Thus does Melville subvert Tommo's and the whites' claims for narrative truth or factuality. Indeed, *Typee* includes many such claims: the preface, the appendix, the sequel, the specific historical references, the strict superficial adherence to the conventions of the narratives of facts—all claim to substantiate the truth of the narrative, a truth Melville slyly asserts in his letters. This is perhaps Melville's most effective joke in *Typee*, a joke he plays out completely on his publishers and his audience. His technique gives full reign to his humor; incongruity, exaggeration, sexual innuendo, and satiric irony are all parts of Melville's subversion of the historical narratives. In the scene in chapter 2 taken from Stewart, we laugh first at Tommo's silly imagination, then at his prudish distance as the orgy breaks out on board. When we compare Melville's account to Stewart's, the comedy becomes clearer, for we can then perceive the satiric butt of Melville's barbs. The stock comic situation—a man totally out of place yet trying in vain to apply his own values to the situation—is one Twain will use to great effect in *A Connecticut Yankee*. In Melville as in Twain, at the heart of the joke is wordplay, for Tommo's (or Stewart's) language is simply incongruent.

Melville's humor, partly a relief from what might otherwise be an overly serious polemic against the evils of progress, rarely lacks a serious message even in the most humorous scenes. Beneath Tommo's comic description of his first sight of the native women lies his hypocrisy and prejudice, and Melville ends the chapter lamenting "the poor savages" when they are "brought into contaminating contact with the white man" (15).

Tommo does not realize that he, too, is as much a cause of the natives' destruction. His condescending narrative, which labels the natives "poor savages" who are "unsophisticated and confiding," does as much as the sailors' promiscuity to foster the "contaminating contact." The whites' narration of encounters with the South Seas natives, Melville demonstrates through his deconstructive tactics, is a stumbling block to a truer perception of the natives and thereby promotes racism.[66] Recognizing the deception of such language, Melville presents Tommo's "anxious desire to speak the unvarnished truth [that] will gain for him the confidence of his readers." Narrative "truth" is the final con-game, and Tommo prefigures in a small way the Confidence-Man. The final tension in the novel, then, is between Tommo's words and the Typee's world, between *Typee* and Typee, between the narrative and the facts.

The dynamics of facts and narrative in *Typee* thus encompass more than an application of source to the narrative: it forms a vital part of the narrative itself. Through Tommo Melville calls into question not only the naive and indiscriminate application of the historical facts Tommo and Western civilization have founded their beliefs upon, but also the historicity of the facts themselves. The history of the white culture's exploration, grounded in the dubious concepts of progress and primitivism, is itself fiction, every bit as much a romantic tale as Tommo's *Typee*. Melville's *Typee*, however, by exposing these fictions is thus more than a fiction drawn from history; it is an account of the collective fiction that is the white culture's history and a plea for a tolerant, relativistic perception of this historical reality.

[66]On racism and narration see Joyce Sparer Adler, *War in Melville's Imagination* (New York, 1981), 111–32.

3

Omoo

Comparative Mythology
of the Religious Elite

"THOUGH I wrote the Gospels in this century, I should die in the gutter," Melville told Hawthorne in 1851, when he was well on his way toward literary obscurity.[1] Although Melville's reputation today exposes what may be a wry self-mockery in this statement, his second "Gospel," *Omoo*, often remains slighted. Critical appraisals of the book have typically included condemnation of it as an incoherent and defective narrative and condescending recognition of it as a straightforward and sunny autobiography. Even Edwin M. Eigner and William B. Dillingham, who present detailed analyses of the novel, call attention to its "digressive" narrative, its "light" tone, and its lack of compelling ideas.[2] It is as if, in the canon of works sacred to Melville scholars, *Omoo* holds a peculiar place as the one novel completely simple and profane: not harboring "the

[1]*Letters*, 129.

[2]Eigner, "The Romantic Unity of Melville's *Omoo*," *Philological Quarterly* 46 (1967): 95–108, describes the psychological development of the narrator, particularly concerning his relationship to society; Eigner, though, concedes that the *Julia* and Tahiti themes are "digressions" (although they comprise half the book) and that the ending is "contrived." Dillingham, *Artist*, 79–102, focuses on the relationship with Long Ghost and shows the narrator in the end learning the responsibility of work.

highest truth, shoreless, indefinite as God,"[3] but nevertheless
(or therefore) a welcome relief for the scholar toiling over Melville's usual inordinate complexity and intellectuality.

Read thus in comparison to other Melville texts or according
to conventional novelistic criteria, *Omoo* does seem to deserve
its reputation as a particularly humorous but inconsequential
work. I believe that the shortcomings of criticism thus far lie
not in failing to evaluate the book according to traditional
categories or in relation to other Melville works, but in failing
to consider the text within the context the book itself suggests:
in the novel Melville refers to a large number of other books,
primarily narratives written by South Seas missionaries such as
William Ellis, Charles S. Stewart, and others. Although the
thorough scholarship of Charles R. Anderson, Harrison Hayford and Walter Blair, and Gordon Roper has demonstrated
how fully Melville made use of the details in these narratives
for *Omoo*'s descriptions and events,[4] one must recognize as well
the extent to which Melville made use of the intellectual content and generic forms of these largely Calvinist narratives.
Only then can one realize that *Omoo*'s peculiarity and its humor
arise from deep, complex issues typical of Melville at his finest.

Just as the narratives of encounters with natives form the
basis of *Typee*'s analysis of progress and primitivism, that is to
say, so the narratives of missionary experiences form the basis
of Melville's analysis in his second novel of the concept of a
religious elite. This latter issue is as well a natural development
from the former, for exploration and the consequent contact
with the natives led not only to a coalescence of the white
society's idea of history but also to an increased study of comparative mythology, to an increased desire or even need to
examine the myth systems of those newly encountered cul-

[3]*Moby-Dick*, 97.

[4]I use only those narratives Melville mentions in the novel and those that
criticism has determined he knew. See in particular Anderson, *South Seas*, 199–
323; Harrison Hayford and Walter Blair, "Introduction" to *Omoo: A Narrative
of Adventures in the South Seas* (New York, 1969), xvii–lii; and Gordon Roper,
"Historical Note" to *Omoo*, ed. Hayford, Parker, and Tanselle (Evanston and
Chicago, 1968). All references to *Omoo* will be to this latter edition and will be
cited parenthetically in the text.

tures. The missionaries Melville read and referred to in *Omoo* were not merely curious about the natives' myths; they felt that they must, for the preservation of Christianity, either refute them as "superstition" or conflate them as decayed forms of a basic Judeo-Christian mythology. Melville, who had observed firsthand the importance of myths in the lives of the natives among whom he had lived, thus had an additional vantage point from which he could form his own comparisons.[5] His perspective also enabled him to see that the consequences of the missionaries' contempt for the natives' religion involved a general destruction of the natives' culture.

I

From youth Melville had grappled with Calvinism, as T. Walter Herbert, Jr., has argued.[6] In *Omoo* his comment upon the Calvinism of the missionaries is particularly vehement: "Tahiti as It Is" viciously attacks the missionaries' hollow faith, political maneuverings, and destruction of the natives. Outraged not only by these abuses but by the religious press back home, which had urged him to expunge offensive passages from *Typee*, Melville strikes out with a vengeance in his second novel. His attack on the missionaries, however, encompasses more than direct criticism, just as his use of the missionaries' narratives encompasses more than borrowing of details. Most obvious, Melville structures his novel along the path, however wandering, described in the missionary narratives. "Paul," as Melville eventually christens his narrator,[7] and his companion Long Ghost clearly echo the missionaries as they rove from

[5]On the issue of acculturation in the novel, see Stephen de Paul, "The Documentary Fiction of Melville's Omoo: The Crossed Grammars of Acculturation," *Criticism* 28 (1986): 51–72.

[6]*"Moby-Dick" and Calvinism: A World Dismantled* (New Brunswick, N.J., 1977). Herbert also examines Melville's quarrel with the missionaries in *Marquesan Encounters*.

[7]Because the term "narrator" is awkward, "Typee" is confusing, and "Omoo" may be inaccurate, I use the term the narrator gives himself upon leaving Tahiti for Imeeo (199).

settlement to settlement and from island to island, following no strict itinerary, but stopping where they find people to talk to, meals to share, places to stay. As Hayford and Blair indicate, Melville's characters follow the course particularly of Ellis, who records his wanderings to and around Tahiti and Imeeo in his *Polynesian Researches*.[8] Melville's title gives further evidence of this generic similarity: "The title of the work," Melville says in the Preface, "is borrowed from the dialect of the Marquesas Islands, where, among other uses, the word signifies a rover, or rather, a person wandering from one island to another, like some of the natives, known among their countrymen as 'Taboo kannakers'" (xiv). That is to say, an "omoo" is a "sacred man" ("Taboo kannaker") who wanders about the islands—a missionary—and *Omoo* is the narrative of such sacred wanderings.

This generic echo further clarifies as well the insidious humor in Melville's characterization, for his protagonists are typical of many of the South Seas vagabonds found in the missionaries' narratives; in fact, they are the group of white men whom the missionaries most abhor and condemn for their totally profane behavior. Ellis again and again attacks these sailors' debauched morals and their selfishness; Stewart calls them "wanderers on the earth, the very dregs and outcasts of society."[9] Melville not only parallels their acts to those of the missionaries, he obviously enjoys his protagonists' unmissionarylike, reckless immorality. Moreover, in a comic travesty of the missionaries, Melville portrays Long Ghost and Paul as sacred wanderers. The natives refer to "Peter" (as Long Ghost calls himself at one point) as "maitai," which means both "good" and "sacred";[10] to Paul he is "an absolute godsend" (12), whose name evokes the Holy Spirit. Indeed, "spirit" is the word Mel-

---

[8]For example, see George Bennet and Daniel Tyerman, *Journal of Voyages and Travels*, ed. James Montgomery (Boston, 1832), 1:47–238. For a summary of the missions see Wright and Fry, *Puritans*; and Gunson, *Messengers*. Anderson, *South Seas*, 297, notes Ellis's wanderings; Hayford's and Blair's footnotes fully record Melville's borrowings from Ellis's *Polynesian Researches*.

[9]*Journal*, 160.

[10]Jean Charles Buschmann, *Aperçu de la langue des Isles Marquises et de la langue taïtienne* (Berlin, 1843), 108, lists the primary meanings of "maitai" as *bon* and *saint*.

ville most often uses, ironically and punningly, to describe "the pious youth," who is constantly "saying masses" while working for the planters (228—typical of Melville's irony). Melville's narrator, whose name also has apostolic associations, is likewise "something of a 'mickonaree' [missionary]" (164), as one of the natives describes him. Of the round-robin Paul concocts, "some present, very justly regarding it as an uncommon literary production, had been anticipating all sorts of miracles therefrom" (79)—closely resembling the many occasions when the missionaries produce some writing for the natives, who immediately regard it as a divine miracle. It is little wonder, then, that when Long Ghost tells Paul of his plans for settling in Tamai, he describes a comic version of the process, from teaching English to establishing industry, typically adopted by the missionaries (245).[11]

By defining his vagabonds in terms that parody the missionaries, Melville develops not only a calculated affront to them, but also a challenge to their sense of spiritual superiority. Their narratives inflate their own mission to heroic and even cosmic proportions: Ellis, adopting a typical millennial tone, calls the conversion of the Tahitians one of the greatest events in the history of mankind.[12] A similar arrogance marked their relations with the natives, for as W. S. Ruschenberger states, "The missionaries are placed in a position entirely above the everyday concerns of this world, and have only to declare their wants to a fiscal agent of the Board of Missions to have them supplied. . . . This arrangement is defective, because it abstracts them too much from the world."[13] Melville's protagonists also consider themselves intellectually, morally, and socially superi-

[11]Ellis, *Polynesian Researches*, 1:11, lists among the missionaries' goals "the progress of civilization"; see Wright and Fry, *Puritans*, and Gunson, *Messengers*, for a summary of what this progress involved.

[12]Ellis, *Polynesian Researches*, 1:9–12, and 3:300; Michael Russell, *Polynesia* (Edinburgh, 1842), 426–31; and John Williams, *A Narrative of Missionary Enterprises to the South Sea Islands* (London, 1842), v. De Paul, "Documentary," 52, says, "The authority of the 'facts' functions generally in Melville's South Seas writings as a pervasive ethnocentric voice of certitude attempting to peg with decidedly Western terms the elusive character of the Polynesian world."

[13]*Narrative of a Voyage Round the World* (London, 1838), 2:343.

or to both the natives and the crew; throughout the novel they feign illness to avoid work, until finally they seek a sinecure in Queen Pomaree's court. Particularly in these instances they resemble the missionaries, who always ingratiated themselves with the Pomaree in power, got food, land, servants, and protection from the ruler, and only then extended their mission to the common people.[14] Such egoism might perhaps be justified, if the mission were indeed sacred; however, Melville, in pointing out these profane similarities, diminishes the importance, seriousness, and sanctity of the mission.

Melville's likely source for this mocking deflation was the Reverend Michael Russell's *Polynesia*, the chief history of the mission to the South Seas. Russell tells of two pairs of suspect wanderers whose actions tended to undermine the authority of the Polynesian mission. In the first case, "two individuals, laying claim to plenary inspiration, announced themselves as the sole medium of communication with heaven; and under the influence of fanaticism or fraud . . . produced in some of the stations great irregularities, and a very general defection from evangelical truth." In the second, "the missionaries observed two English sailors, who boasted that they had in their train no fewer than two hundred proselytes," whom they had comically "converted" and baptized—all without the natives understanding anything.[15] Melville's protagonists, at once heightened parodic versions of the heretics of the first passage and the sailor-"missionaries" of the second, expose the often absurd ineffectuality and unjustified optimism of the historical missionaries. Through their efforts, Melville says, "any thing like a permanent religious impression, is seldom or never produced. . . . [However,] all this was deemed the evidence of the power of the Most High; and, as such, was heralded abroad" (174–75).

Melville's method in these appropriations—joking, to be

---

[14]See F. W. Beechey, *Narrative of a Voyage to the Pacific and Beering's Strait* (1831; rpt. Amsterdam and New York, 1968); and Kotzebue, *New Voyage*. See Dillingham's description (*Artist*) of Long Ghost's and Paul's avoidance of work.

[15]Russell, *Polynesia*, 176–77 and 275n.

sure, but with serious points to his satiric barbs—involves comparing the missionaries not only to those white men they abhor, but also to another group of sacred wanderers found in the missionaries' narratives. Melville's protagonists, who are "like some of the natives" (xiv), closely resemble the most common group of Tahitian sacred wanderers, the Areoi Society.[16] James Wilson describes them as "constantly wandering about from island to island. They are the finest people we have seen. . . . Wherever they go they exercise power to seize what they want from the inhabitants. . . . They never work; live by plunder; yet are highly respected, as none but persons of rank are admitted among them."[17] This description, reiterated in passages in Ellis, Russell, and George Bennet and Daniel Tyerman, accurately applies to Long Ghost and Paul, who on Tahiti and Imeeo go from settlement to settlement, feast to feast, living not merely off the land but off the natives' generosity. Moreover, the areois are also "numbered among the inferior deities" and command "a corresponding degree of veneration by many of the vulgar and innocent."[18] Russell explains:

> Perhaps it was owing in no small degree to the solemnity now described, as well as to the legend which respects the origin of their institution, that the areois passed their lives, esteemed by the people as a superior order of beings, closely allied to the gods, and deriving from them a license to perpetuate the various enormities which disgraced their whole body. Free from labour and care they roved from island to island, supported by their chiefs, or feasting on the plunder taken from the grounds of the poor husbandmen.[19]

Thus they can be wanderers *because* they are sacred: like Long Ghost and Paul, they receive tithes from the chiefs and the populace. "Prompted by the direct inspiration of the gods,"[20] the areois are the Tahitian version of the elect of God.

[16]Melville mentions them on 125.
[17]Wilson, *A Missionary Voyage to the Southern Pacific Ocean* (1799; rpt. Graz, Austria, 1966), 174.
[18]Ellis, *Polynesian Researches*, 1:183 and 189.
[19]Russell, *Polynesia*, 88; see also Ellis, *Polynesian Researches*, 1:189.
[20]Russell, *Polynesia*, 87.

Most observers note that the areois' religious status is signaled by their outlandish dress, which Russell says indicates divine possession. Long Ghost in his rura, boots, and panama hat, and Paul in his blue-and-red suit, turban, and sandals—not clerical collars but functional equivalents—seem to be similarly possessed. More important are the areois' habits of drinking, feasting, playing pranks, and having promiscuous sex.[21] The missionaries, of course, compare the areois' feasting to the descent of a swarm of locusts, condemn their "wild, disorderly behaviour," their "drollery," and their "abusive merriment which they carried with them," and stress, without directly citing their sexual practices, their "lewdness."[22] Perhaps most typically, Ellis describes the society: "Many of the regulations of this body, and the practices to which they were addicted, cannot be made public without violence to every feeling of propriety. . . . In some of their meetings they appear to have placed their invention on the rack, to discover the worst pollutions, of which it was possible for man to be guilty, and have striven to outdo each other in the most revolting practices."[23] Indeed, the areois often put on highly obscene dramatic productions, for sex was an integral part of their religious rites. As Russell points out, their elect status gave them the right publicly and ceremonially to perform acts which anticipated the sexual "Elysium which their mythology taught them to believe was provided in a future state of existence, for persons so distinguished by the favour of heaven." Sex was moreover connected to spiritual possession: the Tahitian word for the Spirit also means "genitals." [24] In their own inverted way, the areois too serve as missionaries, in Ellis's words, "travelling from island to island, and from one district to another, exhibiting their pantomimes and spreading a moral contagion throughout society."[25]

[21]Wilson, *Missionary*, 181 and 349; and Bennet and Tyerman, *Journal*, 1:239.

[22]Ellis, *Polynesian Researches*, 1:182.

[23]Ibid., 1:192.

[24]Russell, *Polynesia*, 88. Wilson, *Missionary*, 343, says that "spirit" in Tahitian is "Taroa, Manoo te Hooa"; Buschmann, *Aperçu*, 107, says that "*houa*" means "*les genitoires.*"

[25]Ellis, *Polynesian Researches*, 1:185.

Melville appropriates these characteristics wholesale into his own "missionaries," who most enjoy those native practices that the historical missionaries most censure. He describes Long Ghost showing "true piety" only when "getting tipsy" (274), when blessing a pig he is about to consume (282), and when playing "capers" or "pranks" (chap. 11). Part of his and Paul's capering, like the areois', is simultaneously sexual and religious: for example, they desire to see the hevar at Tamai not only to see true paganism but also because there "dwelt the most beautiful and unsophisticated [i.e., willing] women in the entire Society group" (234). The doctor—as both his names, Long Ghost and Peter, indicate[26]—is a particularly phallic character, but also religiously so: his seven-day suit for Loo is a parodic creation myth (293). He is a character particularly calculated to offend the sensibilities of Calvinist missionaries as much as the historical areois offended them.

The lawless exploits of *Omoo*'s protagonists, when viewed in this context, thus become more consistent and significant: the idea of the sacred wanderer found in the missionaries' narratives both heightens the parodic humor and unifies the actions and descriptions in the novel. At the center of the idea is the apparently enigmatic term "omoo"—signifying both the characters and the narrative—which also has its source in the missionary narratives. Melville's prefatory definition of the term is spurious, Hayford and Blair point out, for no such word seems to exist in Marquesan.[27] But "omoo" does have a place in the vocabulary of the Tahitian sacred wanderers. Bennet and Tyerman describe the areois as follows: "During the former period [before the advent of the missionaries], there was a description of persons, called *Papaiaomu(Areois)*, a kind of strolling players, who went about the country, from one chief's district to another, reciting stories and singing songs for the entertainment of the people. These stories were called *Aamu*."[28]

[26]Edward H. Rosenberry, *Melville and the Comic Spirit* (Cambridge, Mass., 1955), 23–24, includes an account of Long Ghost as "amorous trickster," as part of his analysis, 23–26, of *Omoo*'s sexual humor. Melville likewise associates his narrator with a phallic pun, as noted by Miller, *Melville*, 134.

[27]Hayford and Blair, "Explanatory Notes" to *Omoo*, 347.

[28]Bennet and Tyerman, *Journal*, 1:69.

Both "*Papaiaomu*" and "*Aamu*" signify myth, the songs and stories of the Polynesians, and the areois are the mythmakers. Whether "*-omu*" or "*-aamu*" (or omoo), at the core of the Tahitian concept of the sacred is the basic phoneme "*mu*," or myth. Combined with other Polynesian vocabulary, "*mu*" yields these results: "*Papai-a-o-mu*" means "writing-of-the-myth" and "*Aamu*" means "here-is-the-myth," according to linguists contemporary to Melville.[29] Both terms, then, indicate that the areois are the presenters of their version of the sacred, just as the missionaries claim to be. Melville, in choosing a Tahitian title which translates as *The Myth*, thus conflates his protagonists with others who partake of and narrate their involvement with the sacred. Yet the result is not to say that Long Ghost and Paul are, like the missionaries or even the areois, genuine spiritual figures, but rather to say that the missionaries, like Long Ghost and Paul, may be no more than parodies of that which they claim to be.

II

The structure of *Omoo* also reinforces this comic reduction of the sacred to the profane, for Melville places his "sacred" wanderers into a profane world dominated by secular concerns and political relationships. Power and superiority are the motivations for virtually all actions; nature is dark, chaotic, almost Hobbesian in its hostility and struggles—definitely not the world most critics of the novel describe. Melville carefully sets Long Ghost's and Paul's wandering within the historical context of the imperialistic struggle of France and Britain for the control of Tahiti, and more generally the Western powers' attempts to subdue and colonize the South Seas.[30] As the *Julia* sights Tahiti, the crew is struck by the *Reine Blanche*, the *White Queen*, "which loomed up black and large; her two rows of teeth proclaiming a frigate" (69). Melville later reveals that the osten-

[29]Buschmann, *Aperçu*, 102 and 113; and Mosblech, *Vocabulaire*, 1.
[30]See Strauss, *Americans*, chap. 6.

sible religious reason for the intrusion of this ominous emblem
of imperialist politics, to protect the French priests, is but a
pretext for the seizure of the island (122–24). Melville's excla-
mation, "what is the welfare of a spot like Tahiti, to the mighty
interests of France and England!" (124), reiterates the crew's
impression of being dwarfed by the huge impersonal machin-
ery of the imperialist powers. In their short incarceration in the
frigate, the crew experience at firsthand the workings of this
war-machine, from its exterior calculated to intimidate to its
interior of brutal force. It is indeed a machine, "a complex
arrangement of the pulley, lever and screw" (109), in which
men are bolted in irons, starved, flogged "without mercy," and
pressed into service—all motivated by a politics of self-interest.

On a smaller scale, Melville presents a similar self-interest
motivating the characters' interrelations. Like the *Reine Blanche*
the *Julia* itself is a political state in miniature, as Paul's first
impressions of the "ill state of affairs" (5) on board show.[31]
Behind all actions on board are the interests of those in power:
for example, Paul realizes that he was saved from the Typees
not out of any "great compassion for me . . . [but only] to have
the benefit of my services as soon as possible" (6, 140); and the
others are kept on short rations to gratify the pocketbook of
the owners, rations "purchased by the owners at an auction sale
of condemned navy stores" (14) at that. Internally, the authorities are concerned during the mutiny only with retaining
command and profits, while externally, the maneuverings in
Papeetee harbor are designed to retain the captain's command.
Indeed, the compulsion for authority, for one man to hold
power over another, rules most of the actions on board, though
it surfaces most clearly in incidents such as Jermin's fight with
Beauty (16–18) and Bembo's attempt to destroy the ship (88–
90). Jermin, the most physically powerful man on board, must
rescue the ship from Bembo; but even Jermin is ruled by Captain Guy. "Miss Guy"—superficially weak, cowardly, ineffectual—is firmly in control of the affairs of the ship, for he is the

[31]"Julia" is the feminine form of "Julius"; Paul's birth into this profane political world is somewhat Caesarian.

consummate politician. To get Paul to sign on, he first gets him drunk; to save his authority when the crew's mutiny and his own illness threaten to make him a commander of an un-manned ship, Guy concocts a complex yet effective plan.

All is politics, too, on Tahiti, which is ruled by the desire for profit: Johnson uses his collusion with Wilson to pad his fees (133); the missionary ends his sermon with a plea for money (174); and even Kooloo jilts Paul for another sailor "quite flush from a lucky whaling-cruise" (158).[32] At the root of this avarice is the conviction that property can be used for political power. The historical missionaries strove to create in the natives the desire for European goods ostensibly to force them to work and thereby rid them of their "indolence" and its attending sins, a process that also enabled the missionaries to control the natives.[33] But as Melville states (chap. 49), this ploy failed and fostered the destruction of the Tahitians. A second conse-quence of the missionaries' policies is a social class system based upon economics, as is evident from the very first glance at Tahiti in chapter 27: "The village of Papeetee struck us all very pleasantly," Melville says ironically. "Lying in a semicircle around the bay, the tasteful mansions of the chiefs and foreign residents impart an air of tropical elegance. . . . The squalid huts of the common people are out of sight, and there is noth-ing to mar the prospect" (101).

Those in authority on the *Julia* and on Tahiti codify their power through law, which the "Farce of the Affidavits" (145) shows to favor them at the expense of the common people: it threatens the latter with extradition, imprisons them, black-balls them, and finally disowns them—all because they refuse to bow to the authority of the men in power. The relations on board are correspondingly fraught with violence, clandestine plots, collusion, and moral decay. Historically, Tahiti was the missionaries' grand experiment in Mosaic law: acting as "ad-visors" to the chiefs, in 1819 they instituted laws that would,

[32]On commercialism in the historical Tahiti see Ellis, *Polynesian Researches*, 2:174 and 210.
[33]Melville refers to this process in chap. 49, which is also evident in *Typee* (see the previous chapter).

they said, "tend to the good of the community, and the stability of [King Pomaree II's] government."[34] That is to say, the laws were used to secure political power in the hands of the ruling class, through whom the missionaries carried out their will and from whom they received a sinecure. Melville demonstrates that these laws, based on the Ten Commandments and covering virtually every aspect of the natives' lives, create a sense of constriction and consequent desperation in all the characters in the novel. Politics, the law, is everywhere, and everywhere it is repressive.

The profane world of *Omoo* is accordingly a Darwinian struggle without the corresponding evolution. Even on this insular Tahiti, Melville presents nature—and human nature—as "the universal cannibalism of the sea; all whose creatures prey upon each other, carrying on eternal war since the world began."[35] In the Calabooza Paul and his fellow sailors, who have been preyed upon by the authorities, are themselves "driven to acts of marauding," stealing from the natives, who "had little enough for themselves" (197). Yet those naturally selected to survive are quite the opposite of a higher species: the "fittest" here include the shrewdly degenerate, such as Guy; the viciously powerful, such as Jermin; and the "unprincipled and dissipated," such as Wilson. Moreover, everyone seems to be physically debilitated, the crew from malnutrition and scurvy, the natives from venereal disease and Fa-Fa. Even the ship itself "was in a most dilapidated condition; but in the forecastle it looked like the hollow of an old tree going to decay" (39). "Decay" is a key term describing the world of *Omoo*, and more acutely the Tahitians themselves. "Far worse off now, than formerly," they and their civilization are dying, Melville laments poignantly (chap. 49). Nor is any hope to be placed in the white society on the islands, for it brings not betterment but further corruption.

By including the chapter "The Coral Islands" (chap. 17), Melville calls attention to this issue of evolution, for the contro-

[34]Ellis, *Polynesian Researches*, 3:105.
[35]*Moby-Dick*, 235–36.

versy over coral island formation was the primary pier from
which Darwin launched his career.[36] Melville has a short and
seemingly innocuous passage on the subject:

> The origin of the entire group is generally ascribed to the
> coral insect.
> According to some naturalists, this wonderful little creature,
> commencing its erections at the bottom of the sea, after the
> lapse of centuries, carries them up to the surface, where its
> labors cease. Here, the inequalities of the coral collect all float-
> ing bodies; forming, after a time, a soil, in which the seeds
> carried thither by birds, germinate, and cover the whole with
> vegetation. Here and there, all over this archipelago, number-
> less naked, detached coral formations are seen, just emerging,
> as it were, from the ocean. These would appear to be islands in
> the very process of creation—at any rate, one involuntarily con-
> cludes so, on beholding them. (62–63)

This passage condenses a huge body of conflicting arguments,
which are present in virtually every narrative that Melville
mentions in the book and which center upon whether or not
the islands could be "in the very process of creation."[37] If so, it
would argue for an evolution of geology that would negate (or
at least modify) the Christian concept of creation. The missionary John Williams roundly attacks the theory by saying that
there is no evidence of "animal agency at work adequate to the
formation of a reef or island of any extent."[38] God is not a coral
insect. In the last line of the passage Melville, more a naturalist
than a missionary, stresses the "involuntary" or natural conclusion that new islands are indeed being created. The natural
world of *Omoo* is evolving just as the world of *Moby-Dick*, in
which "Pip saw the multitudinous, God-omnipresent, coral insects, that out of the firmament of waters heaved the colossal
orbs."[39] To Melville god is in a very real way a coral insect.

[36]Melville was familiar with Darwin from his reading of *The Voyage of the
Beagle* (1845; rpt. New York, 1909); Darwin discusses the formation of coral
islands (491–97).
[37]E.g., Russell, *Polynesia*, 23–29.
[38]Williams, *Narrative*, 9.
[39]*Moby-Dick*, 347.

To counter such evidence many Christians echoed the position of the protoevolutionist Robert Chambers, who argues that "the chronology of God is not as our chronology. See the patience of waiting evinced in the slow development of the animated kingdoms, throughout the long series of geological ages."[40] These Christians and other chronologers tried to integrate the evidence, gleaned from coral island formation, about the age of the earth and man with the time scheme outlined in the Old Testament, some biblical scholars going to absurd lengths to do so. To use Melville's terms in *Pierre*, they wished to separate chronometricals—God's time scheme—from horologicals—nature's.[41] In *Omoo* Melville comically asserts that the chronometer on the *Julia* "stood stock-still; and by that means, no doubt, the true Greenwich time—at the period of its stopping, at least—was preserved to a second" (61). The biblical time-system, Melville is saying, is irrelevant, inapplicable to the present; but Jermin drunkenly still relies upon his "Dead Reckoning," finds the longitude religiously "by the Rule of Three, or else by special revelation," and generally sees double. Melville thus parodically represents the method of the chronologers, who indeed had to see double to make secular events fit into their sacred time scheme.

To Melville Christian chronology is inapplicable, but he also qualifies the naturalist view of evolution. Describing the *Julia*'s voyage, Melville might as easily be describing the course of history as he sees it; he says, "Forever advancing, we seemed always in the same place, and every day was the former lived over again" (34). Like the life in the Typee valley and the history its Stonehenge reveals, in *Omoo* evolution may occur—islands are formed—but the conditions of life never advance, and the destination is ever "uncertain." Melville's nature of universal cannibalism or universal politics is most accurately characterized as a chaos that defies teleology or form. With everyone at each other's throat, with illness and decay rampant, with little direction or plan to one's life, it is little wonder

---

[40]*Vestiges of the Natural History of Creation*, 2d ed. (New York, 1845), 256.
[41]*Pierre*, 210–15.

that the struggle for survival dominates the characters' minds and actions. "Thus went the world of waters with us" (49), Paul says, an allusion to *Paradise Lost*, Book 3, that brilliantly summarizes Melville's natural world, the inchoate world of total darkness just before God lets there be light. This portrayal heightens the contrast between the profane world and any attempt, however comic, to pursue the sacred; yet at the same time, this all pervasive secularity raises the possibility that any missionary enterprise, however sincere, may be ridiculously futile.

In contradistinction to this profane state of affairs are the few moments in which Paul, like Melville's narrators from Tommo to Ishmael, can lose himself in his "reveries." Recalling the dreamlike descriptions of explorers such as Bougainville, he envisions Tahiti, for example, as a place where "such enchantment . . . breathes over the whole, that it seems a fairy world, all fresh and blooming from the hand of the Creator" (66). Similarly, Ellis first perceives Tahiti as follows: "such has been the effect of the scenery through which I have passed, and the unbroken stillness which has pervaded the whole, that imagination, unrestrained, might easily have induced the delusion, that we were walking on enchanted ground, or passing over fairy lands."[42] To Ellis and the other missionaries such reveries are "delusions," for the Christianized Tahiti is the only genuine object of rapture; that is, the missionaries, like Long Ghost and Paul in reacting against what they perceive as a decadent situation, attempt to realize a romantic, idealistic dream. Melville, by reversing the categorizations of the missionaries, for whom nature represented all that was evil and civilization and Christianity all that was good, thereby gives the lie to the perception of Tahiti as a diabolical wilderness and asserts the possibility that what is truly sacred may be found in nature rather than the Ten Commandments.

The mutiny on board the *Julia* can thus be perceived not simply as a farcical rebellion against "the cruelty and injustice of what Captain Guy seemed bent upon" (73), but also as a

---

[42]Ellis, *Polynesian Researches*, 1:29.

parallel to the missionaries' struggles against profane natural and political structures. Long Ghost and Paul again play the part of parodic spiritual leaders, shepherding their motley flock out of captivity and into the promised land. Melville describes the mutiny, accordingly, as at least partly an attempt to "diffuse the right spirit among the crew" (73), who "had been anticipating all sorts of miracles" (79) from the efforts of Long Ghost and Paul.[43]

By the end of Part One, Melville's protagonists have escaped from the profane world of the *Julia* and in the Calabooza have set up an apolitical, communal society reminiscent of a primitive religious group.[44] In these scenes Melville specifically parodies the religious brotherhood which Christ ordained and which the missionaries attempted to realize. In describing Captain Bob, he recalls the Sermon on the Mount (Matt. 6:31): "Beside, we heartily loved the old gentleman, and could not think of leaving him; so, telling him to give no thought as to the wherewithal we should be clothed and fed, we resolved, by extending and systematizing our foraging operations, to provide for ourselves" (150). Indeed, the Calabooza is literally as a city on a hill; its "dazzling white" color makes it, if not the "light of the world," at least so bright that it "cannot be hid" (Matt. 5:14). Following a similar directive, the members of the crew have decided that "no man can serve two masters" (Matt. 6:24), and thus have abandoned the political authorities to follow not Christ but their own antinomian whims. In doing so, they swear no vows but merely answer Wilson yea or nay (Matt. 6:24). For Long Ghost, Paul, and the crew, the Calabooza is the ideal Christian society—without the Christianity.

Although Paul's and Long Ghost's actions follow closely the example of the missionaries, their purposes here, Melville always reminds us, are highly profane. In one of Melville's most

[43]The biblical Paul was struck blind on the Damascus road as he received his calling; Melville's Paul is struck with a sickness in the forecastle as he is about to begin his mission on board.

[44]A. N. Kaul, *The American Vision: Actual and Ideal Society in Nineteenth-Century Fiction* (New Haven, Conn., 1963), 238, cites Melville in connection with this issue.

fully developed metaphors, the "spirits" they diffuse, in the mutiny and in the Calabooza, are more liquid than sacred. Throughout *Omoo* Melville puns on the word, in each case carefully relating liquor to religion. When, for example, "there was no end to my long comrade's spirits," the natives pronounce him "sacred," but only after he has consumed "a couple of flasks of white brandy" (223). The pun clearly illustrates Melville's profaning of the sacred: the very absurdity of Melville's reduction generally calls into question the possibility of spiritual manifestations and particularly attempts to outrage the teetotaling, prohibitionist missionaries.[45] Melville further complicates this profanation by using "spirits" in its most common signification as "good feelings" or "vivacity" (e.g., 266, 276), a meaning neither religious nor alcoholic but encompassing both. That is, spirit of either kind manifests itself in the feelings and produces an increase in the quality of emotion. This similarity is the underpinning not only of Melville's pun but of his profaning the sacred in *Omoo* as a whole: the sense of vibrancy and exuberance that critics have praised in the novel likely arises from Melville's conviction that missionary zeal is better expressed by a sheer joy in drink, in movement, in play—in life.[46]

In Part Two, Melville repeats the pattern of his protagonists' attempt to escape from the profane world and to pursue their own exuberant whims, for their Calabooza brotherhood collapses as soon as it begins. The very structure of the natural world, even on this insular Tahiti, precludes realizing an apolitical, religious society, just as in *Moby-Dick* Fleece's sermon shows that the "natural woraciousness" of the sharks precludes Christianity. Melville's satire in this part of *Omoo* is likewise directed toward a naive Christianity. Like the crew, the missionaries came to Tahiti to institute a sacred society outside the

[45]Both Wright and Fry, *Puritans*, and Gunson, *Messengers*, extensively discuss the missionaries' opposition, for moral and for political reasons, to "ardent spirits."

[46]Rosenberry, *Comic Spirit*, most fully describes Melville's humor in the novel, but his naive categorizing of the book as comically exaggerated self-portraiture ignores much of the complex resonance in Melville's humor.

profane world: "the missionaries were prompted by a sincere desire for good," Melville says; "but the effect has been lamentable" (183). The "Tahiti as It Is" chapters document this effect, which encompasses the decay of the natives' customs, religion, and environment. To state briefly the change Melville presents: the sacred has become profane. The missionaries have become little more than representatives of the imperialist powers: Wilson the elder, a missionary to whom Melville refers with respect, has given way to Wilson the younger, a "dissipated" British consul whom Melville abhors. The sermon Paul hears (173–74) is accordingly little more than a political diatribe against the "wicked Wee-Wees" and a paean to the glories of "Beretanee," plus a plea for provisions for themselves. From this situation, as from the *Julia*, Long Ghost and Paul escape once again, as they continue to do throughout the remainder of the novel.

At one point in the book, when they reach Tamai, they seem to have completely escaped the profane world of the missionaries, their laws, and their military police. Melville deliberately altered the location of the settlement from its actual place to one on a mountain top at "the very heart of the island" (237) to emphasize its transcendence and centrality.[47] It is also one of the few places where native religious rites are still held. The Tamaians themselves, unlike the politicized Tahitians, are not degenerate but are "much more healthful," "more retiring and modest," "and far fresher and more beautiful" (238). Nowhere do Long Ghost and Paul see evidence of a political structure, although the people do act "in concert" in gathering for the hevar:

> "Ahloo! ahloo!" Every link of the circle is broken; and the girls, deeply breathing, stand perfectly still. They pant hard and fast, a moment or two; and then, just as the deep flush is dying away from their faces, slowly recede, all round. . . . Presently, raising a strange chant, they softly sway themselves, gradually quickening the movement, until, at length, for a few passionate mo-

[47]See Hayford's and Blair's footnotes to this passage, "Explanatory Notes," 410–12.

ments, with throbbing bosoms and glowing cheeks, they abandon themselves to all the spirit of the dance, apparently lost to
every thing around. But soon subsiding again into the same
languid measure, as before, they become motionless; and then,
reeling forward on all sides, their eyes swimming in their heads,
join in one wild chorus, and sink into each other's arms. (241–
42)

The girls' chant "Ahloo! ahloo!" captures succinctly the connection of the sexual and the sacred which is typical of Melville's omoos but anathema to the missionaries, for it means
both "ravish" and "revere,"[48] an ambivalence Melville reinforces by punningly calling the girls "backsliding." The dance
itself amplifies this ambiguity, for at the most orgasmic moment the girls are filled with "all the spirit of the dance." The
orgiastic dance represents the transcendence of earthly restrictions essential to participation in the sacred, reinforced here by
the repeated image of the circle. Tamai, Melville may be indicating, is the primitive realization of a desire present in many
missionaries, however strongly their dogma suppresses it: the
urge to cast off civilization entirely and to participate fully in
the sacred.

The desire cannot be sustained, Melville indicates, for the
missionaries' economic system (in the "Mysterious" chapter)
and police force intrude, and consequently the Hegira—a term
that retrospectively makes Tamai Mecca, the sacred city—begins. The term signifies the start of time, but for Melville's
characters the Hegira is only the beginning of the end, for
their goal is now exclusively and unabashedly profane.[49] In
seeking a post in Pomaree's court they seem to have accepted
the political world and to have cast their lot with the mission-

[48]Mosblech, *Vocabulaire*, 6–7, lists among the meanings of "*alu*" both "*faire la
révérence*" and "*ravir.*" Sexual rituals, in so far as they depict procreation, also
function as mythic representations of the cosmogony, the actors in the ritual
thus emulating the divine creator.

[49]Melville likely learned of Mecca and the Hegira from Rev. George Bush,
The Life of Mohammed (New York, 1831); or Edward Gibbon, *The History of the
Decline and Fall of the Roman Empire* (Paris, 1840), vol. 6. Dorothee M. Finkelstein, *Melville's Orienda* (New Haven, Conn., 1961), 166–67, establishes Melville's knowledge of Bush and Gibbon.

aries they hate, missionaries who likewise tried to ally themselves with the profane rulers in their efforts to promote their
"sacred" mission.[50]

Even this final attempt fails, and Paul decides to leave Long
Ghost and his wandering by making a "covenant" to ship out
on a whaler, the *Leviathan*. Hobbes—of whom Long Ghost
talks (12)—provides a gloss for Paul's final actions. Paul has
come into contact with the very Hobbesian natural world, composed of continual, violent, and selfish struggles for power,
and the antithesis of the sacred. As the solution to the problems
of this world, Paul chooses the *Leviathan*, the highly organized
political system. Hobbes, a notorious opponent of Calvinism,
was often denounced as an atheist, a view Melville's allusion
here supports. The captain of the *Leviathan*, the sovereign, is
not God's representative on earth, but "the man of little faith"
(314), he whom Christ condemns in the Sermon on the Mount
for taking too much thought for the means of his subsistence
(Matt. 6:31). The captain, that is, is the mirror opposite of
Captain Bob, and the ship the mirror of the Calabooza:
whereas the Calabooza attempted to be a sacred association,
the ship is purely profane. In the captain's refusal—for na-
tionalistic reasons—to "believe" (314) in Long Ghost, Melville is
saying that Hobbes's *Leviathan* denies the Holy Spirit, for it
places the religious life of the commonwealth in the hands of a
political leader. Thus Melville reverses Hobbes's argument: in
his Hobbesian world, natural religion is suppressed by the political system and monarchy is atheistic.

At the close of the book Melville's narrator sails off on this
ship of statecraft, "and all before [him] was the wide Pacific"
(316). True, the fallen life of paradise lost lies before him, but
it promises to be in no way pacific. Paul, who has sold his
mentor-wanderer Long Ghost for fifteen pieces of silver, thus
participates in the myth of the Fall, as Melville presents in *Omoo*
a myth in which the sacred becomes profane in virtually every
instance. Through this presentation he again satirizes the mis-

---

[50]Significantly, Long Ghost's and Paul's Medina is Partoowye, which historically was the scene of the missionaries' first overthrow of the pagan idols.

sionaries' narratives, which, while claiming exclusive sacredness for the missionaries, document an ever deeper involvement in profane politics. To Melville this sanctified self-interest
is a ridiculous sham; his hedonistic characters comically exag-
gerate the tendencies of the missionaries until, finally, they can
have virtually no pretense to sacredness.

III

The politicization of Melville's characters' mission thus reinforces his reports of the decay of the historical Tahitian mission. Like Long Ghost's and Paul's, the missionaries' original
goals were relatively apolitical. Williams, for example, cautions
against the "assumption of political authority by the Missionary; for, on the contrary, I am convinced that he should inter-
fere as little as possible."[51] It is this "little possibility," however,
that often became reality, for "whether it be in civil, legal, or
political affairs . . . he should do so solely by his advice and
influence. But there are occasions, especially in newly-formed
missions, where he must step out of his ordinary course."[52]
The missionaries' detractors consequently attacked them for
their virtually dictatorial rule of Tahiti, the missionaries re-
sponding that this "reluctant" involvement results from the
relationship between religion and culture. As Ellis says, "We
considered an improvement of their circumstances and a
change in their occupations necessary to their consistent profession of Christianity."[53] This connection, which echoes
throughout their narratives and which depends upon a culturally biased idea of progress, is to Melville as insidious as the
primitivism of *Typee*.

While the missionaries dismiss or excuse their own political
roles, they condemn just such politicization in other religions.
Their prime example is one Melville presents in his version of a

[51]Williams, *Narrative*, 37.
[52]Ibid.
[53]Ellis, *Polynesian Researches*, 2:251.

missionary's sermon (chap. 45): the Catholics' actions are, they suppose, exclusively and deviously imperialistic. Virtually all other religions—Tahitian, Moslem, Hindu, Greek—the missionaries dismiss as purely political associations masquerading under the cloak of religion. The missionaries use this distinction, moreover, to emphasize their own special status, arguing that because all other religions are subject to the decay of the sacred into the profane, which Christianity avoids, one can reasonably and clearly see God's hand pointing to the true religion.[54] They also accordingly see in all other religions elements of this true faith: to Russell traces of primeval belief indicate a knowledge of Mosaic law in the nations from which the Polynesians stemmed; to James Wilson the supreme gods of Tahiti reflect the Jehovan trinity; and to Ellis the Tahitians are one of the lost tribes of Israel and their religion a decayed and perverted form of the one true faith.[55] In short, the missionaries use the techniques of comparative mythology to defend their own faith by dismissing all others.

In *Omoo*, Melville also uses comparative mythology, but to the opposite end, to show that the missionaries' idea of mythology ignores the fact that they themselves fit into the pattern of decay that they narrate. Melville's position, motivated by his sense of their hypocrisy, could be likened to that of the philosophes of the eighteenth century, whom H. Bruce Franklin has so convincingly identified with Melville.[56] Like Melville, the philosophes—of whom Melville probably learned through his association with the Duyckincks and the Young Americans—read travel literature and thereby fostered their interest in comparative mythology. Their interest had a purpose, however: Bayle analyzes pagan myths to expose their fantastic aberration from "natural morality"; the Deists compare myths to show primitive Christianity to be the essence of all religions;

[54]See Russell, *Polynesia*, 93; Bennet and Tyerman, *Journal*, 1:242 and 2:112; Bush, *Mohammed*, 103; and Ellis, *Polynesian Researches*, 2:10.

[55]Russell, *Polynesia*, 63; and Wilson, *Missionary*, 343.

[56]*The Wake of the Gods* (Stanford, Calif., 1963), 1–16; see also Eigner, "Romantic Unity," 98; and Baird, *Ishmael*.

Voltaire uses Bacchus to attack Moses; Hume analyzes religion to show it all "stupidity" and "ignorance."[57]

Melville's comparative mythology further develops his subversive attack on the missionaries, here using their own tactics against them. Like his references to the areois, two seemingly insignificant allusions to Mohammed and his followers exemplify Melville's comparative purposes. He describes Paul in his "Eastern turban" as "the Bashaw with Two Tails" (236)—the headdress of the Moslem mystics—[58] and his and Long Ghost's journey from Tamai to Partoowye as "The Hegira." Mohammed is also a sacred wanderer, even more than the Hegira indicates, for he sprang from the "roving tribes of Arabia" and, like the areois and Melville's protagonists, plundered as he wandered.[59] Mohammed should also remind one of Melville's initial description of Long Ghost: "His early history, like that of many other heroes, was enveloped in the profoundest obscurity; though he threw out hints of a patrimonial estate, a *nabob* uncle, and an unfortunate affair which sent him a-roving" (12—my emphasis). Among the "many other heroes" the doctor resembles is Mohammed, likewise endowed with a patrimonial estate, a rich uncle, and an unfortunate affair in his background. Early orphaned, he too had an obscure early history and developed a superior personal bearing, largely libidinal, or so his historians note.[60] Melville's references to Mohammed, then, reinforce his references to the areois in satirically identifying the missionaries with a group they explicitly condemn as "superstitious" or "fanatical."

The number and extent of these identifications—vagabond

---

[57]Burton Feldman and Robert Richardson, eds., *The Rise of Modern Mythology, 1680–1860* (Bloomington, Ind., 1972), 20; Frank Manuel, *The Eighteenth Century Confronts the Gods* (Cambridge, Mass., 1959), 60; Richard Chase, *Quest for Myth* (Baton Rouge, La., 1949), 13; and Peter Gay, *The Rise of Modern Paganism* (New York, 1967), 20.

[58]Mircea Eliade, *Shamanism*, trans. Willard Trask (1951; rpt. Princeton, N.J., 1964), 402.

[59]Bush, *Mohammed*, 18; and Gibbon, *Decline and Fall*, 6:184–88.

[60]Gibbon, *Decline and Fall*, 6:197–99; on Mohammed's sexuality see: Gibbon, *Decline and Fall*, 6:235; Bush, *Mohammed*, 136 and 161; and Pierre Bayle, *A Historical and Critical Dictionary* (London, 1710), 3:2100.

with missionary with areoi with Mohammed—tends to point
the reader away from the specific attacks Melville makes upon
the missionaries, I believe, and toward a more general portrayal and analysis of the idea of a religious elite. Melville's
deflation of the Tahitian mission is but one aspect of his comparative mythology in *Omoo*, just as the narratives provide a
springboard for his analysis of progress and primitivism in
Typee. The central figure in the myth of the religious elite is
one whom twentieth-century comparative mythologists have
labeled trickster or shaman. Paul Radin characterizes him as "a
hero who is always wandering, who is always hungry, who is
not guided by normal conceptions of good or evil, who is either
playing tricks on people or having them played on him and
who is highly sexed."[61] Like Melville's figures, too, he is often a
comic character who, in satirizing his society, casts off traditional bounds and borders. Long Ghost and Paul—and Melville—in their satiric contempt for society as it is, wander ever
farther from its borders, Long Ghost and Paul toward Tamai,
and Melville toward *The Confidence-Man* and the silence beyond
it, in which he worked, ironically enough, in that institution of
borders, the customhouse.

More important to the trickster or shaman, however, are his
spiritual characteristics. Like Melville's "couple of necro-
mancers" (37), he is often associated with the manipulation of
death and called a "ghost" or "spirit"—the two terms Melville
most often uses to describe the doctor, whose bony frame resembles the skeleton costume of some shamans.[62] Long Ghost
is literally, in one of Melville's most prescient puns, a medicine
man, but more a shamanic doctor than a physician, as he, for
example, induces a trance by taking drugs (chap. 35). Whatever the outward manifestations, a shaman (whether genuine
or sham) is defined primarily by his ability to reach and sustain
a state of religious ecstasy.[63] This characteristic of the religious
elite permeates *Omoo*, for in their appetites, their wandering

[61]*The Trickster* (London, 1956), 155.
[62]Eliade, *Shamanism*, 158–60.
[63]Ibid., 4.

search for a purer experience, in virtually every aspect of their actions, Long Ghost and Paul show this pursuit of ecstasy, this sense of exuberance that the novel's critics often laud. Whether labeled omoos or tricksters or shamans, Melville's protagonists follow the wandering path of the religious elite; but "shaman," calling up an association with "sham" (or trickster in its negative sense), captures the morally ambiguous nature of these characters.

Melville's term "Omoo" nevertheless participates appropriately in this same complex comparative mythology. Melville's word, lifted from Bennet and Tyerman, is, however, more than obscure Polynesian etymology. Erich Kahler traces the etymology of "myth" in the following:

> The Greek word *mythos*, most etymologists believe, goes back to *mü, mu*, which imitates an elementary sound such as the lowing of cattle, the growl of beasts or of thunder, and originally meant inarticulate sounding of all kinds: bellowing, booming, roaring (Lat. *mugire*, Fr. *mugir*), murmuring, humming, rumbling, groaning, *mu*ttering, or in humans, non-verbal utterance with closed lips—and, by derivation, the closing of the mouth, *mute*ness (Lat. *mutus*). From the same root comes the Greek verb *müein, myein*, to close up, to close the eyes, from which derive *mystery* and *mystic*, the secret rites and teachings. Myth and mystery, then, are connected in their origin. . . . Greek *mu* signifying inarticulate voicing with closed mouth, evolved into *mythos*, word.[64]

This explains much. If myths are cross-cultural and if they are language, then they could easily contain cross-linguistic elements as well. Shamanic language, or myth, Mircea Eliade relates, is usually described as animal language, as for example the lowing of cattle—moo. Or the sacred can be indicated by a word signifying the transcendence of rational linguistic and logical categories, as for example the Japanese *mu*.[65] Or the mystical language can be attained by repetition until the pro-

---

[64]"The Persistence of Myth," *Chimera* 4 (1946): 2.

[65]Robert M. Pirsig, *Zen and the Art of Motorcycle Maintenance* (New York, 1974), 314–16.

fane meaning is lost, as for example in the Hindus' *om*(oo). That is to say, in its original signifying of inarticulate voicing, *mu* indicates a sacred language or "myth," but in the Greek came to be *mythos* or "word," too. Myth, then, is literally language, and mystery also.

In all these diverse representations of myth in general and the mythology of the religious elite more specifically—for they are the keepers of the religious word—is a similar movement: religion or myth seems inherently to become politicized. Bennet and Tyerman complain of the areois' influence in both priestcraft and statecraft; Bush says that Mohammedanism "was in fact a political association"; and the shaman elaborates the taboo to include political benefits for himself.[66] This is just as Melville demonstrates in both *Typee* and *Omoo*: the "all pervading taboo" has become the social system itself, just as the Bible-based laws on Tahiti have brought the missionaries to power. In general, extending the sacred into the realm of the profane leads to corruption, for the elite who control the spirits could control the motivations of the people, and thus the political economy.

Melville points to this pattern of profanation in further ways, for many seemingly extraneous allusions refer to historical and literary instances of this phenomenon. Historically, the references to Guy Fawkes and Titus Oates are similarly relevant (33, 180), both concerning attempts by Catholics to disrupt or destroy the British government. More interesting are the implications of what Paul tells us are Long Ghost's intellectual interests: "As for his learning, he quoted Virgil, and talked of Hobbes of Malmsbury, beside repeating poetry by the canto, especially Hudibras" (12). Each employs religion or myth for political ends. The order Melville gives to them is also significant, for they demonstrate a clear progression: Virgil writes myth to justify, in a sense to sanctify the Roman empire; Hobbes condemns myth as absurd yet calls his system "The Christian Commonwealth," thus employing what he condemns to the same ends as Virgil's; and Butler carries this process one

[66]Bennet and Tyerman, *Journal*, 1:88; and Bush, *Mohammed*, 103.

step further by satirizing the tendency of the Puritans to politi-
cize their religion. From Butler it is an easy step to the deconstructive comparative mythology of Melville.

The pattern of the politicization of religion, repeated in
these many variations within *Omoo*, is perhaps a myth itself, the
myth of the Fall. The sacred, by becoming profane, repeats the
archetypal pattern of the fall from paradise into history and
law, the political world but a decayed version of the original
state of nature. Sociologically, for the white race, which considers itself the religious elite of mankind, the fall means the
decay of religion into the imperialist politics Melville describes;
psychologically, for the individual the fall means the loss of
unity with the natural world around him. Paul's readiness to
accept himself as fallen at the novel's end thus further illustrates his distance from Melville; he refuses to dive deeply into
myth, and takes the easy, practical way out by subsuming his
individual will to that of the *Leviathan*. Melville, on the other
hand, always prefers total confrontation with the sacred, even
if the sacred prove to be nothing but a horrible void—annihila-
tion is preferable to servitude. On any level Melville seems to
hold little stock in the company that looks for an easy escape or
a ready paradise.

The last chapter of the myth of the Fall is the reintegration
of the fallen world into the divine—the apocalypse of the historical world and the end of man's fallen condition. The sacred
and the profane, that is, synthesize into the sacred at the end of
the mythic pattern. In *Omoo*, however, the sacred and the profane synthesize into the profane. There is finally for Melville's
white culture no sacred but the profane; all is the natural,
political world, here as in *Typee*. "Myth" in its original meaning
as "a story embodying religious truth" Melville transforms to
"myth" in its more colloquial meaning as "something untrue."
Melville's narrative of facts asserts that the white culture's myth
is merely mythical, that their shaman is a sham.

Like *Typee*, then, *Omoo* is deconstructive: Melville begins with
the basic concept of the sacred wanderer, embedded in the
texts of the missionaries' narratives, exposes the contradictions within the concept, then amplifies them until the narra-

tive collapses. As in *Typee*, too, Melville centers upon the self-contradictory significations of a single term, spirit, then moves to those who possess and control it, then to the most general level of myth itself. That Melville reduces myth to a natural level also indicates that *Omoo* may be as much about the origin of myth as about its devolution. That is, if myth proves to be nothing more than natural, it has no special transcendental origin. Here, too, Melville criticizes the missionaries, implying that they trumped up ordinary events by calling them spiritual—as indeed many of their critics argued—and that they were in reality little more than self-sanctified beach bums. Paul's narrative, which sees spirits everywhere, is not to be trusted, for he attempts to sanctify the profane by covering his and Long Ghost's selfish political motives with the language of the spirit.

There is nevertheless more to the "spirit" of Melville's protagonists, for in them Melville not only criticizes religious elitism but also points to what he feels is essentially religious, to what is not politicized or profaned. Although the difference between enthusiasm and true reverence—the distinction in most religions between the fanatics and the elect—is spurious to Melville, he evinces through his characters a feeling of and for the power of nature, the force of life. Paul and Long Ghost flee from the death and dying around them for anything that will confirm and express life—eating, drinking, sex, movement. This, too, is the power of the coral insects, which create islands by pushing life out from the sea; behind the cocoa-palm, the Tree of Life which provides all that a native naturally needs; behind the "strange shapes of the unwarped primal world" beneath *Moby-Dick*'s ocean. This is the force of *Omoo* that critics such as Lawrence have seen in it. Melville is thus an *un*supernatural naturalist, for his ironic vision sees how life is so much and so often destroyed by the religious elite, whose strivings emanate from this same life-force. The missionaries on Tahiti are forces in opposition to life: in actuality, for they destroy life and love of life; and in principle, for they seek not the natural world but the world that they say transcends it.

Melville's *Omoo*, however, everywhere affirms life: its relentlessly restless movement, its gusto for the pleasures of life, its resistance to strictures and structures, its sheer fun all contribute to the spirit of Melville's theme. Tightly if eccentrically organized around his parodic deflation of the idea of the sacred wanderer found in the missionaries' narratives, *Omoo* thus deserves neither neglect nor condemnation. Yet those elements that critics have pointed to as limiting Melville's achievement—the digression, the light tone, the humor—remain undeniable characteristics of the novel. They are not limitations, however; they are, in fact, vital indications of the process of profanation that is paradoxically an affirmation. *Omoo* is obviously "profane" in its contempt or irreverence for the sacred and in its unrelenting secularity; but it is also "profane" in its deliberate avoidance of the proprieties and rituals of narrative form and in its often disrespectful, abusive, and vulgar comedy. In short, *Omoo*'s flawed narrative, casual tone, and pervasive humor are integral elements of Melville's comparative mythology of the religious elite.

4

Redburn

The Romance of
Laissez-Faire

A "job," Melville called *Redburn*, written to provide for his family after the financial failure of *Mardi*.[1] In his letters Melville always associates Redburn with money and always disparages it on that account: "But I hope I shall never write such a book again—Tho' when a poor devil writes with duns all round him, & looking over the back of his chair—& perching on his pen and diving in his inkstand—like the devils about St: Anthony—what can you expect of that poor devil?—what but a beggarly 'Redburn!'"[2] Melville had previously voiced similar disparagements in his prefaces and descriptions of *Typee* and *Omoo*, which are, as we have seen, by no means so simple as "Melville" protested. When he says to Lemuel Shaw, "I have not repressed myself much—so far as [*Redburn* is] concerned: but have spoken pretty much as I feel," we might therefore

---

[1] *Letters*, 91. See also Hershel Parker, "Historical Note," *Redburn*, 315–52; and William Gilman, *Melville's Early Life and Redburn* (New York, 1951). All references to the novel are to the Northwestern-Newberry edition and are cited parenthetically in the text.

[2] *Letters*, 95. This passage is like an ironic reference to Washington Irving's "The Poor-Devil Author" in *Tales of a Traveler*; see n. 17 below on Irving's relevance to *Redburn*.

suspect that Melville has again considerably and slyly under-
stated the value and complexity of his work.[3]

Indeed, as criticism of the novel, following the pioneering
work of William Gilman, has moved beyond a consideration of
the novel as slightly veiled autobiography, it has accordingly
recognized serious intellectual and aesthetic issues in this "beggarly" offering. Many critics have directed their efforts toward
the question of Wellingborough Redburn's maturation, but the
outcome of his initiation into adulthood and evil has caused
considerable controversy.[4] Others have focused on the book's
social themes: the issues of authority, poverty, cities, and messianic nationalism.[5] The most recent criticism has produced
two notable efforts to unite these psychological and social elements: both Michael Paul Rogin and James Duban deftly use
contextual material to explain the relationship of Melville's
narrator to his themes.[6] Rogin draws convincing connections
between Melville's family politics and the politics of the novel,
while Duban links Redburn's attitudes to theology and politics
contemporary to Melville. Yet both Rogin and Duban leave

---

[3]Ibid., 92.

[4]Newton Arvin, *Herman Melville* (New York, 1950), describes *Redburn* as an
initiation of innocence into evil, a position with which John Bernstein, *Pacifism
and Rebellion in the Writings of Herman Melville* (The Hague, 1964), concurs. H.
Bruce Franklin, "Redburn's Wicked End," *Nineteenth-Century Fiction* 20 (1965):
190–94, says that Redburn matures but becomes what he despises. John
Seelye, *Melville*, and Axel Carl Bredahl, *Melville's Angles of Vision* (Gainesville,
Fla., 1972), see Redburn learning relativism. Edgar Dryden, *Melville's Thematics*, says that Redburn gains a new level of awareness by accepting guilt. In
opposition are: Terence Lish, "Melville's *Redburn*: A Study in Dualism," *English
Language Notes* 5 (1967): 113–20, who says that Redburn's knowledge of evil is
only vicarious; Michael D. Bell, "Melville's *Redburn*: Initiation and Authority,"
New England Quarterly 46 (1973): 558–72, who says Redburn's initiation is of
the most incomplete sort; and John Gerlach, "Messianic Nationalism in the
Early Works of Herman Melville: Against Perry Miller," *Arizona Quarterly* 28
(1972): 5–26, who says that Redburn is always foolish. Three critics concen-
trate on the narrative voices in the novel: Lawrance Thompson, *Melville's Quarrel with God* (Princeton, N.J., 1952); Dillingham, *Artist*, 33; and Merlin Bowen,
"*Redburn* and the Angle of Vision," *Modern Philology* 52 (1954): 100–109.

[5]See Bell, "Initiation"; Bernstein, *Pacificism*; Gerlach, "Messianic Nationalism"; and Harold McCarthy, "Melville's *Redburn* and the City," *Midwest Quarterly* 12 (1971): 395–410.

[6]Rogin, *Subversive Genealogy*; and Duban, *Melville's Major Fiction*.

unanswered a crucial question of tenor and vehicle: If Melville's ultimate aim is political, why then does he use the form of the initiatory sea voyage narrative to present those ideas?

Like *Typee* and *Omoo*, *Redburn* shows Melville again alluding to and following definite narrative of facts categories, again reacting to the ideology of those narratives. Viewing *Redburn* in that context, one can consider more precisely the politics of the novel in relation to Redburn's psychology and can see more clearly a unity which ties together the themes and narrative forms of the book under the concern Melville himself most often associated with *Redburn*, economics. That Melville wrote *Redburn* for money is obvious, but that he wrote it about money is, though less obvious, certainly no less important.[7] Perhaps the duns in Melville's pen managed to find their way onto the page, as certainly—Gilman has amply demonstrated—the matters of Allan Melvill's bankruptcy and Herman Melville's consequent sea voyage found their way into the novel. This focus should not be surprising, for much in Melville's personal life in the Spring of 1849 indicates that economic issues were on his mind as he was writing *Redburn*.

Melville's reading in contemporary periodicals, likely spurred by Gansevoort's involvement in politics and aided by access to Duyckinck's library, revealed an 1849 America and Europe similarly preoccupied with issues arising from political economy.[8] Newspapers and journals reported the results of the 1846 Irish potato famine—the poverty, death, and emigration similar to but more extensive than what Melville pictures in *Redburn*—and often stressed that the Irish poverty resulted from repressive British economic policies. Even more than the famine, the revolutions in Europe in 1848 called America's

---

[7]Immediately before discussing *Redburn* in the letter to Lemuel Shaw (*Letters*, 91), Melville, about to set sail for Europe, says, "Economy, however, is my mottoe." Both Franklin, "Redburn's Wicked End," and Gilman, *Melville's Early Life*, deal briefly with economic issues in the novel; Duban, *Melville's Major Fiction*, 51 and 58–60, more clearly establishes a link between *Redburn* and Smithian economics.

[8]Duyckinck's holdings are catalogued in *Lenox Library Short-Title Lists*, nos. 8 and 12 (New York, 1887 and 1890), which list many contemporary periodicals among the holdings.

attention to the consequences of what had been a decade dominated by the policy of free trade.[9] America itself witnessed in 1846 the Anti-rent War, in which tenants fought to abolish feudal tenures held by landlords in New York state and on which Cooper's Littlepage trilogy centers.[10] In 1848 America faced not a revolution but an election, yet one described by the magazines of the time in rhetoric almost more suitable to the events in Europe.[11] Again, political economy was a crucial issue: the Democrats urged America to abandon any Federalistic trade restrictions and to embrace a free trade policy. In early 1849 the California Gold Rush began and led both Democrats and Whigs to envision a consequent American commerce with Asia and the rest of the world.[12] More negatively, in May of that year class consciousness led to the Astor Place riot between the "codfish aristocracy" and the "mob"—an incident in which Melville himself was tangentially involved.[13]

Melville read about these issues not only in the magazines available to him but also in those narratives he had used in writing *Typee*, *Omoo*, and *Mardi*. Establishing markets was a primary, if not *the* primary concern of the explorers, who since the time of Columbus had as "the main object . . . to open a direct path to India, the grand source of commerce and wealth."[14] Following discovery, commerce and colonialization and further commerce became the rule—for Cook, Bougainville, Porter, Wilkes, and even missionaries such as Stewart and Ellis, whose narratives often read like a marketing primer or an inquiry into the nature and causes of the wealth of newly colonized nations.[15] In *Redburn*, though, Melville is reacting pri-

[9]See "Foreign Gossip," *United States and Democratic Review* 22 (1848): 186; "Old Ireland and Young Ireland," ibid. 23 (1848): 149–52; "Financial and Commercial Review," ibid. 22 (1848): 464–66; "The French Republic," ibid. 23 (1848): 61–62 (hereafter *Democratic Review*); and "The Social Condition of England," *North American Review* 65 (1847): 461–504.

[10]McCarthy, "*Redburn* and the City," 397, applies these issues to *Redburn*.

[11]Rogin, *Subversive Genealogy*, 70–72.

[12]"California Gold," *Democratic Review* 24 (1849): 3–5; and "California—Its Position and Prospects," 24 (1849): 412.

[13]See *Melville Log*, 1:302–04.

[14]*Historical Account of Circumnavigation*, 22.

[15]See Strauss, *Americans*.

marily to those narratives of a slightly different kind of exploration: semifictional narratives of the personal experiences of sailors going to Europe, particularly those of Charles Frederick Briggs; and narratives and guidebooks for travelers in Europe, particularly *The Picture of Liverpool*.[16] In both, economics plays a leading role, for Briggs narrates continual struggles to make a living and *The Picture of Liverpool* describes the nineteenth century's archetypal commercial city. The ideology behind both comes from the other guidebook that Redburn takes with him: Adam Smith's *An Inquiry into the Nature and Causes of the Wealth of Nations*. Although the naive Redburn dismisses it as "dryer and dryer," the perceptive Melville knows better. He perceives Smithian economics responsible for many contemporary problems and structures his novel around it. *The Wealth of Nations* may indeed be "something like a philosopher's stone, a secret talisman," that Redburn fancies it to be (86), for it can turn Melville's "pitch and tar" *Redburn* into a "silver and gold" artistic whole.

I

As a child Redburn loved to look at the many guidebooks in his father's library: he "never tired of gazing at the numerous quaint embellishments and plates, and staring at the strange title-pages, some of which I thought resembled the mustached faces of foreigners" (141). This "reading," as Melville's headnote says, makes his protagonist "intolerably flat and stupid" and causes him many problems throughout the course of the novel. Nor did Redburn read these volumes carefully: interested more in the imaginative flights they occasion than in what they say, he obtains from his half-read literature a typical nineteenth-century romantic desire for the exotic world of the Arabian Nights and for the storied places of England and the continent. Redburn's reading, that is to say, is responsi-

[16]See Willard Thorpe, "Redburn's Prosy Old Guidebook," *PMLA* 53 (1938): 1146–56. More generally, American fiction of the 1840s is infused with economic themes, ranging from pirate adventure stories to tales of life in the city.

ble for his sentimentality, for he wishes to follow the adventurous path of authors such as Frederick Marryat, Nathaniel Ames, Richard Henry Dana, James Fenimore Cooper, and Washington Irving.[17]

These authors, moreover, have given him a basic pattern of initiation which augments his dreams. The young hero of their works—whether like Dana going to sea to become physically a man or like Cooper's Miles Wallingford going to sea to follow in his dead father's footsteps—feels he will gain maturity by traveling; in undertaking his voyage he intends as well to discover his heritage and his place in the world. For him, then, as for Miles and for Irving's Geoffrey Crayon, England and Europe, our old home, must be the goal of his voyage of initiation. Bayard Taylor, in terms very much like Redburn's, sounds the typical romantic tone of this desire: "An enthusiastic desire of visiting the Old World haunted me from early childhood. I cherished a presentiment, amounting almost to belief, that I should one day behold the scenes, among which my fancy had so long wandered."[18] Upon his visit to the Old World, the typical romantic youth comes home mature and successful: Miles returns with a clear perspective about his relation to his family and society and as master of his own ship, and Marryat's Peter Simple returns as a hero and with a wife. That is, the lesson that these narratives have taught Redburn reinforces his romanticism, confirms that his "reveries" about his father, the Old World, adventure, and maturation can indeed be fulfilled.

Also like a motif in these narratives, Redburn's romanticism centers upon his regaining the upper-class status his father

[17]Frederick Marryat, *Peter Simple* (Leipzig, 1842); Nathaniel Ames, *A Mariner's Sketches* (Providence, R.I., 1830); Richard Henry Dana, Jr., *Two Years before the Mast* (1840; rpt. New York, 1965); James Fenimore Cooper, *Afloat and Ashore* (1844; rpt. New York, 1883); and Washington Irving, *The Sketch Book* (1820; rpt. New York, 1961). On Dana and Melville see Robert Lucid, "The Influence of *Two Years before the Mast* on Herman Melville," *American Literature* 31 (1959): 243–56; on Cooper and Melville see Christine M. Bird, "*Redburn* and *Afloat and Ashore*," *Nassau Review* 3 (1979): 5–16.

[18]Bayard Taylor, *Views A-Foot* (New York, 1848), 1. Duban, *Melville's Major Fiction*, 37–39, gives a clear summary of the Old World/New World issue in *Redburn*.

lost, for like Peter Simple, he looks always to win back his inheritance from Lord Privilege.[19] In short, Redburn desires to be, as his speech and the novel's subtitle emphasize, a "gentleman." It is of course de rigueur for the aspiring gentleman to cap his education with a tour of Europe in the manner of "Geoffrey Crayon, gent.," as Mr. Jones tells Captain Riga and as Redburn's sisters tell the people back home (75).[20] This conviction that travel will bring others to regard him with "reverence and wonder," with a sense of his superior social status, encompasses not only his love of Europe but also his wish to emulate his father. Redburn is a "Son-of-a-Gentleman" who hopes by following his father's path to acquire the social status his father once had.

The symbol of all his romantic dreams of traveling, of gentility, of maturation, and of his father is of course the glass ship:

> But that which perhaps more than any thing else, converted my vague dreamings and longings into a definite purpose of seeking my fortune on the sea, was an old-fashioned glass ship . . . which my father, some thirty years before, had brought home from Hamburgh as a present to a great-uncle of mine: Senator Wellingborough, who had died a member of Congress in the

[19]James Schroeter, "Redburn and the Failure of Mythic Criticism," *American Literature* 39 (1967): 279–97, sees the novel as Melville's rejection of gentility. Melville could find many models for his narrator's attitude here, for the *Literary World* of 1847–48 notes and reviews numerous gentleman's handbooks. For a later analysis of the attitudes Melville's narrator exemplifies here and throughout the novel, see Thorstein Veblen, *The Theory of the Leisure Class* (1899; rpt. New York, 1953); Veblen's discussion of the attitudes and practices of the leisure class is startlingly appropriate for Redburn. To analyze and satirize (and deconstruct?) the leisure class "institution" (or "habit of thought") Veblen coined the phrases "pecuniary emulation," "conspicuous leisure," and "conspicuous consumption," which describe the basic concepts upon which his critique of American society rests. Both his concepts and his more specific observations were anticipated by Melville in *Redburn*, though Veblen's *Theory* can be helpful in seeing the coherence of Melville's criticism.

[20]Also see Taylor, *Views*. If Redburn seems similar in this respect to the Melville of "Fragments from a Writing Desk," the older Melville is clearly no aspiring gentleman. At the time of writing *Redburn*, he was also making notes for a story: "(Devil as a Quaker) . . . gentlemanly &c—D begs the hero to form one of a '*Society of D's*' . . . 'Gentlemen' &c" (*Melville Log*, 1:297).

days of the old Constitution, and after whom I had the honor of
being named. (7)

It is no wonder Redburn is so fascinated with the ship, for its
name, *La Reine*, testifies to its aristocratic symbolism, which is
amplified by its connection to his patrician uncle. Although
Redburn himself recognizes the "secret sympathy" between
himself and the ship's figurehead, "a gallant warrior in a
cocked hat" (9), to Melville the ship represents not an exotic
and "gallant" romanticism but a very hollow and fragile idealism, which eventually leaves Redburn with his delicate visions
destroyed even as "many of [the ship's] glass spars and ropes
are now sadly shattered and broken" (9). Rogin's passing comment that Melville is here adapting the name from *La Reine
Blanche*, the ship on which Paul and Long Ghost were held,
suggests that Redburn's idealism is imprisoning as well.[21] Certainly, beneath its beautiful exterior, the ship is also as "very
dark" as Tommo's Marquesan "paradise."

Significantly, Redburn peers inside the ship because he has
an "insane desire" for "some gold guineas, of which I have
always been in want," that he fancies may be inside. That is to
say, in the dark interior of Redburn's romantic dreams lies the
more basic desire for money. Redburn's gentlemanly aspirations may be nothing more than glass visions since his family
has fallen on "hard times," and his wish to emulate his father is
at least partly a wish to regain the time when his family was
well-off and son-of-a-gentleman did not also mean son-of-
a-bankrupt. Through the glass ship, then, we can see a poignant irony in the connection of Redburn's economic desires and
his father worship, for the elder Redburn was by no means a
good model, particularly in his economics, an imperfection of
great consequence for his son.

The economic dimension of Redburn's dreams points toward Melville's chief source for *Redburn*, the writings of
Charles Frederick Briggs. Redburn could find in Cooper et al.
a comforting reassurance of the romance of nautical intitations

---

[21]Rogin, *Subversive Genealogy*, 84.

into the Old World, but Melville finds in Briggs a cautionary model to his narrator's attitudes. Briggs's Harry Franco, like Redburn, has been reading too many romances, which to him are "veritable histories" but which to Briggs are "nothing but fictions."[22] Accordingly, Harry grows up "ignorant of every thing around me, and with dreamy, ill-defined apprehensions of the way of the world."[23] Like Redburn, Harry's idealism deepens with poverty: the more he thinks of his father's bankruptcy and disinheritance, the more "came thronging into my brain the many wonderful stories I had read, of good luck befriending the poor and friendless." "Pride and poverty" demand as well that "whatever I did should be done genteelly." On the other hand, Briggs, as much a critic of class as Melville, deplores in the novel's preface "that strange race, called Aristocrats," and frequently shows his narrator's naive gentility leading him to expose his foolishness, deepening his poverty, and causing him tearfully to leave his home on the Hudson for New York. There he, like Redburn, receives a badly learned lesson in economics while staying with a friend of his father in St. John's Park.[24] There Harry is introduced to a commercial system as vicious and inhumane as that which Melville presents in *Redburn*'s New York: Harry is a frequent victim of shysters and con-men, who play upon his assumed gentility. Like Redburn, he remains a dreamer even as he sails out to sea. "It is a blessed thing for the poor wretches who are, by some means or other, defrauded of their rightful portion of the good things which surround them," Briggs says ironically, "that they can wander at will and appropriate to their own use the greenest spots that they can find in the broad region of Hope. This was my privilege, and I was by no means heedless of my prerogative."[25] The only claim Harry has to the "privilege" and "prerogative"

---

[22]Charles Frederick Briggs, *The Adventures of Harry Franco* (New York, 1839), 1:11; on Briggs's influence on Melville see Perry Miller, *The Raven and the Whale: The War of Words and Wits in the Era of Poe and Melville* (New York, 1956), 47–68.

[23]Briggs, *Harry Franco* 1:7.

[24]Ibid., 1:8–10. Miller, *Raven*, 55–57, points out these parallels.

[25]Briggs, *Harry Franco*, 1:161.

of aristocracy is his vapid hope, a poor compensation for his poverty.

Briggs's subsequent novels reinforce this economic caution to romanticism. In *Working a Passage*, the upper-class narrator finds himself in Liverpool without money to get home; therefore, on a drizzly November he signs on as a sailor. *Bankrupt Stories (The Haunted Merchant)* describes the effects of poverty upon an orphan, while *The Trippings of Tom Pepper*, subtitled *The Results of Romancing*, chronicles the economic struggles, compounded by his inveterate "romancing," of an apparently fatherless sailor—until he is found to be "a St. Hugh and a gentleman."[26] Briggs's message in these novels is clear, if not particularly subtle: romantic dreams of wealth and status, in themselves ridiculous, become meaningless and destructive when confronted by economic reality.

Melville, using Briggs as a model, exemplifies these same results in Redburn's romancing, when "sad disappointments in several plans which I had sketched for my future life [and] the necessity of doing something for myself, united to a naturally roving disposition, had now conspired within me, to send me to sea as a sailor" (3). With one part romanticism and two parts economic necessity, that is, Redburn leaves home carrying little but his coat and his gun, emblems of the genteel pastime of the hunt and tangible links with family heritage. Throughout his travels, however, others scorn his coat, whose "fine long skirts, stout horn buttons, and plenty of pockets" (3) suggest the restriction, clumsiness, and absurdity his romantic ideals impose upon his actions. Redburn receives the coat (of not many colors) from his elder brother: Redburn is something of a comic Joseph, sold literally down the river to the nautical Ishmaelites.

His pastoral childhood behind him, Redburn finds his "young mounting dreams of glory" (10) turning quickly to the

---

[26]*Bankrupt Stories (The Haunted Merchant)* (New York, 1843); *Working a Passage; or, Life in a Liner* (New York, 1844); and *The Trippings of Tom Pepper; or, The Results of Romancing* (New York, 1847). The *Lenox Library* catalogues indicate that Duyckinck's library had copies of *Harry Franco*, *Tom Pepper*, and *Bankrupt Stories* (8:7; 11:37).

"desperation and recklessness of poverty" (12) once he sets out. Thus he reacts to the more bourgeois fellow passengers on the Hudson steamboat with what Thomas Carlyle calls the "berserker rage" of the economically disadvantaged. In New York his fondness for gentlemanly ideals allows him to countenance Mr. Jones's trumping up of Redburn's "highly respectable" family connections—a "father, a gentleman of one of the first families in America," and an uncle, a Senator (16)—and to judge Captain Riga solely on his genteel appearance. Consequently, Redburn, getting no advance in his scant wages, "indulg[es] in some romantic and misanthropic views of life" (23); that is, he wishes he were dead and buried in his churchyard at home and at the height of inflated self-pity describes himself eating "the last supper." This incident, like numerous others, follows a clear pattern: the young Redburn begins in an ignorance of the economic world nurtured by his reading, is duped by that world, and ends in an absurd romantic despair.

Melville crystallizes this pattern in his symbolic description of the fort Redburn sees as his ship leaves New York harbor. Redburn recollects the fort as "a beautiful place . . . and very wonderful and romantic, too" (35), an intimation of the happy times of his childhood. He describes the fort in pastoral terms, complete with a "green grove," calves frisking, cattle grazing, and sheep cropping the grass. He "should like to build a little cottage in the middle of it, and live there all my life" (35), presumably happily ever after. Redburn's memories here too are connected with the romance of sailing, for he visited the fort with his father and his uncle, an old sea captain who had sailed with Langsdorff. But Redburn's Wordsworthian reverie is cut short by another memory:

> But I must not think of those delightful days, before my father became a bankrupt, and died, and we removed from the city; for when I think of those days, something rises up in my throat and almost strangles me. . . . Then I never thought of working for my living, and never knew that there were hard hearts in the world; and knew so little of money, that when I bought a stick of candy, and laid down a sixpence, I thought the confectioner

returned five cents, only that I might have money to buy something else, and not because the pennies were my change, and
therefore mine by good rights. How different my idea of money
now! (36)

Then he had the money and leisure time for romantic dreaming, but now he must work for his pennies. Economics is that
black goat (as Redburn himself is a black sheep) with the long
beard and crumpled horns that symbolically points Redburn
out to the dark ocean.

At sea Redburn, like Bulkington, "resolved not to look at the
land any more" (36), but his resolve is equivocal at best, for
soon he "railed at the folly which had sent me to sea" (51).
Often wishing for the lee shore, Redburn allows his romanticism to intrude often during the voyage to Liverpool. Still reliant upon the ideas he gained from travel narratives and unable to learn the lessons of life around him, Redburn whines
about dying of consumption, preaches Sunday-school religiosity and temperance, and attempts to pay a white-gloved
social call upon the captain (chaps. 11, 14, 17, and 18). In each
case Melville confronts his narrator's inflated perceptions, as
he does Tommo's, with a highly deflating reality. Again typical
of Melville, this juxtapositioning is nowhere more significant
than in chapter 18, where Redburn encounters "in dubious
light" two books: Jack Blunt's *Bonaparte Dream Book* and Adam
Smith's *Wealth of Nations*. The former is a parodic compendium
of visionary romance, complete with astrology, the black arts,
and prophecy. Blunt, even more a stereotypical romantic than
Redburn, reveres Napoleon, tries to avoid aging, seeks the
"Balm of Paradise," and utters apocalyptic forecasts. Melville
portrays him as comically, totally absurd. No less absurd is his
narrator's reaction to *The Wealth of Nations*: "a book, from
which I expected to reap great profit and sound instruction,"
bores Redburn to sleep (86–87).[27] Melville by no means dismisses Smith as his narrator does, here using this literary pair-

---

[27]Adam Smith, *An Inquiry into the Nature and Causes of the Wealth of Nations*
(1776; rpt. Chicago, 1976). Bell, "Melville's *Redburn*," 565, says that Redburn is
incapable of understanding Smith.

ing to indicate a more general dichotomy in his reading, the
picture of sailing presented by Cooper and Marryat given the
lie by the more realistic and reformist reports of Briggs.

At the heart of Adam Smith's economic philosophy is an
almost Calvinistic and certainly Hobbesian concept of man as
self-interested. "It is the interest of every man to live as much at
his ease as he can," Smith says; consequently, "in every profession, the exertion of the greater part of those who exercise it, is
always in proportion to the necessity they are under of making
that exertion."[28] Although his reading has made Redburn at
best a grudging victim of that philosophy, Melville's sailors
represent the Smithian self-interest that contrasts Redburn's
romantic egoism. None of them is willing to risk himself to
prevent the drunken sailor's suicide (51), and all rail against
Redburn's going to sea, where he would "take the bread out of
the mouth of honest sailors, and fill a good seaman's place"
(52). In general they work only as much and as often as they
have to, and ship out only when they run out of money. Jackson epitomizes this aspect of the Smithian man: though supposedly weak, "he was very swift on the legs; at least when a
good place was to be jumped to" (59); though his "sogering" is
notorious, he is able to keep the rest of the crew from calling
him to account. Jackson is quintessentially the man who looks
out for himself—and is successful.

When Redburn, unfamiliar with Smith, first confronts an
unabashed and realistic self-interest so alien to his pious anticipation of glass-ship sailors, he can judge them only as "evil" or
"depraved." Jackson, to Redburn the extreme example of this
depravity, is thus to him a total opposite to the picture of a
sailor typical of romantic travel narratives, the "Handsome
Sailor." Melville's Jackson probably had an anti-cedent in
Dana's Bill Jackson, "Our handsome English sailor";[29] unlike
Dana's Jackson, Melville's sailor is decidedly not handsome,
"such a hideous looking mortal, that Satan himself would have

[28]Smith, *Inquiry*, 2:283. Duban, *Melville's Major Fiction*, 51, mentions this
aspect of Smith.
[29]Dana, *Two Years*, 78–79 and 102.

run from him" (57). Like Dana's sailor, though, Jackson had been to sea ever since he was a boy and is the best sailor on board.[30] His accomplishments stem not from physical ability, however—Melville again reverses the stereotype—but from his dark understanding of human nature. In his Jackson, Melville demonstrates that the naive Redburn, expecting a ship of Handsome Sailors, will see the self-interested sailor as the incarnation of the devil rather than as a typical Smithian man.

When Smithian men interact, interests collide and competition for ownership, the stimulus to overcome natural indolence, ensues. Competing, using one's stock and industry to the greatest advantage, is to Smith one "of the most sacred rights of mankind," as it allows for the smooth operation of society. Trade, which Smith defines as mutual self-interest, promotes harmony among groups and individuals and ensures economic growth for society and its constituents. If kept free of regulation, the market, Smith's "invisible hand," thus guides society toward progress.[31] This ideology of laissez-faire is Melville's most pervasive foil to the romanticism his narrator obtains from his nautical narratives and a counterpart to the political world of *Omoo* with which he criticizes Paul's and Long Ghost's spurious spirituality. From the first, laissez-faire economics dictates Redburn's actions: lack of competition increases his fare to New York, competition keeps the pawnshops' prices low, and Redburn starves. On the *Highlander* Redburn is again victimized by laissez-faire, appropriately so, for its name is a reference to a people whom Smithian economics had brought to ruin.[32] In an 1847 article devoted to an attack upon "The English School of Political Economy"—Smith, Thomas Malthus, David Ricardo, et al.—the *North American Review* laments the accumulation of capital and power in the hands of the few as an outcome of laissez-faire economics, an outcome exemplified in the plight of the Scottish Highlanders: "Since the beginning of the present century, the nation of the Highlanders or Gauls,

[30]Ibid., 78.
[31]See Smith, *Inquiry*, 1:78, 132, and 433.
[32]Smith, *Inquiry*, 1:440, discusses the Highlanders as a positive example of commercialism's supercession of feudalism.

the descendents of the ancient Celts, now reduced to 340,000 souls, has been almost entirely expelled from its home." At the same time, "this revolution in the property, the habits, the affections, the whole existence of a little nation has prodigiously augmented the already colossal fortune of the Duke of Sutherland."[33]

This historical drama Melville—to be sure alert to the irony of a Scottish people impoverished and cast Ishmael-like out of their homeland by a Scottish philosophy—replays with his Highlanders, for Smith's hand invisibly guides the ship from the time Redburn signs on. Riga hired Redburn, he later learns, only because Redburn's price is low. To the sailors, too, Redburn is an undesirable commodity, for he can compete with none of the others (38–39). Important to note, the sailors are forced into this competitive situation by the owners and the larger economic forces (i.e., Smith's market), a fact that Redburn fails to take into account. Nathaniel Ames analyzes a similar situation:

> It [is the American merchantmen's] belief to look after their employers' interest first and foremost, and rather to kill a man by hard work and exposure, than to permit him to defraud the owners by his untimely sickness. Besides, when a sailor dies, his arrears of wages avert to the owners, who, (I speak of New-England merchants) always contemplate the word "dead" frequently repeated on a returned portage bill, with that peculiar satisfaction only to be appreciated and understood by those, whose religious, moral and political creed is comprised in the maxim "a penny saved is a penny got."[34]

Melville's attitude, repeated throughout the novel, was likely influenced by his reading of such pro-sailor writers as Ames or Briggs or Dana, but he goes beyond them to identify the ideology that spawns such abuses.

Melville, that is to say, recognizes the Smithian concept of society accountable not only for these abuses but for the

---

[33]"The Social Condition of England," *North American Review* 65 (1847): 492 and 495.

[34]Ames, *Mariner's Sketches*, 33–34. Cf. Briggs, *Working*, 3.

changes in society, like those forced upon the Scottish Highlanders, and in sailing that distress his narrator. "Thus," Melville explains, "the ship that once carried over gay parties of
ladies and gentlemen, as tourists, to Liverpool and London,
now carries a crew of harpooners round Cape Horn into the
Pacific. . . . *Sic transit gloria mundi!* Thus departs the pride and
glory of packet-ships! It is like a broken-down importer of silks
[his father?] embarking in the soap-boiling business" (107).
The change that Melville describes here and indicates through
much of the novel is precisely the "development" Smith lays
out: the evolution from feudalism to commercialism by means
of the freely competitive economic system. Yet as the shipboard society of the *Highlander* shows, Melville conceives
Smith's ideas to result not in the orderly, progressive society
Smith envisioned, but in the sordid trade of the whaler,
"choked up" with blubber and "reek[ing] with oil." As the *North
American Review*'s analysis of the Highlanders' case specifies,
the problem lies in Smith's concept of ownership: the self-
interested man naturally wants to accumulate capital to gain
leisure, but with capital comes power. Power is used to gain
further capital and further power, until a new bourgeois aristocracy is formed, not necessarily based upon lineage but upon
wealth. Smith's classification of society into "three original or-
ders" (proprietors, merchants, and laborers) and his "causes of
subordination" (superiority of personal qualifications, age, fortune, and birth) can be reduced to a simple formulation: capital begets superiority, and capitalism begets a class system. In
Melville's world the owners are so superior and distant that
they do not even appear, while Riga and the mates maintain an
absolute separation above the working class.

Smith does not believe that subordination per se produces
evils or abuses, yet he fails to consider the exploitation inherent
in his system.[35] Like virtually all the captains in Briggs's and
the others' narratives, Riga tyrannizes over Redburn by "actu-

[35]Smith himself condemns the "rapacity of merchants" but explains, "The
violence and injustice of the rulers of mankind is an ancient evil, for which, I
am afraid, the nature of human affairs can scarce admit of a remedy" (*Inquiry*,
1:519).

ally turning a poor lad adrift without a copper, after he had been slaving aboard his ship for more than four mortal months" (307). Redburn can see that there is something wrong with this system, but he himself takes too much part in it to realize why it is wrong; rather than rebelling against Riga and the moneyed class, Redburn wishes only to be more like them. Throughout most of the first part of *Redburn* (and only slightly less so through the rest of the novel) he enviously persists in considering himself a gentleman, an affiliation that precludes his understanding the economic system he is coming to hate.

But Melville escapes the cogs of Smith's economic machine as Redburn cannot, for in his presentation of the sailors' workmanship and brotherhood he foresees an alternative to laissez-faire capitalism. At the helm of genteel society, Melville says, is the sailor, who "has all your lives and eternities in his hand" (117). Redburn complains that he himself is incapable of performing what a good helmsman can, yet he reveals his admiration for his skills: "The business of a thorough-bred sailor is a special calling, as much of a regular trade as a carpenter's or lock-smith's. Indeed, it requires considerably more adroitness, and far more versatility of talent" (120). A true sailor-man is "an artist in the rigging," able to "understand much of other avocations" and be skilled at them all. This concept directly opposes one of Smith's most basic precepts, division of labor, which Smith says is fundamental to efficient development of capital. While Smith's laborer performs the fewest kinds of operations (and therefore can do many more repetitions of them), Melville's sailors perform the widest multiplicity of operations. Smith's laborer is a mechanical operant; Melville's sailor is a practical artist, an Emersonian man.

For Briggs, likely Melville's source for this idea, working is to be valued in itself as a satisfying skill that also helps one mature, become independent, and keep healthy. Briggs's *Working a Passage* amplifies this theme from the earlier *Harry Franco*. While it takes time for the romantic Harry to come to appreciate the sailors' abilities, the narrator of *Working a Passage*, H. C. F., sees himself in no way superior to other men and thus can immediately perceive the sailors as brave, good, and thoughtful workers doing a difficult job under dangerous and oppressive conditions. Briggs's message here attacks the "soft-handed" aristocracy and extolls the glory of work: "that it is possible to endure hard labour, and be happy with no other refreshment than potatoes and salt, provided they are honestly earned."[36] His sailors are accordingly united by their dedication into a sort of brotherhood. H. C. F., from the moment he comes on board, sees the sailors passing a jug of beer around and says, "There was a fraternal kindness in that little act that impressed me very favourably towards my shipmates."[37] In their circle around the pot of burgoo, Melville's sailors are also an emblem of cooperation, a quality that, despite the competition, extends to most aspects of their work. When the order is given, they spring in unison into the rigging (255); when they come across a former sailor reduced to beggary, they give him alms (187–88); when they find a young stowaway, they "received him with open arms" and take care of him (112). Max the Dutchman (like Marx the Deutschmann) is the most positive example of the workman Melville presents: he "manifested some little interest in [Redburn's] welfare," conspires in a Garibaldian red shirt against the tyranny of Jackson, and "prided himself greatly upon his seamanship" (79). Redburn, like Briggs's narrator, does grow from his earlier blanket condemnation of the sailors, including Red Max, but nevertheless he clings to the notion of their depravity without fully understanding either the economic forces affecting their behavior or the positive aspects of their actions.

Therefore, as the ship nears the coast of Ireland, Redburn still occupies himself with the same romantic dreams as at the outset, but his images of storied and noble places, of the essential *difference* (or *différance*) of the Old World, are quickly shattered (or deferred).[38] The geography "was nothing remarkable"; the Irish fishing boat is "very ordinary looking"; and the English pilot is "very common-place." From the Irish fisher-

---

[36]Briggs, *Working*, 108.
[37]Ibid., 25.
[38]Cf. Taylor, *Views*, 7.

man's confidence game Redburn sees that self-interested people, like the institutions of commerce such as the Liverpool
warehouses, are the same, Old World or New (125). "To be
sure, I did not expect that every house in Liverpool must be a
Leaning Tower of Pisa, or a Strasbourg Cathedral," Redburn
says; "but yet, these edifaces I must confess, were a sad and
bitter disappointment to me" (127).

In Liverpool, Redburn, "meditat[ing]" on the Englishness of
the inn and rejoicing in the realization of his dreams, examines
his surroundings and finds them rather commonplace, if not
vulgar. He then wonders where all the storied places and nobility are, for "not the most distant glimpse of them was to be
seen" (133). There is no aristocracy for Redburn, who can only
lament, "Alas! Wellingborough, thought I, I fear you stand
but a poor chance to see the sights. You are nothing but a poor
sailor boy; and the Queen is not going to send a deputation
of noblemen to invite you to St. James's" (133). Redburn is
"poor"; economics again precludes the realization of his romantic dreams.

Deepening and coalescing this disillusionment is Redburn's
"prosy old guidebook," *The Picture of Liverpool*, which epitomizes to Melville the ineffectuality of the romantic and aristocratic guidebooks—both literal and figurative—that Redburn
has been following.[39] It has nursed his imaginative excursions,
filled him "full of brilliant anticipations" (not a positive term to
Melville, as *Typee* illustrates), and given him a model for his
inept poetic outpourings. It is significant that Melville added
"and Gentleman's Pocket Companion" to his "fac-simile" of the
title page, for the book also represents the height of gentility to
his narrator. The anonymous author, whom Redburn calls "a
scholar and a gentleman," himself says that the poem he quotes
"will no doubt be highly acceptable to the cultivated reader"—whom
Redburn undoubtedly thinks himself.[40] When he tries to use
this "business-like" guidebook, though, he again finds that the
age of gentility has passed. He wants to see the changing of the

[39]See Thorpe, "Redburn's Guidebook," on Melville's borrowings.
[40]Melville added this statement also.

guard at a castle but finds it has become a tavern (152–53); he goes "under a cloister-like arch of stone, whose gloom and narrowness delighted me, and filled my Yankee soul with romantic thoughts of old Abbeys and Minsters," but emerges "into the fine quadrangle of the Merchants' Exchange" (154); and he tries to find the mythic "pool" from which the city got its name but finds it drained and replaced by a "Custom-house" (158). The "Gentleman's Pocket Companion" is no guide to the modern commercial world, so Redburn, sadly disillusioned, must "follow [his] nose throughout Liverpool," which seems "no older than the State of New York" (159).

Redburn has to some degree matured by recognizing the ineffectuality of his guidebook, a process which also entails his abandoning his search for his father. The guidebook, from his father's library, used by his father in his trip to Liverpool, bearing his father's notes, *is* virtually all Redburn has of his father and certainly symbolizes his father to Redburn. He in fact treats the book with the same quasi-religious worship he shows for his father. He has "abounding love" for it, folds it "reverentially," and refuses "by [his] father's sacred memory, and all sacred privacies of fond family reminiscences" to quote from it (143, 145, and 150).[41] Redburn's father worship here, but a part of his emulation of the leisure class, exposes another dimension to James Duban's convincing analysis of Redburn's Christ-like attributes: Melville is indicating that the aspiring gentleman must treat his father's guidebook as if it were a Bible if he is to carry the tenets of pecuniary emulation and aristocratic lineage to their fullest.[42]

Redburn does seem to realize that "the thing that had guided the father, could not guide the son" (157) and checks his pursuit of his father's path "when remembering that he had gone whither no son's search could find him in this world. And then I thought of all that must have happened to him since he paced through that arch. What trials and troubles he had encoun-

---

[41]Thompson reads *The Picture of Liverpool* as an ironic Bible.

[42]Duban, *Melville's Major Fiction*, 39–43, presents much sound evidence of the religious dimension to Redburn's experience in Liverpool, but in referring to the book as an "allegory" he presses his case too far.

tered; how he had been shaken by many storms of adversity, and at last died a bankrupt. I looked at my own sorry garb, and had much ado to keep from tears" (155).Redburn's psychological maturation is marked here not by his rejection of his father as a role model but, more important, by a realization that the facts of economic life preclude his following his father's path through Liverpool. As that last sentence ironically shows, Redburn has followed his father's economic path to poverty, an irony Melville deepens by showing that the elder Redburn was far from worthy of the worship his son feels. The "memoranda" in the guidebook show the elder Redburn noting every little pence spent, reading the preromantic Thomson, watching a tasteless combination of "Richard III. and new farce," and calling on Irving's Roscoe, the fortunately forgotten poet and banker (144). Redburn's father, in short, was a typical, imperfect, bourgeois man of the sentimental enlightenment. That Redburn cannot see or admit his shortcomings shows that he is not yet "on his own."

Redburn's psychological development obviously depends largely upon recognizing the inability of guidebooks to give an accurate picture of reality: the irrelevance of his *Liverpool* guidebook forces Redburn to lose some of his reliance upon preconceived models of experience. Less obviously, *why* the guidebook is no longer applicable—the changes in Liverpool itself—bears significantly upon Melville's purposes. As noted above, Redburn's observations of the discrepancies between the guidebook and reality center upon commerce; indeed, *The Picture of Liverpool* itself emphasizes "the changes that are every year taking place in a town remarkable beyond any other in the Empire, or perhaps, even in Europe, for the rapidity of its improvements and the increase of its commerce."[43] From this increase in trade came the need for socioeconomic institutions equipped to deal with it: specifically, Liverpool responded to the huge increases in commerce in the early nineteenth century by passing the Municipal Reform Act in 1835, building the Custom-house Redburn sees, and constructing the dock in

[43]*The Picture of Liverpool* (Liverpool, 1808), iii–iv.

which the *Highlander* is moored. The decline and fall of Redburn's father, who may symbolize the patrimonial social system
of feudalism, reflects these changes, just as Redburn's movement away from a reliance upon his family coincides with the
change in Liverpool itself, the change around which Adam
Smith built his view of economic history.[44] With the growth of
commerce came the rise of cities, the decline of feudal manors,
and the need for laissez-faire.

Historically, Liverpool was the cardinal city built and maintained by and for commerce. As Redburn reads in the guidebook, "*In every clime her prosperous fleets are known, / She makes the
wealth of every clime her own*" (148). Redburn does well to refer to
the poetry in the guidebook as "epic": to many the history of
Liverpool *is* the epic of commercial progress, and Redburn
could have quoted many lines from the guidebook to say just
that. The anonymous author goes so far as to say that what
Homer's "imagination feigned, is here [in the docks] chiefly
realized by art."[45] Not without reason does Melville stress that
Roscoe is the poet laureate of Liverpool, since "the modern
Guicciardini" combined the arts with banking and represents
the kind of man Liverpool was famous for, the so-called "Liverpool gentleman," an ennobling euphemism for "merchant."
For Redburn, certainly, there is something epical about the
city: the docks remind him of "the old Pyramids of Egypt"
(161); these "noble docks," he says, might be "most fit monuments to perpetuate the names of the heroes, in connection
with the commerce they defended" (162). All the world, he
exclaims later, seems to be brought together "under the beneficent sway of the Genius of Commerce" in the Liverpool docks.

Commerce does indeed rule *Redburn*'s world, but to Melville
its sway is by no means "beneficent."[46] Although in Liverpool,
"all climes and countries embrace," it is far from the "brotherly
love" his narrator claims (165). Melville comments upon Liverpool's economic progress most clearly in his portrayal of the

[44]See particularly Smith, *Inquiry*, 1:420–45.
[45]*Picture of Liverpool*, 50–51.
[46]Similar criticisms can be seen in "The Revolutions in Europe," *North American Review* 67 (1848): 196.

effects of commercialization, for when Redburn wanders through the city, he finds not only that his guidebook does not work but also that the conditions of the city are far from what his gentlemanly morocco has claimed. He sees "Poverty, poverty, poverty, in almost endless vistas: and want and woe staggered arm in arm along these miserable streets" (201). Many of Melville's Liverpool scenes reiterate the misery Redburn summarizes here, misery most movingly portrayed in the Launcelott's-Hey chapter. It is the emotional center of the novel and one of the finest passages in all Melville. Here the poverty confronts Redburn most vividly and personally: here, too, the laissez-faire economics of Smith father their most terrible offspring. Smith believed that under a laissez-faire system, poverty, if not eliminated, would be greatly reduced. Despite the inequities of a leisure class which consumes much more than it produces, "the produce of the whole labour of the society is so great, that all are often abundantly supplied, and a workman, even of the lowest and poorest order, if he is frugal and industrious, may enjoy a greater share of the necessaries and conveniencies of life than it is possible for any savage to acquire."[47] In Melville's Malthusian rejoinder to Smith, Betsey Jennings and her children "were dumb and next to dead with want" (181)—and they remain so from literally a laissez-faire policy. Wherever Redburn seeks help, he is told to "let them be." The law, in fact, supports this insidious laissez-faire and "would let them perish of themselves without giving them one cup of water" (184). The capitalist may read or smoke in a better Lyceum, Melville shows, but the life of the lower class is still a peasantlike misery, still fraught with all manner of vice and dehumanization. The outcasts in Launcelott's-Hey are forced to live, or rather die in the ground like animals; in the vicinity

[47]Smith, *Inquiry*, 1:2. In opposition to Smith's logic, the *North American Review*, in "The Social Condition of England," 65 (1847): 465, states: "Labor is the only article the supply of which seems to increase without any reference to the demand. Its price therefore tends constantly to fall, competition acting on it with the accelerating force of gravity on a falling body; it is miserably paid at best, and much of it can find no employment whatever." Historically, there is more support for this latter view; Redburn's visit coincides with the worst poverty in English history.

of the glorious docks is "depravity . . . not to be matched by any thing this side of the pit that is bottomless" (138); "horrid old men and women" search for bodies around the docks in order to claim rewards (179); and the Booble-alleys "are putrid with vice and crime; to which, perhaps, the round globe does not furnish a parallel" (191). What Malthus demonstrates with his statistics, Melville accomplishes with his own "records"— vivid, powerful, realistic portrayals.[48] Both show the results of the Smithian economic system, in which sympathy for other human beings is "none of my business" (181), and in which "there seems to be no calamity overtaking man, that can not be rendered merchantable" (179).

Everywhere in the Liverpool scenes Melville describes the poverty with business terms—money, selling, peddling—to emphasize that the commercial greatness of the city interlocks with the misery of a large proportion of its people. Melville accurately dramatizes the condition of the city Gilman shows to be one of the most squalid in the 1840s world: "In 1844 an observer found the extremes of poverty and wealth in Liverpool 'hardly credible,' with ordinarily industrious people forced to pawn clothes for bread and live in crowded cellars and often reduced to beggary and crime."[49] The sharp differences in wealth in Liverpool comprise a class system almost as vigorous as feudalism but based on money, not family. Briggs's novels, largely a protest against this economic stratification, are representative of a widespread attitude. The *Democratic Review* explains the process by which the employer-employee relationship becomes just such a class system, then concludes, "Every year evinces a more marked distinction between the poverty of the employed and the limitless wealth of the employer; and aristocracy, already existing, is the results operating upon the elections and the movements of governments, by the direct

[48]Malthus's ideas are summarized in numerous articles in the journals of 1846–49; Melville may also have encountered his works in Duyckinck's library (*Lenox Library*, 8:39). On Melville's use of Malthus elsewhere, see Beryl Rowland, "Sitting Up with a Corpse: Malthus according to Melville in 'Poor Man's Pudding and Rich Man's Crumbs,'" *Journal of American Studies* 6 (1972): 69–83.

[49]Gilman, *Melville's Early Life*, 136. See also John Gross, "The Rehearsal of Ishmael: Melville's 'Redburn,'" *Virginia Quarterly Review* 27 (1951): 593.

application of wealth derived from the labor of others."[50] Melville would agree with such ideas, for he by no means supports Smith's view that the improvement of the bourgeois will ultimately help the worker. "It is too much the custom, perhaps," he says, "to regard as a special advance, that unavoidable, and merely participative progress, which any one class makes in sharing the general movement of the race" (139). When we look more closely at the poor man, we find that "he has made no individual advance of his own" (139).

II

As Redburn loses his romantic attachment to the Old World, he consequently and no less idealistically attaches himself to American messianic nationalism, which he voices in often-cited passages such as this: "The other world beyond this, which was longed for by the devout before Columbus' time, was found in the New; and the deep-sea-lead, that first struck these soundings, brought up the soil of Earth's Paradise. Not a Paradise then, or now; but to be made so at God's good pleasure, and in the fullness and mellowness of time" (169). Redburn thus seems to have made a literal about-face in his attitudes as well as his geographical orientation. As Cushing Strout points out, Redburn's disenchantment with the poverty, vice, and oppression of the Old World cities and his consequent turning to the innocence and promise of the New World are, in fact, typical of the spirit of the 1840s in America, as proclaimed particularly by the *Democratic Review*: "The vivid imagination of Napoleon was ever haunted with the visions of Eastern splendor, but he looked in the wrong direction with the wrong means. His face was set *eastward*, with arms in his hands; "young Democracy" looks *westward*, with the arts of peace as a means to attain the same end, and will be successful where he met only disaster and disgrace."[51] Like Napoleon, the hero of many romantics,

---

[50]"Economic Progress," *Democratic Review* 24 (1849): 104.
[51]"California—Its Position and Prospects," ibid., 427. Cushing Strout, *The American Image of the Old World* (New York, 1963), 5–23; see also Rogin, *Subversive Genealogy*, 70–76.

Redburn traveled east with dreams of aristocratic and Arabian splendor, fowling piece in his hands; he returns westward like Young Democracy, with peace and America in his mouth. The hastiness of his turnabout and the overblown rhetoric he adopts—fathered, no doubt, by similar statements in the American press—do nevertheless lead one to suspect that Redburn's idealistic, romantic tendencies may merely be appearing in different guise.

Deepening these suspicions, Melville presents his narrator's launching into such millennial rhetoric only immediately after Redburn has failed to retrace his father's path; only when fatherless can he say, "We are not a nation, so much as a world; for unless we may claim all the world for our sire, like Melchisedec, we are without father or mother" (169). Redburn's nationalism, then, is partly compensatory: his patriatism is another effort to find his father by adopting America as his father. On another level, in Redburn's realization that his ancestry can no longer be found in the Old World, Melville makes his narrator the personification of Young Democracy or Young America, breaking away from its English parentage to an independent national maturity.[52] Most particularly in Melville's 1840s, America saw itself growing up, finally casting off the last vestiges of aristocratic federalism.

To Redburn, America, "settled by the people" and therefore abhorring aristocracy, engenders a love for the common man, for equality and fraternity—an attitude again typical of the egalitarianism of the time. Redburn accordingly sharpens his criticism of Captain Riga's "despotism": with the voice of a true democrat he complains that, "as at sea no appeal lies beyond the captain, he too often makes unscrupulous use of his powers." He also criticizes more sharply the cabin passengers, one of whom particularly typifies everything now repulsive about the upper class:

> He was an abominable looking old fellow, with cold, fat, jelly-like eyes; and avarice, heartlessness, and sensuality stamped all

[52]Rogin, *Subversive Genealogy*, 66, sees this change as Gansevoort's shift of allegiance from his father to Polk.

over him. He seemed all the time going through some process of mental arithmetic; doing sums with dollars and cents: his very mouth, wrinkled and drawn up at the corners, looked like a purse. When he dies, his skull ought to be turned into a savings' box, with the till-hole between his teeth. (261)

This description shows Melville's powers of caricature at their best and Redburn's newly found democracy at its most rhetorically incensed. The old fellow, like Briggs's merchant Mr. Garvey, is a parodic exaggeration of the Smithian man, exclusively self-interested, completely absorbed in counting his money. In Briggs's words, "The life of a merchant . . . is the most purely selfish and least ennobling of all human pursuits, because it is the most mercenary."[53]

Redburn's democratization is never complete, however, for throughout the novel he holds a more than vestigial attachment to his gentility, personified in Harry Bolton. Harry is the stereotypical gentleman, small, "feminine," "courtly," well dressed. He comes from a storied place, has Byronic adventures and associations (277, 281), gambles, and drops the names of nobility. Although Redburn harbors some suspicions of him and is disgusted by the decadence of his haunts in London—scenes that are the upper-class equivalents of Liverpool squalor—Redburn nevertheless cherishes his friendship. When Redburn says, "And perhaps there is no true sympathy but between equals" (279), he refers not to the crew but to himself and Harry, who are both ecstatic to be called "Gentlemen" by a waiter in New York (303). It is as if Redburn's democratic ideals were little more than a ploy to placate the crew, whom he quickly casts off at the end. Harry, who resembles the Redburn of the voyage out, is also similar to the Redburn of the voyage back; he *is* Redburn's brother, for both conceive of themselves as gentlemen.

Thus Melville's attitude toward his narrator and toward Young America becomes clearer: Redburn's nationalism exists more in words than in actuality, much like that of both the Whigs and Democrats in 1848. Arthur Schlesinger notes that

[53]Briggs, *Bankrupt*, 151.

"the vocabulary of Whiggery had nothing to do with actu-
alities . . . [for the Whigs] intended to serve the business
classes, but the revolution in political values forced the Whigs
to talk as if they intended primarily to serve the common
man."[54] According to Glyndon Van Deusen, a similar duality
pervaded Jacksonian democrats, who on the one hand voiced
the interests of the common man while on the other promoted
through their economic policies the rise of a capitalistic elite.[55]
Through his narrator's association with Harry, Melville shows
his contempt for this hypocrisy widespread in the politics of the
1840s.[56]

As Rogin and Duban have argued, Melville's criticism of
Jacksonian politics may also surface in his characterization of
the sailor Jackson.[57] "A near relation of General Jackson," Melville's Jackson is a common man who holds "extraordinary dominion" over the common sailors, just as the historical Jackson
was caricatured as King Andrew by his opponents. In the brilliant description of Jackson's evil, Melville relates his reign on
board to democracy: "For there is no dignity in wickedness,
whether in purple or rags; and hell is a democracy of devils,
where all are equals" (276). Fortunately for those over whom
Jackson holds sway, his "democracy" is coming to an end. Similarly, during the 1840s Jacksonian democracy was dying, destroyed from within by the division between the Van Buren
and the Southern factions and from without by the slavery
issue and the growing Free-Soil party. When Jackson died in
1845, the party could no longer maintain its cohesion and
power. To one disenchanted with Democratic hypocrisy, the
death of Jackson could maliciously—and Melville is not beyond
malice—be considered the "deliverance" of the common man
(297).

[54]Arthur Schlesinger, Jr., *The Age of Jackson* (Boston, 1945), 279.
[55]Glyndon Van Deusen, *The Jacksonian Era, 1828–1848* (New York, 1959),
262–66.
[56]Rogin, who reads very little irony in the novel and relies rather heavily on a
Melville-Redburn conflation, disagrees.
[57]Rogin, *Subversive Genealogy*, 66–68; and Duban, *Melville's Major Fiction*, 53–
57.

Through both Jackson and Harry, then, Melville exposes the unegalitarian policies underlying his narrator's rhetoric and thereby distances himself from Redburn's position. Through both, too, Melville points to Smithian economics, which is a vital component of the messianic nationalism Redburn espouses. It is perhaps more than coincidence that Smith's theory and the American nation were both born in 1776, for, as George Bancroft stressed, the breaking away from colonization also meant the adoption of laissez-faire.[58] As America asserted its right to nationhood through the unrestricted trade with other countries, free trade continued to represent an essential component of the American self-image and by 1849 had become an important mechanism of the manifest destiny of the country.[59] Internally, too, laissez-faire was considered characteristic of American democracy, in which each man could, in theory, freely pursue his individual economic inclination unhindered by governmental restrictions. The Yankee peddler, free and shrewd, became a symbol of the national identity. During the 1840s, Van Deusen says, this identification was particularly appropriate, for "gone was the era of rigorous, authoritarian control, whether by church or feudal lord or state, over the economic life of the community. In its place had come the day of Adam Smith, of Thomas Malthus and David Ricardo, of Jeremy Bentham and Jean-Baptiste Say."[60]

With the discovery of gold in California, laissez-faire Americanism became a virtual religion, as if God had revealed the gold at precisely the right time and place for the millennial-minded Americans to capitalize upon it. This spiritual side of laissez-faire economics, perhaps originating in Smith's concept of the sacredness of the property of one's labor, is also echoed in Redburn's language when, for example, he foresees the New

[58]George Bancroft, *History of the United States of America, from the Discovery of the Continent*, 10 vols. (1834–1874; rpt. New York, 1885), 5:217; see also 5:110–11, on Adam Smith. In opposition to Bancroft's idea, the *North American Review*, in "The Past and the Present of the American People," 66 (1848): 433, laments the element of greed in the American Revolution.

[59]"The Past Administration," *Democratic Review*, 24 (1849): 204.

[60]Van Deusen, *Jacksonian Era*, 13.

World as "Earth's Paradise . . . to be made so, at God's good
pleasure, and in the fullness and mellowness of time." Redburn, who thought of himself as something of a Christ-figure
on the voyage out and in Liverpool, finds an adequate vehicle
for his religious aspirations only when he climbs aboard the
bandwagon of American millennialism. Like the political parties of the time, Redburn finds in millennial Christianity a sanction for his ideals of the common man, progress, and reform;
to him, as to the Whigs and Democrats, the redeemer nation
would progressively reform the world, giving "God's good
pleasure" a push toward "the fullness and mellowness of time."
An article in the April 1849 *Democratic Review*, "Human Rights
vs. 'Divine Rights,'" traces the development of "the democratic
principle" from the Jews through contemporary America and
stresses again and again the interconnection of free government, free trade, and Christianity, which "has aided materially
in the advancement of democracy." Near the end, the author
summarizes, "Free trade and free religion constitute the very
essence of freedom."[61] Briggs, on the other hand, rails con-
temptuously against those "fanatics" who quote the Bible to
support repressive economic policies.[62]

Melville himself was no stranger to a philosophy that combined religion and economics. Of Allan Melvill, Gilman says,
"No Puritan could have found a better solution to the problems
of keeping one's vessel of virtue pure while amassing wealth
and reputation."[63] And certainly Melville's acquaintances within the Young America movement gave reinforcement to this
picture; Rogin states, "Gansevoort filled the spirit world of
politics with Christian symbolism."[64] That is to say, from his
observations both personal and historical Melville presents in
Redburn the economic substructure of American democratic
millennialism. Smith's laissez-faire underlies all the attitudes
Redburn voices on the voyage homeward, just as it exposed his
ineffectual ideals on the voyage away.

[61]"Human Rights vs. 'Divine Rights,'" *Democratic Review* 24 (1849): 295–97.
[62]Briggs, *Tom Pepper*, 127–29.
[63]Gilman, *Melville's Early Life*, 16.
[64]Rogin, *Subversive Genealogy*, 70.

Through the other subject of the last half of *Redburn*, the emigrants, Melville voices more completely his criticism of this nexus of messianic nationalism and economics and reinforces his picture of the vicissitudes of the Smithian world. Redburn's melting-pot nationalism presupposes the immigration of diverse peoples to the New World; therefore, the Irish emigrants on the *Highlander* are both components of and actors in the pursuit of the American dream. One of them is a dreamer much like the early Redburn: he "would stand for hours together, looking straight off from the bows, as if he were expecting to see New York city every minute" (260). This also sounds quite like the later Redburn, looking westward not for New York but for the destiny that is manifest. The emigrants, too, play their part in this glorious future, for "if they can get [to America], they have God's right to come" (292). Although God's hand, through the American millennial ideal, is to Redburn responsible for the emigrants' voyage, to Melville Adam Smith's invisible hand of the market also points them westward. They can sail west, Melville indicates, because ship owners can reap huge profits bringing them to America:

> Owing to the great number of ships sailing to the Yankee ports from Liverpool, the competition among them in obtaining emigrant passengers, who as a cargo are much more remunerative than crates and bales, is exceedingly great; so much so, that some of the agents they employ, do not scruple to deceive the poor applicants for passage, with all manner of fables concerning the short space of time, in which their ships make the run across the ocean. (240)

Smithian competition determines which ships will carry emigrants and indirectly, through their advertisements, causes the emigrants' overly optimistic "fables" of America. Historically, as in *Redburn*, the Irish typified the plight of immigrants to America, since more left that country for England and America than any other nation in the 1840s. The Irish, also the most conspicuous example of a people torn by famine, oppression, and misery, had been kept firmly under the thumbs of neofeudal British landowners, who ruthlessly implemented Smithian policies that starved, killed, and drove out a huge portion of the country.[65]

Thus the Irish emigrants, a fictional addition to Melville's own ship, are an appropriate subject for Melville to use to point out the inadequacies of both laissez-faire and messianic nationalism. And the problems he exposes are many. As a result of being considered "cargo," the emigrants can be treated inhumanely—as long as at the end of the voyage all traces of abuses can be burned or discarded. On the *Highlander* they are stuffed into bunks that "looked more like dog-kennels than any thing else" (239) or "stowed away like bales of cotton, and packed like slaves in a slave-ship" (241). It is little wonder that, in consequence of this environment and of their insufficient rations (itself brought on by those misleading advertisements), their actions become animalistic at times (e.g., 284). The overcrowding on board also suggests the conditions of the historical Irish, to which Melville ironically refers as "the fertility of an island, which, though her crop of potatoes may fail, never yet failed in bringing her annual crop of men into the world" (199).[66]

On board the *Highlander* Melville presents a microcosmic picture of another disaster occasioned by British economic policies, the Irish potato famine he refers to in the above passage. Even when the emigrants have enough food, their cooking is hampered by "the despotic ordinances of the captain" (263) and becomes a Smithian "wrangling and fighting together for the want of the most ordinary accommodations" (264). When the food itself runs low, their "destitution [is] demonstrable": "all day long, and all through the night, scores of the emigrants went about the decks, seeking what they might devour" (284). The decrease in supply, according to Smith's competitive system, leads to an increase in demand, resulting in increased

[65]In "Ireland and Its Condition," *Democratic Review* 20 (1847): 424–30 blames the capital/labor struggle for Ireland's economic problems.

[66]In "Mill's *Political Economy*: Population and Prosperity," *North American Review* 67 (1848): 370–419 argues against the Malthusians' idea that overpopulation could cause Irish poverty and blames instead British laws that protect the aristocracy.

competition; but to Melville the plight of the emigrants is not theoretical but very real and very poignant. Like Briggs, he feels that the economic system, in which self-interest can drive men to hunger, then to theft and violence, is more to be faulted than the individuals themselves, who—as the "Horatii and Curiatii" chapter shows—normally value Christianity, family, and loyalty.[67]

One of the primary mechanisms furthering the oppressive misery of the emigrants is a strictly enforced class system based exclusively upon money. The "ladies and gentlemen in the cabin" have all the advantages: "nice little state-rooms," stewards to wait on them, meals prepared for them. On the other hand, "the emigrant passengers are cut off from the most indispensable conveniences of a civilized dwelling" (241). On the *Highlander* they are literally cut off by the ropes which "protect this detachment of gentility [the cabin passengers] from the barbarian incursions of the *'wild Irish'* emigrants" (242). This class system, as rigid as any feudal hierarchy, exists solely because the cabin passengers could pay three pounds while the emigrants only twenty guineas; "Such is the aristocracy maintained on board some of these ships" (242), Redburn states. Nor will this aristocracy be alleviated once they reach America:

> How, then, with these emigrants, who, three thousand miles from home, suddenly found themselves deprived of brothers and husbands, with but a few pounds, or perhaps but a few shillings, to buy food in a strange land?
>
> As for the passengers in the cabin, who now so jocund as they? drawing nigh, with their long purses and goodly portmanteaus to the promised land, without fear of fate. (290–91)

It is Redburn's strongest indictment of the class system and leads toward his statement on emigrants' rights. Money, he is saying, can indeed buy a passage to the American dream, as Jay Gatsby was also to learn.

---

[67]To Briggs poverty is lamentably one of the chief causes of crime; the economic system, not the criminal, is to blame (e.g., *Bankrupt*, 13–14 and 186, and *Tom Pepper*, 127–28).

The most devastating effect of this caste system is the fever, which again parallels the condition of the historical Irish. In 1837–38, near the time *Redburn* takes place, and again in 1847 typhus epidemics called "Irish fever" broke out in Liverpool, caused largely by the squalor in that city.[68] The "Irish fever" on the *Highlander* likewise begins out of the squalor of the hold, which Redburn chronicles extensively. The result, other than death, is an even greater separation of the classes, an elemental, barbaric tribalism. The "alleged physician" denies his profesion to avoid contact with the emigrants; "these last deaths brought the panic to its height," Redburn says; "and sailors, officers, cabin-passengers, and emigrants—all looked upon each other like lepers" (289). This is Smithian self-interest carried to its extreme, a world similar to that forecast by Malthus and Ricardo, the prophets of "the dismal science."[69]

In the last half of the book, then, Melville is suggesting that the subject of the emigrants and the subject of messianic Americanism are in deadly conflict.[70] In Redburn's America (and its microcosm the *Highlander*), where laissez-faire is an essential freedom, the poverty, misery, and death of the immigrants must follow, as historically it did. Van Deusen notes that once in America "both Irish and Germans, being poor, often congregated in slum sections, there to be viewed askance by the surrounding natives, whose alarm and disgust increased with the menace of job competition."[71] Like the New York slumlords, the unseen owners of the *Highlander* have the capital, and thus the power, to enforce such oppression, all in the sacred name of free profit. In the face of the millennial dreams of Young Democracy, Melville waves the pale yellow flag of contagion (300)—contagion caused and spread by the policies of laissez-faire.[72]

[68]See Eric Midwinter, *Old Liverpool* (Newton Abbot, Eng., 1971), 86.

[69]See "Mill's *Political Economy*," North American Review 67 (1848): 370–419.

[70]Cf. Duban, *Melville's Major Fiction*, 52: "Their [the emigrants'] misery aboard the American ship represents a more institutionalized form of the Redeemer Nation's neglect for humanity."

[71]Van Deusen, *Jacksonian Era*, 15–16.

[72]The term "contagion" was commonly use to indicate revolutionary activity; see Bernard Bailyn, "The Contagion of Liberty," in *The Ideological Origins of the American Revolution* (Cambridge, Mass., 1967), 230–319.

This conflict, not only a historical analysis, is as well a fundamental aspect of Redburn's psychological growth. To test Redburn's new and supposedly mature faith in democracy, Melville poses the problem of Harry Bolton.[73] As "the prospective doer of the honors of [his] country," Redburn "accounted him the nation's guest" (279), an immigrant for whom Redburn is personally responsible. Keeping his promise to find Harry a job is indeed a test of faith, for everywhere Melville describes Redburn's relationship to Harry in religious terms: can he believe in "his immaculate friend" and "ever [cherish] toward Harry a heart, loving and true," as a true Christian and democrat should? (223). Can Redburn put into concrete action those ideals he has been voicing throughout the voyage home? Despite evidence that Harry may be a liar and a rogue, Redburn keeps "confidential communion" with him (chap. 56) and promises to redeem him, just as the Redeemer Nation is to save the poor and the tired whom the tempest tosses upon her shores.

Melville's reference to Harry as a "prodigal" (217 and 218)— a reference directed toward this test of his narrator's faith— therefore relates very specifically to the story of the prodigal in Luke 15. Harry, "the son of a *man*" (281), has "wasted his substance with riotous living" and seeks refuge with Redburn's father-land. The second part of the biblical parable is more pertinent to Redburn himself: Should his brother complain about the prodigal's fatted calf or should he "be glad" and Christian at being reunited with his brother? Redburn has an equivalent choice: he can stay in New York and help his "brother" (the Christian choice), but he chooses instead to leave for the security of home (the selfish, economic choice). Melville ironically applies the parable at a more general level, too, for in the first part of his parable, the father, America (the same as God to Redburn), certainly does not bring the prodigal Harry his best robe, ring, and shoes and kill the fatted calf upon his

---

[73]With respect to these messianic and economic issues, Duban (*Melville's Major Fiction*, 46–51 and 59) examines Redburn's betrayal of Harry in the context of Luke's parable and Burton's explanation, in *The Anatomy of Melancholy*, of that parable's relation to ideas of "unmerited grace." See also McCarthy, "Melville's *Redburn*," 406–10.

homecoming. On the contrary, America takes no notice of Harry at all: its economic system strips off all but the clothes on his back and starves him into his desperate, suicidal act in the end. Redburn is no Christian brother, Melville is saying; nor is America a fatherly Christian ideal toward the unfortunates seeking refuge under its roof.

This conflict between economic and Christian choices is as well a conflict in definitions, for "prodigal" in *The Wealth of Nations* refers to one who is guided by "the passion for present enjoyment" and is consequently the greatest public enemy in Smith's system.[74] Redburn, faced with choosing between treating his prodigal brother according to Christ's or according to Smith's model, fails his mission to Harry. In Redburn's ear Adam Smith whispers words of wisdom, "Let it be." And Redburn literally lets Harry be. With little more than a cursory good-bye and a perfunctory explanation, he abandons Harry in New York, where he himself saw little more than confidence games, poverty, and desperation on his trip eastward. Redburn has "no doubt, Goodwell will take care of [him]"; his faith, that is, is nothing but a generalized goodwill, and little good or will at that. All is not good and well with Harry, though: laissez-faire once again fails to fulfill Smith's promises. Upon the implementation of a laissez-faire system, Smith says, "though a great number of people should . . . be thrown at once out of their ordinary employment and common method of subsistence, it would by no means follow that they would thereby be deprived either of employment or subsistence."[75] Yet in Smithian America, Harry cannot find a job: his attempts to become a Bartleby fail—the supply of copyists exceeds the demand (311)—and he becomes an Ishmael instead.

Briggs's Harry also arrives in New York from his first voyage and seeks a job copying in a countinghouse; however, the different outcome of his fortunes shows Melville's final reaction to Briggs and the other narratives *Redburn* has been following. Unlike Harry Bolton, Harry Franco obtains full wages from his

[74]Smith, *Inquiry*, 1:360–62.
[75]Ibid., 492.

captain, for he has come to recognize some of his vapid aristocratic pretensions for what they are and has done his work well.
He gets the job, works hard, and in the end achieves success.
Even the antiromantic Briggs, that is, believes it possible to
survive despite poverty and pretensions during a time of economic panic. In his Harry, Melville reverses this ending, for he
cannot give his assent to Briggs's Smithian idea that working
one's way out of "pecuniary embarrassments . . . is to have
tasted one of the greatest enjoyments of life."[76] In Redburn,
too, Melville departs from Briggs's narrative pattern. Both Harry Franco and H.C.F. begin their voyages as naive members of
the "soft-handed" order of society, work closely and sympa-
thetically with the crew, and arrive back home proclaiming,
"How changed was I." Briggs ends, that is, by proclaiming his
narrators' maturity and independence through the joy of
working.[77] It is a pattern, perhaps mythic, prevalent among
many nautical narratives from Smollett to Dana, but one Melville subverts. Redburn, though he has admired the artistry of
the sailors, wants only the money and status it could bring; nor
is he mature or independent, summarily sloughing off his responsibility to go home to mother.[78] If Redburn was "forced"
to give Harry up, as he says, he was forced by his own imma-
turity, which has changed colors but retained the same form
through the course of the book, and by the Smithian economic
system, which impoverishes him but keeps him ever dreaming
and thus precludes his development.

III

Through the character of Redburn and the ideology he voices
and represents, Melville gives the novel a tight yet complex
unity; his critique of the romance of laissez-faire involves just

[76]Briggs, *Working*, 3.
[77]Ibid., 106, 5, and 107–8.
[78]Redburn retains, that is, the almost infinite capacity for dreaming that
Briggs warns against: "bear in mind, young reader, [that you do not] pine after
luxuries, that do not happen to be within your reach" (*Working*, 108).

the sort of multiplicity of voices and intertextuality that to Bakhtin characterizes the novel as a literary genre. Redburn follows very clearly the path of the nautical bildungsroman by Briggs, Ames, Cooper, et al., essentially a pattern of progress to maturity through experience of the world. Whether an experience of the genteel culture in the Old World or of the difficult labor in a sailing ship, the youthful narrator undergoes an organic development that (re)integrates him with society at the end. Through his narrator, though, Melville shows the pattern in either case to be a romantic idealization in problematic conflict with the realities of the economic world. Both Redburn's Irvingesque quest for gentility and his Briggsian celebration of the possibilities of democracy are little more than a veil for an economic ideology that supports yet undercuts each: laissez-faire spurs his desires for money and status but dictates that he will get neither; it bankrolls his democratic nationalism but subverts it from within.

This technique of subversive juxtapositioning Melville uses to similar effect throughout the novel. Harry, a double of the Redburn of the first half of the novel, makes the same initiatory mistakes and has the same aristocratic pretensions, but Redburn cannot see these similarities which expose both Harry's and his own flaws. At the other extreme, Jackson, an outcast and a victim of the economic world, is also Redburn's brother, whom he again fails to recognize and learn from.[79] Melville reinforces this twinning—repeated in numerous contrasts of characters and scenes—most largely in *Redburn*'s structure, a movement from west to east and from east to west. At the outset of the former movement, Melville places as a marker the suicide of a drunken sailor, while at the beginning of the latter movement, he describes the "animal combustion" of another sailor. Thus beginning in death, each movement follows an almost mythic path, but backward, away from death, not from adolescence. At the poles of these movements, the scenes Redburn encounters (and at the end those Redburn and

[79]Cf. Schroeter, "Failure," 293–96; Dillingham, *Artist*, 41; and Rogin, *Subversive Genealogy*, 66–68.

Harry encounter) in New York and Liverpool are strikingly similar in their depiction of poverty, depravity, ruthless competition, and oppression—again all economically based. In this structuring Melville indicates, for his narrator and his readers, that the initiatory voyage is a dubious pattern, one that seeks unsuccessfully to escape economic reality. Redburn, no less than Tommo or Paul, follows a false path to the end.

Superimposed on this structure is the narrator Redburn, who years later realizes his youthful desire to "be telling my own adventures to an eager auditory" (7). This Redburn, emulating those beloved travel and guidebook narrators, humorously chronicles his past naïveté, commiserates with himself about the often painful maturation process, and relives the significant moments of his past. In writing his Rousseauvian "Confessions" he tries to accomplish in narrative what he has failed in life: to discover a pattern of growth, of progress in his experience. Redburn the narrator, however, is often as silly and ignorant as the young Redburn he thinks he has grown beyond. He lectures in favor of temperance, for example, and he admits, "I am sometimes by nature inclined to indulge in unauthorized surmisings about the thoughts going on with regard to me." He is, perhaps most stupidly, trying to write a guidebook just like the useless guidebook that, even as he writes, is still his favorite book (chap. 30).

Although this narrative voice continues throughout the book, in narrating the Liverpool scenes Redburn tells his readers to drop their books of travel, for his adventure-guidebook is becoming irrelevant even as he is writing it—although he himself never consciously abandons it. In telling of Liverpool, Redburn is confronted with *facts*, like those Jackson narrated (57–58), that are in their compelling horror more significant than his own trite story. In short, realism threatens to usurp his romance. To a degree the character of his narrative alters as a result, Redburn the narrator becoming something of a Dickensian reformist, all the while obliviously continuing his own adventures. These two tendencies in his narration are often in conflict through the last half of the book: Redburn wishes at once to continue his adventure story but also to give vent to the

realistic social criticism that forces itself upon him. Redburn
the character therefore fades in and out of the narrative as the
narrator wavers between these two purposes, one demanding
the narrative of personal experiences, the other the description
of social conditions. Melville, whose attitudes Redburn occa-
sionally seems to voice in moments of more mature understanding, knows that Redburn's story, "The Sufferings of
Young Wellingborough," is unimportant in the light of the
sufferings of the emigrants and the emigrant Harry, knows
that the true story is America's and more generally Western
man's economic inhumanity to man. Melville shows that Redburn, no Ishmael, grew up neither in the course of his adventures nor in the course of writing them, perhaps largely because he failed to look beyond his models of narration to the
ideology that lay beneath them. Ishmael, who could abandon
Ahab's quest and his own Christian categories and could embrace Queequeg's paganism, is saved; but Redburn can end
only in the confused eddies of his troubled mind.

Melville does not use Smith merely as a subversive counter-
point to the romantic pattern his narrator has been reading
and following, however; Smith's guidebook, to a large degree
responsible for Redburn's romancing, is itself infused with romantic elements. The wealth of nations, Smith indicates, most
basically depends on a "continual increase" in capital and a
"perfect liberty" in trade, that is, upon a highly idealistic faith
in progress and freedom.[80] This romantic component of
laissez-faire is revealed most strikingly in Smith's virtually
Gothic central trope, the invisible hand of the market, reminiscent of the hand of the giant specter that haunts Horace Wal-
pole's Otranto or of the hand of Providence in George
Bancroft's romantic history. The romance of laissez-faire in
Smith is thus the ideological equivalent of the personal romance of sailing in Ames, Cooper, and Briggs, and is the
largest example of Melville's subversive juxtapositioning. This
progressive and romantic conflation of the ideological and the

[80]These phrases are repeated throughout Smith (e.g., *Inquiry*, 1:136 and
344–45).

personal, typical of American typological history and of Smithian economics, does not cohere, Melville indicates.[81] Laissez-faire economics, like the primitivism Melville attacks in *Typee* and the missionizing in *Omoo*, not only collapses from conflicts inherent in the concept, but leaves the individual as "sadly shattered and broken" and "pitch[ed] head-foremost down into the trough of a calamitous sea" as Redburn's beloved glass ship.

[81]Ibid., 1:26.

5

White-Jacket

The Cloak of the Millennium in the Ark of State

As he is trying to auction off his white jacket, Melville's narrator remarks that "it behooves me once again to describe my jacket . . . this jacket of mine, undergoing so many changes, needs to be painted again and again, in order truly to present its actual appearance at any given period."[1] Melville's *White-Jacket*, too, seems to require repainting, for it similarly has undergone many changes in its season of critical wear and tear. Like White-Jacket's duck frock-shirt-quilt-jacket, the book itself lends one to ask, What is it? Critics have proposed it to be an autobiography, a propaganda tract, a historical document, a romance, an anatomy, a novel. Adding to the confusion, critics have interpreted the title symbol as the psychic self, a mask of innocence, protection from evil, military existence, the palsied universe beneath, patched-up theological beliefs, isolation, and the narrator's family.[2]

---

[1]*White-Jacket; or The World in a Man-of-War*, ed. Harrison Hayford, Hershel Parker, and G. Thomas Tanselle (Evanston and Chicago, 1970), 201; all further references will be cited parenthetically in the text.

[2]Anderson, *South Seas*; Thompson, *Melville's Quarrel*; Vincent, *Tailoring*; Rosenberry, *Comic Spirit*; Paul McCarthy, "Elements of Anatomy in Melville's Fiction," *Studies in the Novel* 6 (1974): 38–61; Priscilla Allen Zirker, "The Major and Minor Themes of Melville's *White-Jacket*" (Ph.D. diss., Cornell University, 1966); George Creeger, "The Symbolism of Whiteness in Melville's Prose Fic-

Each coat of critical paint has, nevertheless, somewhat clarified the outlines of the book. Beginning with Anderson's work
and culminating in Howard P. Vincent's *The Tailoring of Melville's White-Jacket*, criticism has traced the numerous sources of
the book to find that Melville, departing from autobiography
and urging reform of naval abuses, exaggerates the style and
content of his source material, making the book more "mili-
tant" than the originals. Other critics, while continuing to grant
that reform is the major issue, expand Anderson's perspective
by focusing on the narrator. Several perceive White-Jacket, like
a hero of a nautical bildungsroman, going through the process
of psychological growth from innocence to experience by
means of a confrontation with evil.[3] Other critics highlight
Melville's points by sketching in details of the background of
the book. Most themes that they explain are fairly obvious:
egalitarianism, reform, messianic nationalism, whiggism, the
man-of-war microcosm.[4] Yet Melville's presentation of these
themes, laced with ironies, undercut with contradictions, com-
plicated by an unreliable and shifting narrator, is apparently
neither clear nor coherent. Melville's *White-Jacket* is often as
abused and maligned as his narrator's white jacket.

In these diverse issues is nonetheless a discernible pattern:
like the sailor-narrators Melville consults as sources for this

tion," *Jahrbuch für Amerikastudien* 5 (1960): 147–63; James E. Miller, Jr., "*Redburn* and *White-Jacket*: Initiation and Baptism," *Nineteenth-Century Fiction* 13
(1959): 273–93; Robert Albrecht, "White-Jacket's Intentional Fall," *Studies in
the Novel* 4 (1972): 17–26; Seelye, *Melville*; Dryden, *Melville's Thematics*; and
Dillingham, *Artist*.

[3]For a list of the primary sources Melville used see Vincent, *Tailoring*. Also
see Willard Thorpe's "Historical Note" to *White-Jacket*; Miller, "*Redburn*";
Seelye, *Melville*; and Martin Pops, *The Melville Archetype* (Kent, Ohio, 1970).
Albrecht, "Intentional Fall," sees White-Jacket confronting not evil but the idea
of a utopian society; Dryden, *Melville's Thematics*, sees him as another young
artist; and Wai-Chee S. Dimock, "*White-Jacket*: Authors and Audiences," *Nineteenth-Century Fiction* 30 (1981): 296–317, stresses his shifting relationship with
the reader.

[4]Zirker, "Themes," sees the themes of the book as egalitarianism, flogging,
and war; Rogin, *Subversive Genealogy*, relates these themes to Melville's family;
Duban, *Melville's Major Fiction*, sees Whiggism as unifying the major themes;
and Paul McCarthy, "Symbolic Elements in *White-Jacket*," *Midwest Quarterly* 7
(1961): 309–25, presents the typical view of the book's disunity.

novel, White-Jacket voices a strong concern for those issues, egalitarianism and reformism, typically promoted by those narrators. Like them, too—and like Redburn—White-Jacket seeks sanction for his positions in the tenets of American democracy and Christian millennialism, but this political and religious philosophy undercuts those reforms White-Jacket seeks to effect. The novel thus follows the same structure of contradiction and collapse evident in the earlier narratives of facts. In *White-Jacket*, then, Melville's narratives of facts are in many ways "Homeward-Bound." Melville has been moving increasingly toward American themes, and none is more typically American than millennialism. Moreover, this central issue in *White-Jacket* has been peripherally yet importantly present in *Typee*'s description of the progress of history toward paradise, in *Omoo*'s description of the mission of a chosen people, and in *Redburn*'s description of the conflict between millennial dreams and economic reality. Thus *White-Jacket*, more than a preparation for *Moby-Dick*, is a culmination of Melville's early narratives of facts; it is the longest, most complex, and richest of these novels. In it Melville brings the issues of progress, missionizing, and messianic nationalism together in a devastating critique of the dominant ideals of America in 1849. The millennial theme is, obviously, a most appropriate capstone for these narratives, for it is the teleology driving all those narrators of facts whom Melville read and all those whom he created.

I

At the beginning of *White-Jacket* Melville describes extensively and in detail the organization of the *Neversink*, through which he develops the metaphor of ship as social microcosm.[5] In his presentation of every order and occupation of society—from the Sheet-Anchor-Men, described in terms suggesting the

[5]On the issue of community in the novel see Kaul, *American Vision*; Albrecht, "Intentional Fall"; and Gerlach, "Messianic Nationalism," 5–26.

clergy, to the Waisters, peasant *"sons of farmers"*—Melville may have been developing an idea he read in Samuel Leech's narrative:

> A vessel of war contains a little community of human beings, isolated, for the time being, from the rest of mankind. This community is governed by laws peculiar to itself; it is arranged and divided in a manner suitable to its circumstances. Hence, when its members first come together, each one is assigned his respective station and duty. . . . each task has its man, and each man his place. A ship contains a set of *human* machinery, in which every man is a wheel, a band, or a crank, all moving with wonderful regularity and precision to the *will* of its machinist— the all-powerful captain.[6]

This passage, which implies that the description of life on shipboard is essentially a political description, suggests many of the issues Melville develops in the first part of his book. In the redundancy of the title to chapter 3, "the principal Divisions . . . divided," Melville stresses "this endless subdivision of duties in a man-of-war" (11). *Neversink* society, "a state in itself" (23), is highly organized, by what work one does, by when and with whom one eats, and by where one sleeps. The social hierarchy is not only horizontally extensive but vertically oriented as well. There is a strict order of rank on board: in the great chain of naval being, the Commodore, a godlike personage who neither speaks nor deigns to associate with the people, occupies the top link of this society (194), while his more down-to-earth representative, the captain, "is its king" (23). The various lieutenants and midshipmen form the gentry; and "forming the first aristocracy above the sailors" are the various subordinates—stewards, corporals, and so on.[7] The men, themselves arranged in a hierarchical structure from main-top-men to landsmen, are the unprivileged masses: they eat only after the nobility have eaten, sleep in four-hour shifts while the

---

[6]Samuel Leech, *Thirty Years from Home* (Boston, 1844), 39–40.

[7]See Ibid., 59–60; and J. Ross Browne, *Etchings of a Whaling Cruise* (New York, 1846), 504. Zirker, "Themes," distinguishes sailor narratives from officer narratives; Duban, *Melville's Major Fiction*, 69–71, discusses aristocracy.

nobility sleeps all night, and fight wars while the nobility gets all the glory (28, 84, 208). Thus the shipboard society is composed of "two essentially antagonist classes in perpetual contact" (208), an amplification of the class issue in *Redburn*.

Into this society Melville places his narrator, a typical sailor who feels a strong need to assert his individuality. When he comes on board, "White-Jacket was given the *number of his mess*; then his *ship's number* . . . then, the number of his hammock; then, the number of the gun to which he was assigned; besides a variety of other numbers" (11). This mechanistic social system, like that Leech pictures, threatens to make White-Jacket little more than a mathematical point, threatens to deny his individuality and humanity. He complains, for instance, about much of the forced communality on board, for he cannot have his own wash-pail (85–86); and about specific eating and sleeping hours, for they seem unnatural (28–30, 35). He sees no reason for "the uniformity of daily events," other than that *"precedents are against"* any change.[8]

Even as White-Jacket tries to assert his individuality, though, he tries to assert his humanity by belonging to the brotherhood of his fellow sailors. Like Redburn, he constantly laments the ostracism his jacket brings him. He moves almost desperately from area to area throughout the ship, seeming to search for a place for himself but unwilling to accept the position the authorities have dictated. In the *"Forty-two-pounder Club,"* however, White-Jacket comes to satisfy his desire both for belonging and for individuality.

White-Jacket gratifies these urges in another and more important way: he perceives and describes himself as a typical sailor like those sailor-narrators he has been reading—Leech, Henry Mercier, William McNally, Nathaniel Ames, and J. Ross Browne. They, too, as Mercier says, read nautical narratives and spun nautical yarns to give themselves and their work a

[8]Russel B. Nye, *Society and Culture in America, 1830–1860* (New York, 1974), 38, shows this attitude to have been typical of Americans in Melville's day; see also Alice F. Tyler, *Freedom's Ferment* (1944; rpt. New York, 1962), 25. Rogin, *Subversive Genealogy*, 89, argues that White-Jacket rejects social stratification.

sense of importance and continuity.[9] White-Jacket, who follows their example and thinks of himself as the representative voice of his fellows, calls for reform of the many abuses the repressive officers and the hierarchical naval system inflict upon the sailors. In this respect he resembles particularly McNally, whose *Evils and Abuses in the Naval and Merchant Service Exposed* is just what the title indicates, an exposé, with little or no thread of narrative. Even in the accounts by Mercier, Leech, Ames, and Browne, much more narratives than propaganda tracts, reforming the sailors' life plays a prominent role: describing life on board leads these narrators, as it does White-Jacket, to "moralize upon the folly, in all arbitrary governments" (81) and to promote egalitarian reforms.

In the flogging chapters, the central focus of White-Jacket's reformism, Melville most fully acknowledges the prerogatives of his narrator's chosen genre—virtually every sailor's narrative contains at least one flogging scene—but revealingly transforms the typical generic prescription.[10] In the flogging scene itself, taken from Leech, Melville adopts, then exaggerates, the tendencies of his source, thus exposing and undercutting his narrator's position. The rhetorical excesses of White-Jacket, who melodramatically decribes the scene in lurid detail, replete with flailed flesh and seared psyches, indicate that he may be exaggerating the facts in his zeal to promote the sailors' cause. For example, the victim John, whom he has described as a "brutal bully" (136), becomes a stoic hero during the flogging. More revealing is White-Jacket's portrayal of Peter. In Leech, the man's punishment is much more severe—a night in irons and four dozen lashes—but Leech's rhetoric is much less polemical and melodramatic.[11] His sailor, though "robbed of all self-respect," is merely led off bleeding; but Peter, suffering

[9]Henry Mercier, *Life in a Man-of-War* (1841; rpt. Boston, 1927); William McNally, *Evils and Abuses in the Naval and Merchant Service Exposed* (Boston, 1839); and Ames, *Mariner's Sketches.*

[10]See Leech, *Thirty Years*, 48–58.; McNally, *Evils*; Browne, *Etchings*, 221–24; and Vincent, *Tailoring*, chap. 9.

[11]Vincent, *Tailoring*, chap. 9.

the "unendurable torture" of but twelve lashes, is corrupted for life (138). Through White-Jacket, who is milking the scene for all the sympathy it is worth, Melville thus exposes the sailor-narrators' attempts to inflate the issue of flogging (and more generally naval abuses) beyond what a realistic representation of the facts would allow.

Why the narratives tend to dramatize this issue Melville explains in the following chapters, which show the philosophical and political bases of White-Jacket's and the narrators' position. White-Jacket first argues that flogging is illegal, but even in this argument he goes overboard. After saying that the flogging issue is not a "question of expediency; it is a matter of *right and wrong*" (146), he in fact discusses it in the next chapter as a question of expediency. More absurdly, he ends the chapter demanding that every man who believes in flogging should be flogged until he recants—an excellent example of Melville's outrageous irony.

When one looks at them more carefully, White-Jacket's more pragmatic arguments against flogging appear similarly flawed.[12] Quite willing to violate his egalitarianism in order to support his argument, he explains that English and Southern officers are less willing to flog their men unmercifully, for "from their station in life, [they] have been more accustomed to social command . . . [while] a coarse, vulgar man, who happens to rise to high naval rank by the exhibition of talents not incompatible with vulgarity, invariably proves a tyrant to his crew" (141). White-Jacket momentarily forgets his previous diatribes against aristocracy and his previous statement that "every American sailor should be placed in such a position, that he may freely aspire to command a squadron of frigates" (114). Ending the chapter on the "Evil Effects of Flogging" in high and winding flights of rhetoric, he explains in detail how flogging—"a thing between a man's God and himself" (142)—cannot harm a man with true dignity, which seems to imply that

---

[12]Dimock, "*White-Jacket*," 300–301, questions Melville's frankness in these passages; Dryden, *Melville's Thematics*, 70–71, says that all of White-Jacket's arguments are untrustworthy.

the evils of flogging result not from the system doing the punishing but from the individual's reaction to that punishment. Then he seems to recollect himself and summarily says that the sailor who feels shame will be grievously tortured.

Nor is his case against the necessity of flogging any more successful. As a purported example of flogless rule, White-Jacket cites Collingwood, who "began by inflicting severe punishments, and afterward ruling his sailors by the mere memory of a by-gone terror" (148)—not suggesting the efficacy of total abolition. Earlier, too, White-Jacket has shown that the groggy sailors do not easily learn by example. Near the end of the chapter he contradicts the Collingwood example again, saying that "flogging has been, and still is, the law of the English navy. But in things of this kind England should be nothing to us, except an example to be shunned" (150). He concludes an argument based upon past examples, that is, with the sentiment that "the Past is dead."

Melville's rhetoric in these passages is brilliant, so brilliant in fact that many readers have been as swayed by them as his narrator wishes, demonstrating that Melville might have made as effective a politician as his brother. But his *narrator's* arguments—and this is perhaps the most brilliant aspect of Melville's persuasive powers—all fall apart. Comically fall apart, one might add, both here and elsewhere. In his ardent desire to identify himself with the sailors' cause, White-Jacket, like the sailor-narrators he emulates, often proposes the pettiest of reforms, exaggerates the most trifling of abuses. In grandiose rhetoric, for example, he calls on God, Congress, and the Secretary of the Navy to better the sailors' meal times, sleeping hours, and damp working conditions (chaps. 7, 20–22).[13] In short, White-Jacket's desire for brotherhood, as strongly voiced as Redburn's and as similarly suspect, leads him to repeat the sailor-narrators' condemnation of flogging; however, Melville's undercutting of his narrator's argument raises serious doubts about his narrator's (and the other narrators') motives.

[13]Here Melville is parodying Leech, *Thirty Years*, 116–20, and McNally, *Evils*.

The philosophical basis for White-Jacket's reformism is, as James Duban has argued, American Whiggism, which was also the party of Mercier's "Galley Politicians."[14] Like Mercier, who makes the analogy between the skill of "a good steersman" on his *U.S.S. Constitution* and William Henry Harrison's ability to pilot the nation, White-Jacket relates shipboard politics to American politics. As authoritative corroboration for his arguments against flogging, he therefore cites all the typical Whig authorities: Blackstone, Collingwood, the Law of Nature, the Declaration, the Constitution. The last of these, the "eternal principle" for White-Jacket's arguments and perhaps an acknowledgment to Mercier, was the Whigs' ultimate authority, from which any deviation brought evil. They contended, for example, that the Democrats held that "the restrictions of the Constitution are fetters to the free," a policy that initiated the hated Mexican War.[15] Mercier's paean to Harrison is little more than another aspect of "Life in a Man-of-War"; but Melville's portrayal of White-Jacket's Whiggism more astutely identifies and examines the ideology behind the reformist stance of sailor narratives.

White-Jacket's identification with the Whigs, more than a citation of authorities, allows him to perceive the situation on board, which his reforms are directed to correct, as stemming from the compulsion of those at the top of the ship's hierarchy to maintain forcibly their authority. The captain censors the theatrical production "to see whether it contained any thing calculated to breed disaffection against lawful authority" (93); the officers "scruple not to sacrifice an immortal man or two, in order to show off the excelling discipline of the ship" (197). This authoritarianism is endemic to the naval system, particu-

---

[14]Mercier, *Life*, 138–39. Duban's argument, *Melville's Major Fiction*, 61–81, does not connect White-Jacket's Whiggism to Melville's nautical narrative sources, though he ably details Melville's use of other works.

[15]"Executive Usurpations," *American Review: A Whig Journal of Politics, Literature, Art and Science* 5 (1847): 224. Duban, *Melville's Major Fiction*, 71–74, argues for Melville's familiarity with the journal. On the Whig tradition see Caroline Robbins, *The Eighteenth-Century Commonwealthman* (Cambridge, Mass., 1959), 381; Ernest L. Tuveson, *Redeemer Nation* (Chicago, 1968), 58–74; and Tyler, *Freedom's Ferment*, 3, 265–66.

larly the executive branch of shipboard government. "That the king, in the eye of the law, can do no wrong, is the well-known fiction of despotic states," White-Jacket says; "but it has remained for the navies of Constitutional Monarchies and Republics to magnify this fiction, by indirectly extending it to all the quarter-deck subordinates of an armed ship's chief magistrate" (217).

This issue of executive authority was readily familiar not only to readers of nautical narratives—Leech, Mercier, McNally, and Browne each condemn this aspect of naval discipline[16]—but to any American in 1849, for it was the crucial issue of the Whig party, who had adopted their name in 1833 to link their criticism of Jackson's "executive usurpation" to the Revolutionary Whigs.[17] According to the Whigs, the "Democratic organization," as they called it, had led the country into an illegal, immoral, and unnecessary war against Mexico, a sister republic. The issue to them, though, was not the war per se but Polk's conducting an unpopular war by bending the Constitution. The *American Review* summarizes: "The great doctrine which gave us our party designation was that of opposition to Executive usurpations. We hold it to be essential to the success of our free form of government that the President should be kept strictly within the limits of his proper Constitutional authority."[18] Even when the election of their candidate, Zachary Taylor, made such comments unnecessary, the Whigs continued to stress the need for executive limitations, for men tend to "arrogate a superiority over those who are less favored, and form themselves into a separate class."[19] Like that on the *Neversink* or what the Whigs accused "King Andrew" Jackson and his followers of forming, the executive aristocracy would

[16]Leech, *Thirty Years*, 37; Mercier, *Life*, 2 and 8; McNally, *Evils*, 71; and Browne, *Etchings*, 35–50.

[17]See William R. Brock, *Parties and Political Conscience* (Millwood, N.Y., 1979), 6.

[18]"The Whigs and Their Candidate," *American Review* 8 (1848): 222; see also "The President's Message: The War" and "Executive Usurpations," 5 (1847): 2, 13–15, and 217–18.

[19]"Origin of the Two Parties," *American Review* 9 (1849): 16, argues against veto power on this ground.

engender a class struggle similar to what White-Jacket describes; the Whigs consistently stress that Polk's incursion into
Mexico most harmed "the people" of America. "The whole
ultimate authority of the government, under the Constitution,"
the *American Review* says, "is in the hands of the People—this is
our system. And yet we have here a doctrine which withdraws
from the people all authority, and gives the whole power, present and ultimate, over to the government, or the existing administration."[20] The Whigs thus saw the American government during the election of 1848 much as White-Jacket and
the other nautical narrators see their ships' governmental conditions: as a struggle between those who believe in hierarchy,
aristocracy, and executive authority on the one hand, and the
victimized people on the other.

To oppose the executive usurpations of the officers, then,
White-Jacket uses the Whig identification with "the people"
(28–30). More than a common reference to sailors, this term
was a catchword by which the Whigs allied themselves with
their political heritage, a deliberate echo of the rhetoric of
eighteenth-century radical libertarianism and revolutionary
egalitarianism.[21] Melville makes a similar, but parodic analysis
of this rhetorical move when White-Jacket says, "*the people,
keep up their constitutions, by keeping up the good old-fash-
ioned, Elizabethan, Franklin-warranted dinner hour of twelve*"
(28). This passage not only traces Whig rhetoric back to its
sources in England, the Enlightenment, and the Revolution,
but also puns upon the Whigs' constitutionalism. Later in the
same passage, Melville mocks another commonly claimed aspect of Whig ancestry: when White-Jacket says, "Doubtless,
Adam and Eve dined at twelve; and the first Patriarch Abra-
ham in the midst of his cattle" (29), he resorts to the typical

[20]"Dangers to Be Guarded Against in the Progress of the United States,"
American Review 5 (1847): 622, 624; see also "Opinions of the Council of Three:
The Nature of This Government," 6 (1847): 374, and "Causes of the Success of
the Whigs," 8 (1848): 547.
[21]"Representative Government," *American Review* 7 (1848): 280. Zirker, "Evidence of the Slavery Dilemma in *White-Jacket*," *American Quarterly* 18 (1966):
477–92, analyzes the egalitarian theme in the novel.

Whig ploy of relating "the people" to the chosen people. By the time the American Whigs had incorporated "the people" into their lexicon, then, the term was not being used in the original radical sense. Thus *The American Review* at one moment claims that "there is a right of revolution," but at the next qualifies this assertion, saying, "we must admit that this Age is peculiarly revolutionary; subject to a revolution of opinion slow, gradual, profound."[22] Specifically, they use the term "the people" not for revolutionary purposes but to oust the Democrats and gain political power for themselves. Behind White-Jacket's adopted Whiggism is a similarly self-serving motivation: he wishes to diminish the power of those above him and to ingratiate himself with "the people" by putting his rather trifling shipboard events in terms of the larger events of contemporary American politics.

The Whigs themselves—and White-Jacket along with them—in order to give greater significance to their own positions also identify themselves with a larger American political ideology, at times sounding much like Democrats or even Puritans.[23] Their appropriations begin, as White-Jacket's do, with the placing of their reforms under the aegis of Progress. Reformism is itself obviously an expression of the drive to progress by improving man's conditions: immediately after his flogging arguments, White-Jacket says, "The Past is dead, and has no resurrection; but the Future is endowed with such a life, that it lives to us even in anticipation" (150). "The Future . . . the Future . . . the Future . . . ," White-Jacket chants. Although this is the chant of virtually everyone in mid-nineteenth-century America—witness Whitman—the Whigs claimed it as one of their own traditional tenets. Encouraging an expanding American influence throughout the globe, the Whigs "shout the

[22]"On a Congress of Nations to Settle National Disputes," *American Review*, 5 (1847): 348, and "The Age Is Revolutionary," ibid. 6 (1847): 85.

[23]See Brock, *Parties*; Daniel W. Howe, ed., *The American Whigs* (New York, 1973); and Schlesinger, *Age of Jackson*. On the conservative pragmatism of the Whigs as related to *Moby-Dick*, see Duban, *Melville's Major Fiction*, 92–95, and "'A Pantomime of Action': Starbuck and American Whig Providence," *New England Quarterly* 44 (1982): 432–39.

watchword, *Onward, onward.*"[24] The Whig philosophy of history, thus essentially and absolutely Progressive, divides the world into friends and enemies of Progress and makes each historical event into a struggle between Good and Evil.

This perception tends to cast the idea in a religious light and thus gives it greater status. The Whigs' politics—again appropriating American politics—cannot be divided from religion, for they hold that "we enjoy a form of government whose fundamental maxims differ in no particular from those of . . . the law of conscience—and that to sin against *our* law is to sin against humanity."[25] With this rhetoric, the Whigs alter the terms: law becomes moral commandment and lawbreaking becomes sin. White-Jacket can then present Christ as a model for the head of his ship's government and denounce flogging laws that "dare profane what God himself accounts sacred" (142). The Whigs' spiritualization of politics reflects the intensity of their belief in progress and their other political positions, but it also exposes their tendency to dock at every possible rhetorical port.[26]

It is a rhetorical haven that many of the sailor-narrators resort to as well. Melville's chief source, Mercier, argues that the sailors' nearness to "the verge of eternity" makes them much more spiritually conscious than most would think, then uses this statement to set up his passage on the "Galley Politicians," in which he praises the virtues of Harrison. Mercier later uses his spiritual mantle to call for officers to search their souls and determine "whether your conduct, to the hardy class of men under your command, when braving with you the perils of the unfathomable deep, would call forth a like tribute of warm and disinterested respect to your memories, should the

[24]See Tyler, *Freedom's Ferment*, 1; Nye, *Society*, 28 and 33; Tuveson, *Millennium and Utopia* (Berkeley and Los Angeles, 1949); Herbert Butterfield, *The Whig Interpretation of History* (London, 1931); "Poverty and Misery, versus Reform and Progress," *Democratic Review* 23 (1848): 27; and "The Anglo-Saxon Race," *American Review* 7 (1848): 29.

[25]"The Future Policy of the Whigs," *American Review* 7 (1848): 331; see also "Opinions of the Council," ibid. 6 (1847): 371.

[26]See Butterfield, *Whig Interpretation*, 64–65.

dread fiat of the Almighty snatch you from amongst them."[27] If under Mercier's often inane drivel runs a current of religious reformism, in Leech it is an overflow. Leech is writing a conversion narrative; his Christianity informs every aspect of his life, for "Where is the presence of the meek spirit of Chrisitanity more needed than on the decks of our merchant and naval vessels?" It is the answer to the officers' cruelty and the men's depravity. Leech therefore ends with an evangelical appeal to "rest in His bosom, who says to you, 'Come unto me, all ye that are weary and heavy laden, and I will give you rest.'"[28] Such high-minded Christianity, also vital to McNally's and Ames's narratives, often descends into the most banal pieties and trivial reforms, however. But Melville, closely linking tenor and vehicle, uses this sanctified self-interest as he did in *Redburn*, to question not only his narrator's and the sailor-narrators' idealism but also the Whigs'. In each case reformism is an inflated cloak draped over a desire for personal security and political influence.

At the end point of this idealization is White-Jacket's likening his own mission of reform to that of Christ: "To be efficacious," he says, "Virtue must come down from aloft, even as our blessed Redeemer came down to redeem our whole man-of-war world" (229). This conflation places White-Jacket's self at the highest position and his reforms on the course of redemption for the entire world. In a word, White-Jacket is a millennialist. Just as at the end of his reformism is the millennium, at the end of his passages on flogging is a statement on American millennial destiny:

> And we Americans are the peculiar, chosen people—the Israel of our time; we bear the ark of the liberties of the world. . . . God has given to us, for a future inheritance, the broad domains of the political pagans, that shall yet come and lie down under the shade of our ark, without bloody hands being lifted. God has predestinated, mankind expects, great things from our race; and great things we feel in our souls. The rest of the nations

[27]Mercier, *Life*, 130 and 198.
[28]Leech, *Thirty Years*, 254 and 304.

must soon be in our rear. We are the pioneers of the world; the advance-guard. . . . Long enough have we been skeptics with regard to ourselves, and doubted whether, indeed, the political Messiah had come. But he has come in *us*. (151)

This passage, rightly the most famous in *White-Jacket*, informs all of White-Jacket's positions. In order to be "the advance-guard," "to break a new path in the New World," America must be reformist, must strive to keep its institutions in line with God's directives, or be scourged as God so often scourged Israel. The American, like White-Jacket, constantly must face forward, looking toward his "future inheritance." Millennialism also satisfies White-Jacket's desire for individualism: in order to know what "God has predestinated," we must be able to follow the "great things we feel in our souls," unrestricted by outside forces. "Our own hearts are our best prayer-rooms," White-Jacket says; therefore, "the chaplains who can most help us are ourselves" (158).

Thus central to White-Jacket's millennialism is the belief in and reliance upon eternal principles and models. He cannot accept the laws of the *Neversink*—hierarchy, aristocracy, and all—because they conflict with Divine laws, to him inherently more compelling. Government to him, as to the Whigs, is thus "a partnership, indeed, but of no gross transient character. . . . It is a firm, whose confirmation rests in eternal laws," a cooperative venture between God and man based upon the rules God, not man, has ordained.[29] These rules apply not only in the central tenets of their government, but in each historical event, which Divine Providence guides. Melville, here as in *Redburn*, parodies this providential tendency, for in the chapter that follows the millennial passage, he shows White-Jacket celebrating "an almost miraculous intervention" of "Providence"—a barrel of grog (152–54). This perception of historical events and more largely the course of history itself are, obviously, teleological. To use White-Jacket's metaphor, "Life is a voyage

---

[29]See "Opinions of the Council," *American Review* 6 (1847): 375, and "The Destiny of the Country," ibid. 5 (1847): 232. This attitude is echoed by Mercier, *Life*, 235 and 286.

that's homeward-bound!" (400; see also chap. 2). The home, to which "those magical words" (6) refer and toward which the man-of-war is bound, is that place which Christ has gone to prepare, the heaven beyond the millennium. The "home*ward*" stresses that the ship of history constantly progresses in the direction of the millennium, while "bound" implies the inevitable, "predestinated" chart of the voyage.

Historically the American ship of state likewise conceived of itself as bound for the millennial port. Sacvan Bercovitch shows how, like White-Jacket, the Puritans, "substituting teleology for hierarchy, . . . discarded the Old World ideal of stasis for a New World vision of the future." The vision was of the millennium, as the settlement of New England followed a revival of interest in the Book of Revelation.[30] In the 1840s apocalyptic ideas were particularly prevalent, gaining expression in groups as diverse as the Perfectionists, the Millerites, and the Mormons. The Whigs, who had first opposed the Democrats' Manifest Destiny, realized the popular appeal of millennialism and for the election of 1848 became vocally millennialist. The election of Taylor and the discovery of gold in California led them to muse upon the workings of history:

> Now for what purpose has the providence of God conducted our nation unconsciously through the events of the last three years, to the edge and prospect of such a stupendous, startling future? . . . a Divine idea is ever realizing itself in the historical life of humanity, as truly as in the life of nature. . . . Behind the series of outward events we are made to see the Supreme Disposer touching the springs of human action.[31]

In purely material terms, the development of California would unite the continent, eventually tie America to Asia and all other nations, and thus "draw the world's history into the stream of ours." More abstractly, "the barriers of time and space will be annihilated," and Christianity will come to spiritualize the world.[32]

[30]Sacvan Bercovitch, *The American Jeremiad* (Madison, Wis., 1978), 23 and 70.
[31]"California," *American Review* 9 (1848): 334.
[32]Ibid., 332–39.

In accordance with his millennialism, then, White-Jacket portrays his ship—historically Melville's *United States*—as a microcosm of America (see 20, 114, 374–75).[33] When in the famous millennial passage White-Jacket says that "we Americans . . . bear the ark of the liberties of the world" (151), Melville punningly refers not only to the ark of the covenant but also to Noah's ship of state. It is a significant reference, as Bercovitch notes in tracing "the use of ark for ship of state . . . from Joshua Scottow's *Narrative of Massachusetts* (1694) through Joseph Warren's oration on the Boston Massacre (1775), Melville's *White-Jacket*, and W. E. Arthur's July Fourth speech of 1850."[34] In Noah's case the world (or all its animal life) was truly in a ship, but in Melville's case the metaphorical conjunction of ship as state and ship as world might seem contradictory. To the Whigs, however, who described America as the modern Israel, the American nation *was* the world, composed of all nations and destined to rule over the entire globe.[35] In White-Jacket's similar conflation, as in Redburn's, Melville exposes the inflated egos of his narrator, the Whigs, and America.

White-Jacket's metaphorical American world is a "world in a man-of-*war*," which he often laments. In this respect he follows the course of Melville's sources, who frequently give voice to antiwar sentiments, basing them as White-Jacket does on Christian and moral grounds. Leech, for example, rails against the inhuman contradiction of war perpetuated "by Christian (?) nations," and asks, "What Christian will not pray for the destruction of such a spirit?"[36] Here again White-Jacket also echoes the typical Whig, who in 1848 conceived of Polk's administration as "calculated, in fact, 'to prepare the heart of this people for war.'" At times the Whigs see metaphorically what

[33]The sailor-narrators also use this trope: see McNally, *Evils*, 151; and Mercier, *Life*, 235–44.

[34]Bercovitch, *American Jeremiad*, 104–5n.

[35]See "The Destiny of the Country," *American Review* 5 (1847): 232–33; "The Future Policy of the Whigs," ibid. 7 (1848): 329–32; and "The Whigs and Their Candidate," ibid. 8 (1848): 225.

[36]Leech, *Thirty Years*, 189; see also 130–44, and McNally, *Evils*, 79–81.

White-Jacket sees in reality: that "war, conquest, the lust of dominion—these things become the order of the day."[37] Melville's narrator literally sees a society dominated by the idea of war, the world around him an actual man-of-war, whereas the Whigs only figuratively complain that the Mexican war has made American society little more than a warship of state.[38]

Historically, the navy was itself very much a part of the Mexican war, the problems in Oregon, and America's westward destiny. California and the millennial hopes it excited also needed to be protected. Thus the *Neversink* itself, like Melville's *United States*, is most likely returning from protecting American interests in the Pacific.[39] On the most literal level, then, Melville links tenor (millennialism) and vehicle (ship): his microcosm not only describes American society and exposes White-Jacket's political leanings, it is itself a result of the historical situation it typifies. Moreover, this ship-millennium connection—which Melville emphasizes by the name *Neversink*, which refers to the eternal qualities America saw in itself—has a significant metaphorical history as well. Bercovitch gives two prominent examples: both Mather's General Introduction to the *Magnalia* and David Austin's Advertisement to Edwards's *History of the Work of Redemption* refer to America as an ark of the millennium.[40] Even though it is buffeted by the tempestuous weather of Cape Horn or foundered by the flogging tyrants, Melville's millennial ark also is sailing, never sinking, on the ocean of history—or so his narrator believes.

Just as America's ideals are gathered together on board Melville's ship, so too does the narrator's white jacket symbolically

---

[37]See "The President's Message" and "Executive Usurpations," *American Review* 5 (1847): 1, 227; and "The Whigs and Their Candidate," ibid. 8 (1848): 225.

[38]Adler, *War*, 29–54, sees at "*White-Jacket*'s center" Melville's hatred of war.

[39]In 1849 the *Democratic Review* printed an extract, "Rambles in California (From a Navy Officer's Journal)," which ends with the commodore planting "the stars and stripes over the unresisting Mexican fortresses of the Pacific" (24 [1849]: 75). Anderson, ed., *Journal of a Cruise to the Pacific* (Durham, N.C., 1937), 8–9, notes that the *United States* was protecting American interests in the region.

[40]Bercovitch, *American Jeremiad*, 104.

cover his millennial role.[41] To recognize the symbolic relevance
of the jacket, one must first recognize that what Melville describes is not in the strictest sense a "jacket": "An outer garment
for the *upper part of the body*: orig. the same as or a shorter form
of the jack; now, an outer garment with sleeves, reaching *no
lower than the waist*, worn by boys (as an *Eton jacket*) and by men
in certain occupations; also a short coat without tails (as a *Nor-
folk jacket*), worn in shooting, riding, cycling, etc."[42] Yet the
narrator's "jacket" does not fit this definition, for it is "of a
Quakerish amplitude about the skirts" (3), and only severely
shrunken does it extend above the loins (100). Clearly Melville
has retailored his white "jacket" to fit another figure. In the
Book of Revelation John of Patmos refers six times to the
"white robes" to be worn by the redeemed during the millennium: "After this I beheld, and, lo, a great multitude, which no
man could number, of all nations, and kindreds, and people,
and tongues, stood before the throne, and before the Lamb,
clothed with white robes, and palms in their hands" (Rev. 7:9).
He explains that "these are they which come out of the great
tribulation, and washed their robes, and made them white in
the blood of the Lamb" (Rev. 7:14).[43] In "America: or a Poem
on the Settlement of the British Colonies, addressed to friends
of Freedom and their Country," Timothy Dwight applies this
image to the American millennium. There a personification of
Freedom, dressed appropriately for the mission in "robes of
pure white," gives the poet a vision of the future, when "white-
rob'd Peace [Quakerish?] begins her milder reign, / And all
virtues croud her lovely train."[44] The poet is allowed to see that
when America achieves ideal Freedom, Peace, and Virtue, the
heavenly kingdom will descend. In the 1840s this poetic theme

[41]Thompson, *Melville's Quarrel*, argues that the jacket represents White-Jacket's theological beliefs.

[42] *Oxford English Dictionary*, 1933—my emphasis.

[43]Harold Beaver, "Herman Melville: Prophetic Mariner," in Richard Gray,
ed., *American Fictions: New Readings* (London and Totowa, N.J., 1983), 72,
argues that *Moby-Dick* parodies Revelation.

[44] *The Major Poems of Timothy Dwight*, ed. William McTaggart and William
Bottorff (Gainesville, Fla., 1969), 10 and 12.

became a reality for many Americans: in 1843 and again in 1844, for example, the followers of William Miller gathered, clad in their white robes, on hilltops or in treetops to await the predestinated end of the world.[45]

Or, like White-Jacket, in the main-top. Knowing the background of this symbol, one can more easily see the ironies Melville directs at his narrator, even in the first chapter. "Homeward-bound" from the "last harbor in the Pacific," White-Jacket dons his "outlandish," not to say otherworldly, garment (3). Importantly, it is "of [his] own devising," for White-Jacket's millennialist role, like the Millerites', is self-appropriated; made from bits and pieces of the religious and political ideas he has picked up, it is a consciously adopted patchwork, not a unified, seamless garment. Unlike Dwight's Freedom, White-Jacket is not divinely directed, but acts out of concern for personal security: "to shelter [him] from the boisterous weather [they] were soon to encounter" (3). He knows the tribulations of the end times and needs the spiritualizing protection of a jacket. It undergoes a "metamorphosis" that makes White-Jacket "white as a shroud"; but his sartorial spiritualization has about the same effect as the Millerites' robes had on them, even to White-Jacket's eventual fall.[46] The robe does not bring on a millennial transformation but does almost transform him into a corpse; his consequent ascension is only literal, in his "own proper person" and "in accordance with natural laws."

Nor does he play his role as originally set out but expands it, stuffing and padding his jacket until he becomes a "universal absorber," appropriating everything from flogging to grogging into his role. Like many American millennialists, who became increasingly secularized and preoccupied with an ad hoc series of reforms, White-Jacket thinks he can perfect his jacket merely by painting, patching, and pocketing it.[47] Such extreme re-

---

[45]See Tyler, *Freedom's Ferment*, 70–78.
[46]Ibid., 75, gives an instance of a millennial robe's causing a fall from a treetop.
[47]See Bercovitch, *American Jeremiad*, 93.

formism can only be a "burden" to the millennialist, for he
constantly tries to retailor society and thus lives in the "foul
weather" of seeing too many reforms to be effected in order to
prepare the way of the Lord. To the millennialist reformer it
must seem, as it does to White-Jacket, that progress involves
"dragging myself up, step by step, as if I were weighing the
anchor" (4). Thus White-Jacket, no more than a typical sailor,
cloaks his need for self-importance under the mantle of millennialism; progressing homeward on his ark of state, he sits high
in his religious maintop—a spiritual guide "gleaming white"
for all to see.

II

Although White-Jacket, like the sailor-narrators and the
Whigs, believes that the evils of class and war can be re-formed
or patched up by an appeal to Christianity, Melville is more
skeptical. To contrast his narrator's millennialism, he makes
reference to White-Jacket's own professed standard of conduct, the Sermon on the Mount. As in *Omoo*, here Melville
parodically uses that text to deflate his narrator's pretensions.
Soon after tailoring his millennial jacket, White-Jacket adds
pockets in order to keep all his possessions close to him, thus
ignoring Christ's dictum to "lay not up for yourselves treasures
upon the earth, where moth and rust doth corrupt, and where
thieves break through and steal: but lay up for yourselves treasures in heaven, where neither moth nor rust doth corrupt,
and where thieves do not break through and steal" (Matt.
6:19–20). When White-Jacket tries to lay up material treasures
within his Christian role, thieves break in and steal from his
pockets, and he must sew them up. Melville again exposes
White-Jacket's hypocrisy when the jacket's distinctive light col-
or prevents him from loafing like other sailors (chap. 29), just
as the visibility of the role he has adopted should prevent his
self-serving laziness. In the Sermon Christ calls for his followers to "let your light shine before men, that they may see
your good works, and glorify your Father which is in heaven"
(Matt. 5:16). White-Jacket wants only to paint over his light

jacket, so that he may shirk off some "good works," as everyone else does. He cannot get paint; therefore, he washes his jacket neither in the blood of the Lamb nor to make it whiter than snow, but to darken it. Melville has the last, ironic laugh, though: nothing can lessen the light of the jacket.

White-Jacket therefore cannot help but let his light jacket shine before men, whose reaction is what Christ predicts: "Blessed are they which are persecuted for righteousness' sake: for theirs is the kingdom of heaven. Blessed are ye when men shall revile you, and persecute you and say all manner of evil against you falsely, for my sake. Rejoice and be exceeding glad: for great is your reward in heaven; for so persecuted they the prophets which were before you" (Matt. 5:10–12). The men vituperatively blame the jacket for the crowding in the mess and for the death of three men (333), but White-Jacket is not at all "glad" at the prospect of such persecution. He is no martyr, as Melville's parody of redemption shows: "Jacket," cries White-Jacket, "you must change your complexion! you must hie to the dyers and be dyed, that I may live. I have but one poor life, White Jacket, and that life I can not spare. I can not consent to die for *you*, but be dyed you must for me. You can dye many times without injury; but I can not die without irreparable loss, and running the eternal risk" (78). White-Jacket is the complacent Christian, taking no religious "risk," balancing his spirituality against "loss." Like Long Ghost and Paul, he is no Christ and will not give up his life to his Spirit but would sooner give up his religious role or color it to blend in with the crowd. In short, White-Jacket, desiring his millennial role to provide material comforts—his original intent in making the jacket and adding the pockets—bemoans the very Christian fact that spirituality requires him to cast off personal possessions, comforts, reputation, even warmth.

As White-Jacket's millennial mission carries him throughout the ship he comes increasingly to see that vice abounds in his man-of-war world: the sailors steal (chaps. 9 and 10), fight (chap. 33), smuggle (chap. 44), gamble (chap. 78), engage in homosexuality (chap. 89), and drink. That is, White-Jacket comes to realize "the almost incredible corruption pervading nearly all ranks in some men-of-war" (182) and to question whether reforming the naval system could indeed reform the sailors' character and conditions. When, for example, the release of naval oppression is complete and they are given "Liberty," the results are disastrous. After "all the mad tumult and contention of 'Liberty,'" the sailors return "in all imaginable stages of intoxication" (226). Attaining popular liberty, a key ideal to White-Jacket's and the Whigs' millennialism, thus not only fails to better the conditions of the men, but leads to even more blatant expressions of depravity. White-Jacket then conceives that human nature makes the world "upon the whole, charged to the combings of her hatchways with the spirit of Belial and all unrighteousness" (390). Like Tommo, White-Jacket seems to suggest that man must be either placid, noble, and loving, or ferocious, horrible, and cannibalistic. Melville, who invariably shuns extremes for a middle path, is harshly satirizing his narrator's hyperbolic perceptions. Melville's position becomes clearer if one compares the men returning from liberty "in all imaginable stages of intoxication" to his source in Leech. "When a man of war is in port," Leech says, "it is usual to grant the crew occasional liberty to go on shore. These indulgences are almost invariably abused for the purposes of riot, drunkenness and debauchery."[48] In White-Jacket's description, "imaginable" hints that some of this description may be his own imagination; it is certainly much more inflated. He describes the ship "more like a mad-house than a frigate" (227) and uses this black-or-white perception to support an ever-growing conservatism.

Melville undercuts the validity of White-Jacket's excessive perceptions even more strongly by showing that the reason for his misperceptions lies in a central tenet of his millennialism, the belief that "we Americans are the peculiar, chosen people—the Israel of our time" (151).[49] In the 1840s both Demo-

[48]Leech, *Thirty Years*, 109.

[49]Gerlach, "Messianic Nationalism," 12, calls the millennial passage "a calculated exaggeration which exposes its own foolishness." Bercovitch, *American Jeremiad*, 68–69, explains that as early as the 1650s English millennialists began dissociating their millennial hopes from British history and associating them with American history.

crats and Whigs saw the Anglo-Saxons coming to world supremacy under the American flag, but the Whigs, perhaps
because of the British heritage of the political theory, proclaimed more loudly their racial superiority.[50] In a January
1848 article entitled "The Anglo-Saxon Race. An Inquiry into
the Causes of its Unrivalled Progress, with some considerations
Indicative of its Future Destiny," *The American Review* reasons
that the Anglo-Saxon peoples are superior because of their
moral integrity, their ceaseless enterprise, their intellectual activity, and the social elevation of their women—characteristics
which promote the free and individualistic social institutions in
Anglo-Saxon England and in America.[51] To show the continuity of the race and stress that America has recaptured the
greatness of the race, the author parallels the two societies—
Alfred, for example, becomes Washington—and draws a conclusion that sounds quite similar to White-Jacket's: "In view of
these facts and impressions, we cannot resist the conclusion
that Providence has raised up, and sustained, and qualified the
Anglo-Saxon race, to perform a great work in reclaiming the
world; has guided and protected them from temptation, or
brought them from it *purified*, and ennobled by every scene of
trial; and has given to them—to *us*—the destinies of the
world."[52] As in *White-Jacket*, the overt intent of this passage is
reform, but equally overt is an assertion of racial superiority
and political elitism.

What Melville thinks of such a position is clear from *Mardi*
on. In the Vivenza passage Melville describes the inevitable
decline and fall of all empires; no one nation is the chosen.[53]
Thus "the grand error" of Vivenza is their self-aggrandizing
millennial elitism, which both leads to and is undermined by
slavery. Although black slavery is at most a tangential issue in

[50]"The Constitution; Written and Unwritten," *American Review* 6 (1847): 6;
"The Age Is Revolutionary," ibid., 87, and "The Late Negotiations for Peace,"
ibid., 451.
[51]"The Anglo-Saxon Race," *American Review* 7 (1848): 29.
[52]Ibid., 43.
[53] *Mardi; and a Voyage Thither*, ed. Harrison Hayford, Hershel Parker, and G.
Thomas Tanselle (Evanston and Chicago, 1970), chap. 161.

White-Jacket, Melville's narrator is racist and elitist.[54] His jacket, he tells us in the first line, is "not a *very* white jacket, but white enough"—just as he himself is white enough to be a member of "mess No. 1," which is "principally composed of the headmost men of the gun-deck" (62). This group has special privileges and resembles, more than anything else, a gentlemen's club like that Tommo imagined in Typee. White-Jacket summarizes their position above their fellow men:

> We could do so many equivocal things, utterly inadmissible for messes of inferior pretension. Besides, though we all abhorred the monster of Sin itself, yet, from our social superiority, highly rarified education in our lofty top, and large and liberal sweep of the aggregate of things, we were a good deal free from those useless, personal prejudices, and galling hatreds against conspicuous *sinners*. . . . We perceived how that evil was but good disguised, and a knave a saint in his way. . . . We perceived that the anticipated millennium must have begun upon the morning the first worlds were created. . . . And we fancied that though some of us, of the gun-deck, were at times condemned to sufferings and slights, and all manner of tribulation and anguish, yet, no doubt, it was only our misapprehension of these things that made us take them for woeful pains instead of the most agreeable pleasures. . . . Such, at least, were our reveries at times.
> (186)

The absurdity of these "reveries" is obvious, particularly in light of Melville's strictures on his previous narrators' reveries. Melville's point is simple: placed by his political and religious beliefs literally above his fellow man, White-Jacket condescends to them.[55] Moreover, White-Jacket hypocritically con-

---

[54]See Karcher, *Shadow*; Zirker, "Evidence"; and Rogin, *Subversive Genealogy*, 86–87.

[55]Larry Reynolds, "Antidemocratic Emphasis in *White-Jacket*," *American Literature* 48 (1976): 17, labels White-Jacket a snob and an elitist but ascribes these qualites to Melville as well. Duban, *Melville's Major Fiction*, 73, states: "Quite possibly, then, *White-Jacket*'s emphasis on both an aristocracy of intellect and the necessity of freeing individuals from the tyranny of the majority conforms to Whiggish attitudes that Melville may have harbored when he told Hawthorne, '[i]t is true that there have been those who, while earnest in behalf of political equality, still accept the intellectual estates.'" I read this letter as considerably more ambiguous and inconclusive than Duban does.

demns the vulgarity of others but keeps secret that he, like Tubbs, was a whaler himself (16). Melville plays with this characteristic in his narrator, who, shortly after condescendingly pitying a "poor mulatto" whom the captain scourges, is himself dragged before the mast (chap. 67). At other times Melville portrays his narrator's elitism as a silly romanticism. Now and then White-Jacket climbs up into the top, "give[s] loose to reflection," and blends into "the All."[56] There he can forget the troubles of the world below and intellectualize with the literati. Like the primarily upper-class Whigs, White-Jacket in his "large and liberal sweep" wants to associate with only the gentry.

Reinforcing this elitism is White-Jacket's main-top companion, Jack Chase. To Melville's narrator, "noble Jack Chase" is a "gentleman," most likely a "by-blow of some British Admiral of the Blue" (13–14)—an aristocrat. Appropriately, too, he is English, showing that White-Jacket, for all his Americanism and egalitarianism, readily exposes his Whig tendency to trace his ancestry back through the English race (see also 141–50). To White-Jacket, Jack is the ideal libertarian hero, a friend to his brothers in the top yet always able to commune with naval royalty. His exploits fighting for liberty are epic. These rather grandiose perceptions come through the eyes and words of White-Jacket, however; a closer look at Jack's words and actions will show that Melville's opinion is by no means his narrator's. From his position as First Captain of the Top, Jack literally looks down upon his brother sailors—and morally, too, for he despises Tubbs, who had been a whaler, as "vulgar" (15) and patronizes Lemsford (41). At the same time he, as ambitious as the Rienzi he says he is (225), inflates his own reputation. He alludes to everything (his diction is inflated even for Melville), in one passage equating himself with Homer, Shakespeare, Byron, Shelley, and invoking the sanction of the Bible (270–71). Making his own adventures into epic battles, he describes the battle of Navarino in the highly exaggerated terms of a

---

[56]Cf. Vincent, *Tailoring*, chap. 8. For a more cautious yet similar statement see Melville's famous letter to Hawthorne, *Letters*, 130–31.

typical sailor's yarn, as a comparison with Melville's sources reveals.[57] When he must act, though, Jack fails to live up to the image he cultivates. Melville parodies his "revolutionary" Whiggism in the theatricals chapter (23), in which Jack, with the deliberately silly name Percy Royal-Mast, heroically rescues fifteen oppressed sailors—but it is only playacting. He does, though, secure "Liberty" for the people—but it is only shore leave—by a disgusting obsequiousness to the captain (213–14). Finally, when White-Jacket, Jack's "pet," is about to be flogged, Jack intervenes only after another—and a marine at that—has spoken in White-Jacket's behalf. Snobbish, pretentious, silly, cowardly, hypocritical, Jack Chase is little more than a parody of the hero White-Jacket imagines himself.

In White-Jacket's main-top millennialism, that is, is a latent conservatism; despite strenuously voicing concern for progress, he self-contentedly wishes only to preserve his own place at the top. To trust Providence completely, Melville shows, is to perceive that "the anticipated millennium must have begun upon the morning the first worlds were created" (186). This complacency—Jack Chase is in the main-top and all's well with the man-of-war world—is itself contradictory, for millennium and tribulation are mutually exclusive. It is also abhorrent to Melville, for it denies the reality of pain and suffering. One cannot dismiss the world as "misapprehension" or climb above it into a metaphysical main-top without disastrous consequences. Most immediately, White-Jacket's attitude leads him to deny many of the values he has promoted. For instance, when the visit by the Portuguese nobility offers a chance for him to deride the aristocracy, as a true republican should, he shows himself only "willing to correct the rhetoric of so fierce a republican" as the New England tar who does lash out at Don Pedro (235–36). On the contrary, White-Jacket wants "to yield his tribute of 'A Stanza to Braganza.'" The allusion is telling: Braganza is not only the name of a Portuguese family but also the name of a famous ship, whose crew murdered a tyrannous master and mate. White-Jacket is neither brigand nor Bra-

[57]See Vincent, *Tailoring*, chap. 14.

ganza but every bit as obsequious a "bragger" as Jack Chase.[58]

The most prominent expression of the elitism and conservatism in both White-Jacket and the Whigs is their theory of representative government. The 1840s Whigs evolved their policies in opposition to the Democrats, whose key phrase is "will of the majority."[59] The Whigs stress the representative character of the American republic: to them the right to govern "the people" comes not from the people but from the Constitution to the representatives, who are a sort of political equivalent to the Whig religious idea of a chosen people. *The American Review* explains that, since the electoral sovereignty originates in the Constitution, enfranchisement must be limited. They ask rhetorically whether it is not obvious that this limitation should be the case, since, "every franchise being a trust, or at least involving one; the electoral franchise has been given to such only of the people as are deemed fit and competent trustees of so important a power, and qualified to use it with advantage to the republic? Thus, instead of taking away anything from three-fourths of the community, the Constitution simply imparts to the remaining fourth a right of its own creation, which was never theirs before."[60]

The problems with this philosophy are readily evident in *White-Jacket*, whose narrator recognizes that some restriction is necessary, or "a man-of-war's crew would be nothing but a mob . . . ungovernable" (9)—the typical Whig attack on Democracy. Therefore, he and Jack Chase distinguish between "the public," a monstrous mob of rabble, and "the people," their brothers in the main-top (192). This policy of limited enfranchisement, perhaps little more than an excuse for pseudo-aristocracy, is a rationale for many of the elitist tendencies and condemnations of depravity in Melville's narrator.

[58]McNally, *Evils*, 71. "The Republic," in *American Review* 9 (1849): 399–401, urges a similar caution in making changes, on the ground of the sacredness of American institutions.

[59]"Representative Government," *American Review*, 7 (1848): 280–85; and "The French Republic," *Democratic Review* 23 (1848): 70.

[60]"Representative Government," *American Review* 7 (1848): 282; "Necessity of Party—The Press—The Locofoco Platform," ibid. 8 (1848): 11; and "The Republic [no. II]," ibid. 9 (1849): 478.

The Whig sees two categories, Right and Wrong, the Justly Privileged and the Necessarily Excluded, if he carries his millennialism to the limit. In *Mardi*, too, Melville exposes this problem in Republicanism: the inscription on the Vivenzan deity reads, "In-this-re-publi-can-land-all-men-are-born-free-and-equal," but in very minute characters, "Except-the-tribe-of-Hamo." "'That nullifies the other,' cried Media. 'Ah, ye republicans.'"[61]

Perhaps most hypocritically, White-Jacket is thus guilty of promoting virtually the same system he condemns. Most of his reforms are directed toward the shipboard caste system, which enfranchises the officers at the expense of the crew and, he has said, is responsible for the depraved condition of the men and for the evils on board. Yet he comes to associate himself with an elite every bit as oppressive. As a result, he grows more and more to consider the men, "the people" of the first part of the book, as unworthy of enfranchisement, as too vulgar for social contact, and as too incorrigibly evil to benefit from the reforms he had once so urgently called for.

Consequent to White-Jacket's loss of faith in the efficacy of reforms is a growing otherworldliness, particularly evident in his arguments against the Articles of War. White-Jacket there recognizes war as the cause of the evils he perceives, for it necessitates the discipline that demands he know his place and threatens to flog him when he does not; war reduces even Jack Chase "to the Feejee standard of humanity." Therefore, White-Jacket directs his attacks not toward reform of specific naval abuses, as he had earlier, but toward war itself. His diatribe against the Articles of War, which parallels his earlier flogging arguments, clearly shows a change in White-Jacket over the course of the book. He presents the same rhetorical flourishes, the same patriotic appeals to the Bible, the Constitution, and the "Congress of freemen," the same protest against an unjust authoritarian system, but here White-Jacket ends not with a call to reform the Articles but merely with a statement of their evil. He focuses, that is, not on practice, but on the theory

[61] *Mardi*, 512–13.

behind the practice; his arguments call not for concrete action but for abstract intellection. Although White-Jacket cannot believe that peace will be accomplished "with no other effort on our part than to be strictly honest and strictly just," he does believe that no action can bring peace. "But where the unscrupulousness of martial discipline is maintained," he says, "it is vain to attempt softening its rigor by the ordaining of humanitarian laws" (328). Reform, then, cannot alleviate the evils of this man-of-war world; therefore, White-Jacket comes to a "mind our own business, and let them alone" policy. His pacifism means detachment.

This disengagement from social concerns is perhaps most evident in White-Jacket's emotional reaction to "The Monthly Muster round the Capstan." He appeals neither to reason nor to Christianity nor to the Constitution but to the reader's reaction to three words repeated throughout the Articles: "'*Shall suffer death*!' The repeated announcement falls on your ear like the intermitting discharge of artillery. . . . No reservations, no contingencies; not the remotest promise of pardon or reprieve; not a glimpse of commutation of the sentence; all hope and consolation is shut out—*shall suffer death*! that is the simple fact for you to digest" (293). Clearly, behind much of White-Jacket's intellectual argument against the Articles, and more largely against his man-of-war world, is an abhorrence of the very real, inevitable "fact" of death. In such a world, White-Jacket recognizes in a moment of hysteria, a man has only one right, "the privilege, inborn and inalienable, that every man has, of dying himself, and inflicting death upon another" (280). White-Jacket is coming to feel as trapped within this system as Tommo did in Typee; he fears, if not cannibalism, a similar cycle of murdering and being murdered, which leads him to a panic much like Tommo's.

More than the naval laws occasion White-Jacket's fear of death, for he is coming to perceive in his role as millennialist reformer a dead end. Symbolically, wearing the white jacket brings Melville's narrator increasingly closer to death. When early in the book he is mistaken for a ghost, he almost falls from the rigging (chap. 19); each time a man dies on board, the jacket is peripherally involved, as White-Jacket later laments (333); at the end the jacket very nearly kills White-Jacket himself, who cuts himself free of it and joyously cries, "Sink! sink! oh shroud!" (394). In this recognition of the jacket's connection with death, though, White-Jacket is merely echoing a position Melville has presented from the first: that the jacket of millennial Whiggery has a sinister, even deadly lining. His narrator's increasing preoccupation with war and death—in the latter part of the novel these themes are the concern of over half of the chapters—follows clearly from his recognition of evil as a part of humanity impervious to social and political reform. He sees that "some of these evils . . . like other organic evils, are incurable, except when they dissolve with the body they live in" (375); therefore, death, a part of "the predestinated necessities of things," is the direction toward which his philosophy is tending.[62]

White-Jacket can find a palliative to this nihilism in his millennialism, which itself becomes increasingly idealistic and otherworldly. White-Jacket, for whom throughout the book, "my real acquaintances were comparatively few, and my intimates still fewer" (174), becomes even more isolated near the end.[63] Then he rarely ventures out of the maintop, most likely since his jacket has brought him the scorn of his fellow crewmen, while his isolation, fed as well by his own scorn for them, drives him up into his own mental main-top. A pre-Ahab, White-Jacket encounters evil and becomes something of a monomaniacal egoist who violates the dictum he had stated earlier: "to be efficacious, Virtue must come down from aloft to redeem our whole man-of-war world; to that end, mixing with its sailors and sinners as equals" (229). But White-Jacket is only a silly Ahab: he does not launch out in a quest to destroy the evil but lapses into a complacent idealism. "Ah!" he sighs, "the best righteousness of our man-of-war world seems but an unrealized ideal, after all" (324).

Lest one be tempted to take White-Jacket's philosophy here

---

[62]Cf. Mercier, *Life*, 130 and 205.
[63]Dillingham, *Artist*, 63–66, describes White-Jacket's increasing isolation.

too seriously, Melville presents a more extreme version of this idealism in Ushant, who in the last part of the book parallels Jack Chase's heroism in the first. Jack is the parodic liberator of the people, while Ushant clings parodically to his absurd ideal. One should be suspicious of the distance White-Jacket puts between the man Ushant and the heroic description of him. Resorting glowingly and profusely to metaphor and allusion, White-Jacket tries to force the description of Ushant as a mythic figure, an "oracle" or an "old philosopher"—but it is only for a beard that he lets himself be flogged, imprisoned, demoted, and dishonorably discharged. Even White-Jacket recognizes that Ushant could have caused "the disgrace to the American Navy of a tragical mutiny, growing out of whiskers, soap-suds, and razors" (359). Only White-Jacket's own nihilistic idealism could carry this "pettiest of trifles" to such importance.[64]

Latent within the millennialism White-Jacket appropriates is an Ushant-like idealism that Bercovitch has shown to stem from the Puritans, who had no choice but to explain away events in order to preserve their ideal plan of history. "To condemn the profane is to commit oneself to a spiritual ideal," Bercovitch says.[65] And commit themselves the later Whigs did. The Democrats, calling for reforms that would increase the power of the masses, condemn the Whigs' policies as "merely nominal or theoretical"; while the Whigs themselves, in their belief that "it is not the men, however admirable, but the principles they represent, that give dignity and interest to a war of opinion," lend support to their detractors' accusation.[66] The American Whigs saw history as a progress toward "the Divine ideal"; they looked not to the secular events but to the underlying Divinity and "humbly acknowledge[d] how little we have done for ourselves and how much Providence has done for

---

[64]Rogin, *Subversive Genealogy*, 97, sees the mutiny as a comic anticlimax, a "farce."

[65]Bercovitch, *American Jeremiad*, 69 and 179. Vincent, *Tailoring*, often mentions the idealism/realism dichotomy but does not apply it to a reading of the novel.

[66]"Poverty and Misery," *Democratic Review* 23 (1848): 27; and "The Future Policy of the Whigs," *American Review* 7 (1848): 329.

us."[67] The Whigs want not practical reform but patient awaiting. Just as the Christ of the Sermon on the Mount exhorts his
audience to look not to earth but to heaven, White-Jacket increasingly voices a concern for the next world and a disenchantment with this one. Brave deeds may bring a man glory,
he says, "thereby gaining [him] the name of a hero in this
world;—but what would they have called him in the next?"
(315). His jacket, too, comes more and more to be associated
with the spirit. He sees Shenly's shroud as resembling it, "a
white frock" imagistically transformed into "a snow-white, soli-
tary fowl, which—whence coming no one could tell—had been
hovering over the main-mast during the [funeral] service, and
was now sailing far up into the depths of the sky" (342). Only
near the end can White-Jacket make this identification, for
only then does he look upward toward heaven rather than
down upon his man-of-war world.

As he looks to the Divine at the end of the book, White-
Jacket does not propose laws to solve problems but "supported
by what God has given me, I tranquilly abide the event, whatever it may prove" (385). He has not, though, lost his fervent
faith; his religion has merely become more conservative, more
focused on the Divine control of events and the otherworldly
end of the human course. Thus "the whole present social
frame-work of our world [is] so ill adapted to the practical
adoption of the meekness of Christianity, [and] . . . his gospel
seems lacking in the practical wisdom of earth. . . . But all this
only the more crowns the divine consistency of Jesus; since
Burnet and the best theologians demonstrate, that his nature
was not merely human—was not that of a mere man of the
world" (324). Nor does Melville's narrator wish to be a man of
the world. That is to say, White-Jacket still promotes millennialism, but reduced to its most elemental component. He no
longer believes in an earthly perfection within history and before the return of Christ, yet he still foresees an end time of

[67]"California," *American Review* 9 (1849): 332–36; and "The Destiny of the
Country," ibid. 5 (1847): 231. See also Bercovitch, *American Jeremiad*; and
Tuveson, *Redeemer Nation*, 31 and 88. On providential historiography in *Moby-
Dick* see Duban, *Melville's Major Fiction*, 82–148.

perfection, not on earth but in heaven, after the divine cataclysm. Whether one calls this change a movement from millennialism to millennarianism or from postmillennialism to premillennialism, there remains in White-Jacket's beliefs throughout the book an orientation toward the paradise of the end times.[68] White-Jacket is always Homeward-Bound.

"The End"—out of the sequence of chapters just as its ideology projects a time out of the sequence of history—is White-Jacket's millennarian sermon about The End; paralleling the earlier millennial passage, it summarizes all the beliefs White-Jacket has come to hold in the last part of the book.[69] He continues to stress the problems in his world, but now blames not the system but the individual, since "the worst of our evils we blindly inflict upon ourselves; our officers can not remove them, even if they would" (399). Yet White-Jacket does not dwell pessimistically upon these evils or upon death, for he can believe that "when a shipmate dies . . . never more do we behold him again; though, sooner or later, the everlasting undertow sweeps him toward our own destination." Thus because he believes that "Our Lord High Admiral"—the fact that the American navy had no admirals indicates Melville's skeptical reaction—directs the world in an inevitable progress toward heaven, a pattern beneath the flow of events, White-Jacket can rest assured that he will escape death and evil. "For how can this world-frigate prove our eventual abiding place," he asks, "when, upon our first embarkation, as infants in arms, her violent rolling—in after life unperceived—makes every soul of us sea-sick? Does this not show, too, that the very air we here inhale is uncongenial, and only becomes endurable at last through gradual habituation, and that some blessed, placid haven, however remote at present, must be in store for us all?" (398–99). This Platonic or Wordsworthian dualism, the philosophical counterpart to his millennialist religion, dismisses the

---

[68]See Tuveson, *Redeemer Nation*, 33–34; and Bercovitch, *American Jeremiad*, 94–95.

[69]Vincent, *Tailoring*, chap. 19, describes this passage as a sermon but with no irony; Gerlach, "Messianic Nationalism," 14–15, argues that Melville here is toying with the reader, for the ideals in the passage are Claret's.

political, for his "placid haven" here is not America but heaven. With a cosmic optimism reminiscent of Emerson, White-Jacket concludes that "Whoever afflict us, whatever surround, / Life is a voyage that's homeward-bound!" The triteness of this faith and the ease with which White-Jacket, like the "transcendental" chaplain whom he earlier lampoons, dismisses the world's evil indicate that Melville does not share his narrator's position. Moreover, Melville positions this final statement in the main-top, the scene of romantic reverie and idealistic metaphysics.

Preceding "The End," Melville subjects his narrator to a now-famous fall: immediately "dragged" by "the irresistible law of gravitation . . . toward the infallible centre of this terra-queous globe" (392), White-Jacket experiences Melville's pri-mal element as Tommo did with the Typee women. Although at the bottom he sees death and the "fashionless form" of the deep-sea creatures, he immediately "bound[s] up like a buoy"—like the boyish Tommo, he is no Pip—and is safely back in the main-top minutes later. Through his narrator Mel-ville is saying that for the millennialist who focuses exclusively upon the "placid haven" beyond this world, the Fall is in-consequential, however dramatic it may seem to many at first glance.[70] Since the penalties of the Fall can be so easily dis-missed by the inevitable progress of the world, one can easily gain redemption, as easily as climbing up a mainmast. The Fall from innocence to experience and the baptism back to inno-cence are thus for White-Jacket no more than empty symbols, which he happily casts off with his jacket. The loss of the jacket reinforces the inconsequentiality of symbolism itself for White-Jacket: his idealism precludes realizing the abstract with a con-crete symbol. His casual Christianity is of course fruitless: his last view of the land "*believed* to be broad on our bow" (395—my emphasis) is a "Pisgah" sight, for he will never reach the promised land.

In the end, then, White-Jacket remains in a state of spiritual and psychological adolescence.[71] True, he has come to per-

---

[70]See Vincent, *Tailoring*, chap. 17.

[71]Dillingham, *Artist*, is perhaps most typical of the critics who argue that White-Jacket matures in the end.

ceive evil and has lost some of his naïveté; he refuses, though, to face the fact of this evil even as he perceives it. White-Jacket's "growth" is if anything a retreat: he turns away from a relationship with the natural, adult world, refuses even to tell of his shipmates, shrugs off dealing with his own problems, and dwells in the land of his fantasies. Historically, too, White-Jacket's position is a denial of the fact of secularization: he refuses to see that secular events have become a part of his spiritual mission, indeed always were a part of it. Like the Puritans of the second generation and later, he is trying to deny history, his own and his nation's.[72] White-Jacket's self-important attempts to link himself to larger ideologies, Whig and millennial, expose themselves as veiled and failed elitism, removing him ever further from his fellow sailors—and their narratives—and ever further into solipsism.

III

Just how far White-Jacket's ideology has carried him beyond the sailor narratives and toward idealism is evident in a comparison between *White-Jacket* and Melville's sources. In specific passages that Melville "borrowed" from his sources, Melville perceives the ideological tendencies of the original, exaggerates them, and thereby brings to light these conflicts. For example, Vincent demonstrates that the arraignment of White-Jacket (277–81) was taken from the following passage of John Sleeper's *Tales of the Ocean*:

> Accordingly the offender was lashed to a gun, by the inhuman satellites of tyranny, and his back bared to the lash. Before a blow was struck, he repeated his declaration that he was an American citizen, and the sworn foe of tyrants. He demanded his release—and assured the captain in the most solemn and impressive manner, that if he persisted in punishing him like the vilest malefactor, for vindicating his rights as an American citizen, the act would never be forgiven—but that his revenge would be certain and terrible. . . . The white skin of the young

[72]See Fred Somkin, *Unquiet Eagle* (Ithaca, N.Y., 1967), 82; and Bercovitch, *The Puritan Origins of the American Self* (New Haven, Conn., 1975), 118.

American was soon cruelly mangled, the blows fell thickly and
heavily on his quivering flesh. . . . His bonds were loosened, and
he rose from his humiliating posture. . . . The hapless sufferer
saw [the captain's] smile of exultation—and that moment decided the fate of the oppressor. With the activity, the ferocity,
and almost the strength of a tiger the mutilated American
sprang upon the tyrant, and grasped him where he stood, sur-
rounded by his officers, who for the moment seemed paralyzed
with astonishment—and before they could recover their senses
and hasten to the assistance of their commander, the flogged
American had borne him to the gangway, and then clutching
him by the throat with one hand, and firmly embracing him
with the other, despite his struggles, he leaped with him into the
turbid waters of the Demerara! They parted to receive the tyrant and his victim—then closed over them, and neither was
afterwards seen.[73]

Both Sleeper's anonymous seaman and Melville's White-
Jacket base their actions and words upon their individual
"rights as an American citizen" in opposition to tyranny. While
in Sleeper the tyranny is real—mangled flesh, flayed skin, clot-
ted blood—in White-Jacket it is only anticipatory and mental,
indicating that White-Jacket's hypersensitivity about individual
rights has led him so far into his own imagination that he
cannot perceive events as they are.[74] In Sleeper, the Yankee
acts out of "revenge," probably justified, for a severe physical
punishment, while in Melville, White-Jacket's is not so much
calculated justice as "instinct," a "purpose" that is finally irrational. This sense of purpose—he believes himself "homeward-
bound"—becomes here, as in the book as a whole, an assertion
of the individual's right to die. Expanding Sleeper's portrayal
of the life-and-death importance of reform of naval tyranny
and at the same time recognizing the otherworldly basis of this
reformism, Melville shows the ideas behind Sleeper's narrative
to be nihilistic. White-Jacket's language, straining against this
tendency, is steeped in Christian and in idealistic terminology;
it is inward, ecstatic, crazed, and self-righteous.

[73]Vincent, *Tailoring*, 151–53. Dimock, "*White-Jacket*," compares the author-
reader relationships in these passages.

[74]Vincent, *Tailoring*, says that the power of this passage comes from its
"inwardness."

This overstated language—of both White-Jacket and the narrators of facts with whom Melville connects him—attempts to overcome the contradictions or inadequacies in the ideology it presents. Moreover, it tends to give the rather nondescript narrator more of a sense of mission, of importance, particularly when such inflation is tied to a literary convention, the epic, which both White-Jacket and Melville's sources adopt. Mercier, for instance, is often guilty of stylistic excesses similar to White-Jacket's, as the following invocation demonstrates: "Hail to thee, galley of a man-of-war,—place of frying-pans, grid-irons, and tea-kettles,—*sanctum sanctorum* of thick lips, wooly heads, and countenances as multiform and varied in their hues, as the tints of the dying dolphin."[75] This passage shows many of the tendencies Melville develops *ad absurdum* in his narrator—inflation of trivia to grandiose proportions, pretentious and latinate diction, overdeveloped allusions, and so on—who fills his second jacket, *White-Jacket*, with similar epic conventions. White-Jacket presents extensive catalogues of characters (see chaps. 3 and 6), many of whom he describes with epic epithets like "noble Jack Chase, Captain of the Main-top," or "old Ushant, Nestor of the Crew." Many of his multitude of allusions also refer to epics, to Camoens, Milton, Homer, Virgil, Dante. His epic similes run rampant as well: he uses seven different similes to describe Quoin, for example (42).

This tendency to the epical had been the norm from the time of Columbus: America was not discovered but invented, as Edmundo O'Gorman has said. Part of this invention was the perception of the American experience as epic: the third part of Thomas Morton's *New English Canaan* is a mock epic; Roger Wolcott's *Poetical Manifestations* is a typical seventeenth-century epic of frontier settlement; Mather's *Magnalia* models itself on the *Aeneid*; Joel Barlow's *Columbiad* is modeled on *Paradise Lost*; Dwight's *The Conquest of Canaan* celebrates the epic of the American Revolution.[76] These epics served the very necessary purpose of giving the young and emerging nation legitimacy

[75]Mercier, *Life*, 175; see also 98 and 216.
[76]See Seelye, *Prophetic Waters*, 176 and 336; Bercovitch, *Puritan Origins*, 135, and *American Jeremiad*, 130; and Jones, *Strange New World*, 94.

and stature by linking the American experience to those of the noblest Western nations.

When, like *White-Jacket*, the American epic is infused with a sense of religious mission during a time of reform, a slightly different sort of epic can be seen. To emphasize its most essential idea, I choose to call this epic jeremiad of the American millennium a "millenniad." Mather's *Magnalia* not only celebrates and chronicles America's greatness, but calls for a return to the path toward an even greater destiny; Dwight's *Canaan* "builds on constant crises (rebellion, backsliding, treachery, holy war) toward a celebration of the New World republic— America, the second 'blissful Eden bright, by heaven de- sign'd.' "[77] Thus the millenniad, like *White-Jacket*, incorporates conventions from both epic and jeremiad genres. Like the Is- raelites in the jeremiad model, White-Jacket's people are cap- tives of the Babylonish officers; this situation he describes in epic terms, as not merely a conflict between officers and sailors on a ship, but between the Righteous and the Wicked in the epic amplitude of the world in a man-of-war. In the jeremiad, the captivity was a divine scourge to the chosen guilty of back- sliding or declension; in *White-Jacket* the declension consists in both the sailors' vices and the authorities' sacrilegious laws. Thus the jeremiad is most simply a call for reform, but reform based, as the epic is, upon a conviction of national identity, purpose, and destiny. In the jeremiad, the destiny is God's will; in the epic, it is national greatness; in the millenniad, it is both. White-Jacket invokes Providence to aid him toward this des- tiny, just as a Jeremiah would call on God or an epic poet on the gods. Finally, as the jeremiad must have its Nehemiah and the epic its hero, White-Jacket has not one hero but two, Jack Chase and Ushant, both epic heroes and models for righteous behavior.

Melville, however, undercuts most of the millenniad ele- ments his narrator tries to invoke. White-Jacket's stylistic exces- ses are little more than Melville's parody of the epic and

---

[77]Bercovitch, *American Jeremiad*, 130. Dimock, "*White-Jacket*," 299, links *White-Jacket* and the jeremiad.

jeremiad conventions his rather ordinary sailor-narrator pirates. On the most literal level, the fact is that the world is *not* in a man-of-war, that the *Neversink*, despite its name, is just a ship. To inflate its events to epic proportions, as White-Jacket or America does, is a ridiculous lie. Historical events are to Melville merely historical events, not to be viewed as divinely sanctioned episodes of millennial importance and epic proportions. Although one might laugh at White-Jacket's pretentiousness, if one remembers that his is representative of America's, one can see the seriousness of Melville's point. America is not an epic jeremiad of the world (and the sailors' narratives even less so); to write as if it were leads but to hypocrisy, ignorance, and self-destruction.

As in Melville's previous narratives of facts, *White-Jacket*'s inflations and conflations reveal its narrator's attempt to accomplish in writing what his ideology precluded his accomplishing in actuality.[78] White-Jacket pieces together this millenniad *White-Jacket* in an attempt to compensate for many "dismal times" in the past and for the ineffectuality of his millennialism on board. His propagandistic voice of the people, for example, tries to accomplish a popular rebellion against and reform of the naval system, which he was utterly powerless to effect himself. On board he cowardly tries to hush the Yankee who criticizes the Brazilian nobility, but in his narrative he launches into the same criticisms himself. He can use his narration, too, to try to escape from some of the unpleasant incidents in his memory. After the arraignment scene he writes, "Let us forget the scourge and the gangway a while, and jot down in our memories a few little things pertaining to our man-of-war world" (282). It is as if he thinks he can relegate the scourge completely into the past and dismiss this most unpleasant but memorable event by overbalancing it with trivial data. The fragmentary structure of the chapter that follows, though, indicates that he cannot adequately compensate for the events quite as he wishes.

---

[78]This compensatory aspect of nautical narratives can be seen in McNally, *Evils*, 183–91.

Although White-Jacket fights against this chaos through his writing, it is an irradicable part of the world Melville presents in the novel. Nature here, as throughout Melville's narratives of facts, threatens the man whose ideology denies the disorder. It is a Cape Horn tempest in which "the sense of fear is annihilated in the unutterable sights that fill all the eye, and the sounds that fill all the ear. You become identified with the tempest; your insignificance is lost in the riot of the stormy universe around" (108). Yet for White-Jacket, always concerned with himself, such self-annihilation is unacceptable and he must try to utter the unutterable. Through his narration he attempts almost compulsively to order experience and thereby counteract this natural, entropic chaos. If he could limit the world to a level of complexity he can understand, he feels, he would not have to fear it. He therefore first attempts to classify his world, the ship, by means of metaphor: if he can say what it is like, he can understand it. In trying to define the *Neversink*, White-Jacket compares it to: "the world in its orbit" (115); "the whole earth itself . . . a vast hogshead, full of inflammable materials" (129); "a church" (155); "an insular fortress" (160); "a sort of State Prison afloat" (175); and, in a mad fit of tropic fever: "a city afloat. . . . Or, rather, a man-of-war is a lofty, walled, and garrisoned town, like Quebec. . . . Or it is like the lodging-houses in Paris, turned upside down. . . . A man-of-war resembles a three-story house in a suspicious part of town" (74–75). White-Jacket seems unsure of what metaphor to use, for indeed no one metaphor can encompass the world, which is many, if not all, things. Thus his metaphors often fail, for, "as, in a Chinese puzzle, many pieces are hard to place . . . and thus the whole puzzle becomes a puzzle indeed, which is the precise condition of the greatest puzzle in the world—this man-of-war world itself" (164).

White-Jacket's denomination of the ship as microcosm similarly limits the world and allows him to dismiss everything not on the ship as an instance of the form on board. This world he can then Ramistically divide and subdivide until he can comprehend the pattern and the parts. The failure of this tactic is also clear: White-Jacket must omit much to make his microcosm hold water, as he himself admits. He cannot allow himself to describe Rio, for example, for he must "adhere to [his] one proper object, *the world in a man-of-war*" (160—see also 226). But of course the world cannot be *in* a man-of-war—the part cannot encompass the whole—any more than his book can be the world or the ship. White-Jacket, in trying to limit his world through narration, falls into the trap of believing that literary structure mirrors or, even more bizarrely, acts upon the world.

White-Jacket wishes to divide his world not only to understand but to conquer: he often manipulates events through the order in which he places his descriptions, tales, and narratives of the events, thus subtly coloring them to fit his ideology. After an imagined description of deaths from battle (chap. 16) he narrates the death of Bungs and creates the impression that his death is a result of the literary representation. By setting events in juxtaposition to events more obviously fictional, he blurs the distinction—never clear anywhere in the book—between fact and fiction. He first presents a highly theatrical chapter, in which a fictional rebellion threatens to become an actual rebellion, then follows it with a highly conventional (according to the prescriptions of the narratives of facts genre) and highly false (according to Dennis Berthold) dramatization of Cape Horn.[79] These instances demonstrate White-Jacket's high-handed narrative attempt to restructure the world, as he did with metaphor and microcosm, to restructure it according to the pattern and purpose he imposes. Melville exposes these tactics in the transitions at the beginning of the chapters, which are at best heavy-handed attempts to tie together in logical sequences events that cannot be logically connected (e.g., 350). However, he says:

> What we call Fate is even, heartless, and impartial. . . . Yet though all this be so, nevertheless, in our own hearts, we mold the whole world's hereafters; and in our own hearts we fashion our own gods. Each mortal casts his own vote for whom he will to rule the worlds; I have a voice that helps to shape eternity;

---

[79]"Factual Errors and Fictional Aims in *White-Jacket*," *Studies in American Fiction* 11 (1983): 233–39.

and my volitions stir the orbits of the furthest suns. In two
senses, we are precisely what we worship. Ourselves are Fate.
(320–21)

White-Jacket cannot understand the mishmash of events, so
calls it Fate, but then realizes that in calling it that, he has
helped shape it, and therefore becomes what he describes. This
process works similarly for the book: in trying to understand
the events of his own past, White-Jacket gives them a name by
narrating them, and thereby becomes *White-Jacket*. He has thus
transformed himself into narrative, can understand and control his place in the scheme of things, and can be what he
worships, a hero.

He can as well avoid what he fears most, death, by immor-
talizing himself in his writing. The scenes concerning the death
of Shenly, some of the most powerful in the novel, illustrate
White-Jacket's narrative evasion. He sits up with the dying
man, only "a bit of crumpled paper" in his hand, as if all White-
Jacket can cling to in the face of death is writing. Indeed, after
Shenly dies and the last stitch is sewn, all that remains of him is
his two-letter epitaph in *"Black's best Writing Fluid* . . . meaning
'Discharged, Dead'" (344). A hedge against death and the only
claim to immortality in this man-of-war world, writing provides
the means for White-Jacket to escape his all-too-apparent mor-
tality: "I can not stop to weep over Shenly now," he says; "that
would be false to the life I depict; wearing no mourning weeds,
I resume the task of portraying our man-of-war world" (345).
As long as he can depict life and re-create his world, he can set
death behind him.

To Melville, however, one cannot—whether Tommo or
White-Jacket—so easily flee from death with a well-wrought
narrative. Melville ends the chapter that White-Jacket began as
an escape from Shenly's death with the story of the *Glorieuse*
(348). The name, French for "saints in glory," indicates that the
Professor's lesson is meant for Melville's millennialist narrator
as well as the middies. The ship, like White-Jacket at this point,
is isolated, crippled, oppressed, and, as White-Jacket stresses
all man-of-war's men are, imminently close to death and eter-

nity.[80] The story has no ending beyond death, however; the narrative breaks off; the ship "can *not* be saved." Nor can White-Jacket. Death is a natural phenomenon from which there is no escape, narrative or otherwise.

Thus furthering the distance between himself and reality that his ideology has opened up, White-Jacket perceives events through the medium of language. Before he tells of his own rounding of Cape Horn, for example, he must first mention Orpheus, Ulysses, Dante, and the many historical analogues (chap. 24); while trying to describe Rio, he must compare it to virtually everything in the world (chap. 50). In the course of his narrative, White-Jacket becomes increasingly concerned with these interpolations, stories, tales, and other narratives, at the expense of reality. As part of the traditions of the literary main-top, songs were sung and yarns were spun; as White-Jacket spends more time there, he spends more of his narrative retelling these tales. The battle of Navarino aptly illustrates the novel's increasing involution and fictionality: White-Jacket, narrating from a later perspective, describes himself listening to Jack Chase narrating a highly exaggerated and fictionalized account of the battle, which Melville culled from Leech, Nicol, and A British Seaman.[81] Not surprisingly, White-Jacket comes to prefer such fictions, which he can control, to the facts. As to Redburn, to White-Jacket life becomes little more than a book: the path of the world-ship is indiscernible from the path of the book, as White-Jacket sails on "in the rapid wake of these chapters" (44).[82] He has, he thinks, succeeded in fusing his past into his narrative, obliterating all distinction between past and present, fiction and reality.[83] He thus seems to have effected the millennial goal with which he set out on board: he has indeed re-formed the world, resurrected his white jacket in a more spiritualized form. *White-Jacket* is the second coming of White-Jacket.

[80]Dillingham, *Artist*, argues that *White-Jacket* is about amputation, physical and psychological.
[81]See Vincent, *Tailoring*.
[82]Cf. *Letters*, 93; and Mercier, *Life*, xv.
[83]Cf. Dryden, *Melville's Thematics*, 67–79.

In this involuted and metafictional narrative, one can see
traces of the Melville of the romances, of the poststructuralism
that Edgar Dryden, Harold Beaver, and Rodolphe Gasché perceive in *Moby-Dick, Pierre,* and *The Confidence-Man.*[84] But in the
narrative of facts genre, Melville is quite critical of his and
others' narrators' confusing factual and fictional narrative. In
his review of J. Ross Browne's *Etchings* and Captain Ringbolt's
Sailors' Life and Sailors' Yarns he presents directly his opinion of
this dichotomy.[85] To Melville, Browne's book is "a book of
unvarnished facts . . . [which] unquestionably presents a faith-
ful picture of the life led by the twenty thousand seamen,"
whereas Ringbolt's book "is made up of little stories of the sea,
simply and pleasantly told, and withal entertaining"—but
wrong. Melville clearly comes out on the side of fact and of the
sailors, who are the reality principle in *White-Jacket.*[86] White-
Jacket, though, presents more "little stories of the sea" than
"unvarnished facts," making his narrative and his millennial
goal fall short. He cannot convincingly re-form his world, for
he builds too much upon the sandy foundation of his own
selfish imagination and too little upon the hard bedrock of
facts.

Melville's criticism of millennialism is thus, in *White-Jacket* as
in his previous narratives of facts, fundamentally an issue of
biased perspective. Melville shows that the millennial perspective leads irrevocably toward idealism when confronted by the
facts of the real, natural world. It leads, too, to an attempt to
subsume politics in religion, which *Omoo* and *Redburn* also show
is impossible. This entails in Melville's narrator a preference
for the ideal over the real, for narration over experience, for
fiction over facts. The millennialist narrator of experience,
personal and historical, thus cannot avoid hypocrisy, for the
narrative itself must deny its factuality even as it claims to be a
narrative of facts.

[84]Dryden, *Melville's Thematics*; Beaver, "Herman Melville," 64–79; and Gasché, "The Scene of Writing: A Deferred Quest," *Glyph* 1 (1977): 150–71.
   [85] *Literary World* 1 (1847): 105–6.
   [86]This is a distinction the sailor-narrators also make: see Mercier, *Life,* 215;
Leech, *Thirty Years,* 33; and McNally, *Evils,* 116.

6

Israel Potter

Revolutionary American Narrative

In December 1849, while still occupied with the reviews of *Redburn* and the publication of *White-Jacket*, Melville had in mind "the Revolutionary narrative of the beggar."[1] Fired with *Moby-Dick* and *Pierre*, however, he abandoned the project until 1854. Yet the resultant *Israel Potter* is more closely connected to the former narratives than to the latter romances. Like *Redburn* and *White-Jacket*, Melville's "Revolutionary narrative" is vitally political, showing a similar preoccupation with the themes of democracy and elitism, poverty and Christianity, and the interrelations among them in the American mind. *Israel Potter* is similar generically and tactically as well, for it is a narrative of facts. In it Melville, "with a change in the grammatical person" (vii), uses and reacts to narratives of Revolutionary War experiences—not only the *Life and Remarkable Adventures of Israel R. Potter* but also those of Benjamin Franklin, John Paul Jones, Ethan Allen, and others[2]—and reacts in a "revolutionary" way

---

[1]Walter E. Bezanson, "Historical Note" to *Israel Potter: His Fifty Years of Exile*, ed. Harrison Hayford, Hershel Parker, and G. Thomas Tanselle (Evanston and Chicago, 1982), 174; all subsequent references will be cited parenthetically in the text.

[2][Henry Trumbull], *Life and Remarkable Adventures of Israel R. Potter . . .* (Providence, R.I., 1824); *The Works of Benjamin Franklin*, 2 vols., ed. Jared

by again turning the narratives against themselves to make a vital and prescient comment on the American Revolution.

Many critics have noted the centrality of the revolutionary themes, often linking them to the other major issues in the novel—poverty, Christianity, exile, identity—while others have examined the dominant images, such as clothes, colors, or gardens.[3] Still other critics link the novel to historical events contemporaneous to it: Carolyn Karcher relates it to the slavery question, Michael Paul Rogin to the American political situation in the 1850s, and William Dillingham to figures such as Webster.[4] These last three critics demonstrate a recent—and admirable, I believe—attempt to interpret the novel in light of its sources and historical backgrounds, to interpret it contextually. Yet a reading of Melville's sources here must address not only the specific instances of Melville's borrowings, as Walter Bezanson's "Historical Note" to the Northwestern-Newber-

Sparks (Boston, 1836–40); Robert C. Sands, *Life and Correspondence of John Paul Jones* (New York, 1830); and Ethan Allen, *A Narrative of Colonel Ethan Allen's Captivity* . . . (Philadelphia, 1779). I am using the edition of Potter's *Life* as conveniently reprinted by R. D. Madison in the Northwestern-Newberry edition; see Bezanson's "Historical Note," 184–205, for a discussion of Melville's sources. Melville, again pressed financially and critically, considerably streamlined his use of sources in *Israel Potter*, as becomes evident when one compares it with his other narratives of facts.

[3]Robert Zaller, "Melville and the Myth of Revolution," *Studies in Romanticism* 15 (1976): 607–22, discusses power and revolution in the novel; Dryden, *Melville's Thematics*, 141–48, concentrates on the failure of the author-hero and "the fictions with which man surrounds himself"; Seelye, *Melville*, 111–17, shows that Israel's many identities add up to no identity at all; Adler, *War*, 79–87, concentrates on Franklin, Jones, and Allen in discussing the moral reaction to war; Alexander Keyssar, *Melville's "Israel Potter": Reflections on the American Dream* (Cambridge, Mass., 1969), discusses the theme of unrealized human hopes by analyzing the garden archetype, the pattern of immurement, and the clothes motif; Arnold Rampersad, *Melville's "Israel Potter": A Pilgrimage and Progress* (Bowling Green, Ohio, 1969), discusses the novel's structure and its sources in Dante and Bunyan; and John T. Frederick, "Symbol and Theme in Melville's *Israel Potter*," *Modern Fiction Studies* 8 (1962): 265–75, discusses the organic symbolism of stone, fog, and confinement.

[4]Karcher, *Shadow*, 102–8, relates the Revolution to the slavery issue; Rogin, *Subversive Genealogy*, 224–30, discusses attitudes toward the Revolution in the 1850s, noting Melville's reaction to Lincoln and to Stephen Douglas; and William B. Dillingham, *Melville's Later Novels* (Athens, Ga., 1986), 244–96, analyzes the contrasting issues of liberty and poverty.

ry edition does so thoroughly, but also the totality of Melville's engagement with his sources.[5] That is to say, in *Israel Potter*, as in *Redburn* and *White-Jacket*, Melville does not merely use his sources to generate the themes and images in the novel, he addresses the ideological and generic aspects of those revolutionary narratives as well.

The Revolution was a topic of considerable concern in Melville's 1850s. The highly revisionist history by Richard Hildreth, along with the slavery problems and those resulting from the Mexican War, prompted both worried reevaluation and outrage about that revisionism. More significant, the 1850s also saw the Revolution being used by such historians as Jared Sparks and George Bancroft for purposes that were largely conservative.[6] Bancroft's *History*, each volume reviewed extensively in Duyckinck's *Literary World* as it appeared in the 1850s, presented a romantic and progressive view of the Revolution. Consistently reiterating the divine course of history, Bancroft traces the generation of the American Revolution back through Columbus to the Greeks: "From the intelligence that had been slowly ripening in the mind of cultivated humanity sprung the American revolution, which organized social union through the establishment of personal freedom, and emancipated the nations from themselves."[7] Such an exalted effect was matched in Bancroft's mind with the revolution's "astonishing deeds": "For America, the period abounded in new forms of virtue and greatness. Fidelity to principle pervaded the masses. . . . Heroism, greater than that of chivalry, burst

---

[5]Bezanson ably summarizes Melville's borrowings, but does not examine the ideology of the sources; conversely, John P. McWilliams, Jr., *Hawthorne, Melville, and the American Character: A Looking-Glass Business* (Cambridge, Eng., 1984), 183–89, accurately assesses Melville's critique of the self-serving component in the Revolutionary heroes, but his short reading does not examine Melville's sources.

[6]See Sparks, *Ethan Allen* (1848; rpt. New York, 1902); Bancroft, *History*, 2:319–27; and contemporary periodicals such as *The Literary World*, *Harper's*, *Putnam's*, and *The North American Review*. On Sparks and Bancroft as conservative interpreters of the Revolution see Michael Kammen, *A Season of Youth: The American Revolution and the Historical Imagination* (New York, 1978), 47–48.

[7]Bancroft, *History*, 2:325.

into action from lowly men."[8] To Bancroft, in short, the Revolution was the culmination of white culture and virtually epic in scope and quality. Nor was this view confined to Bancroft; were Melville's readers to consult "the volumes of Sparks," as Melville's narrator says he has, they would find similar views. Sparks and Bancroft—and other lesser lights—were engaged in a concerted effort in the early 1850s to preserve and promote what is perhaps best labeled the myth of the Revolution.

As his previous narratives of facts demonstrate, Melville is highly skeptical of these grand historical claims. Just as Bancroft's Revolution was the culmination of the West's cultural, religious, and political progress, so Melville's *Israel Potter* involves the cultural issues of *Typee*, the religion of *Omoo*, the political economy of *Redburn*, and the political millennialism of *White-Jacket*. To express his skepticism about these aspects of the Revolution, Melville found an ideal vehicle in the *Life and Remarkable Adventures of Israel R. Potter*, which like the other narratives Melville uses tends to glorify America and its Revolution but contains as well elements that deny and subvert that glorification. Just as Potter praises the exploits of the colonists, sounds jingoistic praise for America, and vilifies Britain, he perhaps unwittingly calls into question the ideology and achievements of the Revolution by presenting his own often pitiable and dubious motivations and experiences. Melville, seeing in Potter's narrative these ambiguities, heightens them with some help from the other narratives, and thereby offers a critique of problems—the poverty he personally experienced, the slavery, the acquisitive nationalism, and the rationalizing religiosity—evident in his own day. Ever suspicious of the "advances" of white culture, Melville wryly demystifies the whitewashing of this crucial event in American cultural history. His Israel returns not to acclaim and veneration but to oblivion and further poverty, returns on July 4, 1826, the fiftieth anniversary of the Declaration of Independence and the day both Jefferson and John Adams died, the date Michael Kammen sees as giving rise to "a popular impulse . . . that for a time verged

[8]Ibid., 2:327.

upon being a cult of ancestor worship—still another way of creating a sense of national tradition—but the impulse aroused opposition and soon lost its momentum."[9]

I

Central to Melville's critique of the Revolution and literally central in his *Israel Potter* is his presentation of three heroes of the Revolution in a section he added to the *Life*. Franklin, Jones, and Allen had by the 1850s become major figures in American tradition, if not objects of cult worship: their narratives had been printed and reprinted and they were subjects of voluminous biographies by Sparks and others. Yet Sparks, and each figure himself, consciously forms that tradition, consciously attempts to mold and cast the reputation of revolutionary hero. In each case, the reputation is a response to British aspersions: for instance, Sparks, in his "Continuation" of Franklin's *Autobiography*, controverts "a late English writer" who "insinuates" that Franklin ignored his poor relatives; and in the preface to Jones's narrative, Robert C. Sands attacks the English edition, whose editor reveals "his own monarchical and English prejudices" by impugning the character of Jones. The effect of such histories, Allen worries, is compounded by "some men . . . in these states, who read the history of the cruelties of this war with the same careless indifferency, as they do the pages of the Roman history . . . and so far as such influence takes place, robs us of the victory we have obtained." In a very real sense, then, the war continued to be fought by preserving the reputation and tradition of its "noble heroism, which after having astonished the present age, will continue to be the imperishable object of veneration of future generations." Thus Franklin, writing his *Autobiography* not only to his son but to all the heirs of his revolutionary heroism, constructs a crafty case for his own reasonable, enlightened, public-spirited motivations; and though the book ends before 1775, it is clearly a

[9]Kammen, *Season*, 17–18.

justification—less overt than but similar to Jones's and Allen's—of the representative American revolutionary.[10] Even though Sparks's preface claims that "few writers have been so regardless of literary reputation as Franklin," the autobiographer himself says that he "shall perhaps not a little gratify [his] own vanity" in presenting his life to posterity.

One must be suspicious of the self-serving nature of such justifications, nowhere more clearly evident than in the *Life and Remarkable Adventures*. Most obvious, Potter writes (through Trumbull) to attempt to secure the pension that he sees as "remuneration for services rendered, and hardships endured in the cause of my country."[11] Potter further attempts to promote his case by tying himself to the ample coattails of the good Dr. Franklin:

> My interview with Dr. Franklin was a pleasing one—for nearly an hour he conversed with me in the most agreeable and instructive manner, and listened to the tale of my sufferings with much apparent interest, and seemed disposed to encourage me with the assurance that if the Americans should succeed with their grand object, and firmly establish their independence, they would not fail to remunerate the soldiers for their services—but, alas! as regards myself, these assurances have not as yet been verified! I am confident, however, that had it been a possible thing for that great and good man (whose humanity and generosity have been the theme of infinitely abler pens than mine) to have lived to this day, I should not have petitioned my country in vain for a momentary enjoyment of that provision.[12]

Potter uses Franklin not only as a sanction for the importance of his rather small revolutionary role but also as an authorita-

---

[10]Franklin, *Works*, 1:374; Sands, *John Paul Jones*, 6–7, 195, 288, 395; and Allen, *Narrative*, 2. On Franklin's attempt to claim representative status, see Mitchell Breitwieser, *Cotton Mather and Benjamin Franklin: The Price of Representative Personality* (Cambridge, Eng., 1984); Christopher Looby, "'The Affairs of the Revolution Occasion'd the Interruption': Writing, Revolution, Deferral and Conciliation in Franklin's *Autobiography*," *American Quarterly* 38 (1986): 72–96; and Albert Furtwangler, *American Silhouettes: Rhetorical Identities of the Founders* (New Haven, Conn., 1987), 15–34.

[11] [Trumbull], *Life*, 105.

[12]Ibid., 50–51.

tive mouthpiece for his own case, despite the fact that his use of "seemed" and "apparent" might undercut that authority.[13] Thus he repeats on a far less grand scale the concern for reputation and establishment of tradition so important to Franklin himself.

Melville, taking skeptical note of this tactic in Potter and the others, amplifies to absurdity the grandiose and ridiculously coincidental connections of the insignificant Israel. Furthermore, by introducing more fully Franklin, Jones, and Allen, Melville can ironically subvert the reputation each has tried to secure for himself, often by whitewashing actions that might be construed as derogatory. Potter's self-promotion is transparent—at once pathetic and comic—in both the narrative and the novel; that of Franklin, Jones, and Allen, present though less overt in their narratives, provides Melville an occasion for more significant and subtler satire.

As many critics have noticed, Melville's portrait is clearly critical of Franklin, yet how this picture reflects Franklin's writings has yet to be fully developed. Melville recognized Franklin's proclivity for preserving reputation by repeatedly labeling him "venerable" and "famous" and by linking him with figures from Jacob to Plato to Hobbes. Yet it is not the substance of these figures Franklin resembles but their "style," "mental habits," their practicality and prudence (46–47). Melville's Franklin is a rather shifty and indefinite "personage," frequently described with the "seemed" and "appeared" Melville saw in Potter's description. Indeed, appearance or reputation may be his most important noncharacteristic.[14]

Melville also carefully controverts two important facets of the portrait of Franklin that the Doctor himself promoted and that were firmly a part of American tradition. First, Melville parodies Franklin's reputed altruism by establishing him as the supposedly generous helper who "'every time he comes in he robs me,' soliloquised Israel, dolefully; 'with an air all the time,

[13]Cf. Sands, *John Paul Jones*, 278.

[14]Breitwieser, *Mather and Franklin*, and Furtwangler, *American Silhouettes*, both develop this issue in their analyses of Franklin; for a more positive view of Melville's Franklin, see Dillingham, *Melville's Later Novels*, 260–68.

too, as if he were making me presents'" (53). "Air" indeed, for all Franklin's gifts are mere words, like the "O-t-a-r-d" that vanishes under Franklin's arm (50–51). In his writing Franklin directs his "a penny saved is a penny earned" philosophy toward others' improving their lot, but he himself gained much from it and from his promotion of it. And though he stresses that he refused to profit from his public service and his inventions, there is some question—as Sparks's testy response to British claims indicates—about Franklin's genuine commitment to help the less fortunate in any way other than by dispensing advice. Of particular relevance to *Israel Potter* is Franklin's highly Smithian position on poverty. Bezanson convincingly argues that Melville obtained Franklin's line about Indian corn (40) from an essay in Sparks's edition of the *Works*. Another essay in that volume, "On the Price of Corn, and Management of the Poor," takes a stance typical of Franklin and more relevant to the themes of Melville's novel: "I think the best way of doing good to the poor is, not making them easy *in* poverty, but leading or driving them *out* of it."[15] Here and in other essays in the volume, Franklin urges giving no aid to the poor, for to do nothing will encourage them to work their own way out of poverty. He then uses England as the primary example of a nation that coddles its poor with support, with the result "that there is no country in the world in which the poor are more idle, dissolute, drunken, and insolent."[16] To the Israel of the last part of the novel, who looks to America as a dream of relief from his English poverty, this American philosophy holds cruelly devastating ironies. Franklin's laissez-faire policies, like the man himself, would rob Israel once more. That America has enshrined Franklin's ideal of "God helps them that helps themselves" is perhaps responsible for the callous governmental response that led to the historical Potter's narrative plea for relief.

Compounding Melville's condemnation of Franklin's cloaked acquisitiveness and callousness is what his (literal) cloak sig-

[15]*Works*, 2:358.
[16]Ibid., 359.

nifies. Like the weird dressing gown he wears, Franklin himself is invested in terms suggesting an "astrologer," a "necromancer," terms associating him with *Omoo*'s necromantic con-man, Long Ghost, and with its destructive astrologer, Jermin. Melville's characterization of Franklin obviously affronts the highly rational, pragmatic image Franklin sought to cultivate—nothing would irk Franklin or his followers more than to be considered superstitious—yet Melville is comically exaggerating tendencies evident in Franklin's own works. The charts and checklists central to—and in—the *Autobiography*, like his famous *Almanac*, resemble astrological charts, somewhat domesticated. "Household Plato" does accurately characterize him, but he is the Plato Melville savages in *Pierre*: "Now without doubt this Talismanic Secret has never yet been found; and in the nature of human things it seems as though it never can be. Certain philosophers have time and again pretended to have found it; but if they do not in the end discover their own delusion, other people soon discover it for themselves. . . . Plato . . . and many more belong to this guild of self-impostors."[17] Melville's Franklin, too, is one of this guild: his talismanic secret, pragmatic thought and the work ethic, he holds with such cultlike devotion that he has become blind to the plight of such as Israel. Thus this American sage has become a "practical magian," a lord of the flies (47, 39). Further images of and allusions to death permeate Melville's portrait: he describes Franklin in a "drizzly November" (47) that recalls Ishmael's suicidal urge at the beginning of *Moby-Dick*, and he places him in a setting where "one almost expects to encounter Paracelsus or Friar Bacon turning the next corner, with some awful vial of Black-Art elixir in his hand" (47). In short, Melville indicates that for Israel and for America more generally, Franklin and his philosophy are a pseudo-scientific, dead-end mystification.

Although considerably more heroic than his Franklin, Melville's Jones shows a similar concern for his reputation and a similar ambivalence. Like Franklin, Jones is vain, looking with "pleased coxcombry" (62) in the mirror and making demands

[17]*Pierre*, 208.

"with a look as of a parading Sioux demanding homage to his gew-gaws" (58). Like Franklin, too, Jones's vanity is exemplified particularly in his quest for reputation: for example, Jones proudly boasts of being the first to raise the American flag, but concludes, "if I perish this night, the name of Paul Jones shall live" (113). Melville is here echoing the amply demonstrated tendency in Jones's narrative. Examining such actions, which produced much criticism of Jones, Sands says, "Such is the temperament of those who feel that they are 'born to achieve greatness;' the exhibition of which, until their vision is realized, is laid to the score of personal vanity." Nathaniel Fanning, who served in Jones's main-top, gives further evidence of his captain's often absurdly jealous guarding of his reputation: he attempts to lie and maneuver out of his responsibility for mistreating a passenger who had refused to bow to his authority; and his treatment by the Dutch "so elated him with pride, that he had the vanity to go into the state house, mount the balcony or piazza, and shew himself in the front thereof, to the populace."[18]

Undercutting these displays of self-assurance is Melville's portrayal of Jones's essentially ambiguous or even dubious character.[19] Melville explains that his "pleased coxcombry seemed to mingle with the otherwise savage satisfaction expressed in his face. But the latter predominated" (62). As this last sentence emphasizes, the "savage" is Jones's dominant characteristic: his ambivalence is that of a civilized "bloody cannibal" (91). Melville repeatedly emphasizes this characteristic,

[18]Sands, *John Paul Jones*, 44; Nathaniel Fanning, *Memoirs of the Life of Captain Nathaniel Fanning* . . . (New York, 1808), 91–97, 69. Lewis Leary, "Introduction" to *His Fifty Years of Exile (Israel Potter)* (New York, 1957), vii, argues for Melville's reading of Fanning; Bezanson, "Historical Note," *Israel Potter*, 195n, sees little evidence for Melville's reading of Fanning, but to me the detail about the Man-in-the-Moon and the similarity of Melville's attitudes to Fanning's seem good reasons for agreeing with Leary.

[19]Kammen, *People of Paradox: An Inquiry Concerning the Origins of American Civilization* (1972; rpt. New York, 1973), argues for paradox as a crucial American characteristic; see especially chap. 7 ("Ambiguities of the American Revolution," 225–49).

graphically detailed in his adding to the historical Jones "a sort of tattooing such as is seen only on thorough-bred savages—deep blue, elaborate, labyrinthine, cabalistic" (62). The tattoos relate Jones to the occultishly dressed Franklin, but they also link him to such shifty, sinister figures as *Omoo*'s renegado Lem Hardy, whom Paul gazes upon "with a feeling akin to horror." To Paul, as to Israel, there is something horrible about one who seems to have so markedly rejected his society, so determinedly made himself a renegado.

Also like Lem Hardy, a military leader whose "campaigns beat Napoleon's," Jones with his tattoos shows a primitive violence seen most fully in the fight he leads against the *Serapis*. The historical Jones himself concludes from the battle that "humanity cannot but recoil from the prospect of such finished horror, and lament that war should be capable of producing such fatal consequences."[20] Yet Melville, choosing to emphasize the violence in Jones's character, allows his Jones no such reflection; instead, it is Israel who consequently muses, "Is civilization a thing distinct, or is it an advanced state of barbarism?" (130). Jones, the bloody "crimson thread" in Israel's "blue-jean" career, is not merely an example of revolutionary heroism but of "the primeval savageness which ever slumbers in human kind" (63).

The image of Jones as cannibal carries another implication that further exposes the character of the historical Jones: that his violence is often directed toward his own kind. The historical Jones was early in his career a chief mate in the West Indies slave trade, where his severity toward his men was of such notoriety that Jones himself, his editor Sands, and Cooper all feel called upon to controvert it. Melville's Jones tells Israel, "to this hour they say there that I . . . flogged a sailor, one Mungo Maxwell, to death. It's a lie, by heaven!" (91). Fanning, typically, asserts not that Jones flogged him but that he forced the sailor to sit on a pot of gunpowder, which he then ignited. Moreover, Fanning asserts that Jones commonly filled sailors'

[20]Sands, *John Paul Jones*, 187.

ears with gunpowder and ignited it as "his method of punishing the crew."[21] True or not, these assertions serve to illustrate the common sailors' perception of the captain as inordinately callous. Of more immediate relevance to *Israel Potter* is Fanning's portrayal of Jones's violent rejection of the sailors' poverty. Even as Jones was being wined and dined as the toast of Parisian society, his men were being denied proper winter clothing and adequate rations. Fanning quotes Jones's response to one lieutenant's supplication: "'I do not want your advice. . . . [G]o to your own duty, each one of you, and let me hear no more grumbling.' He said this in a rage." As a result of Jones's failure to give relief, "a number of Americans became beggars in a foreign country."[22] Like Franklin, whose "help themselves" philosophy so attracts him, Jones shows a desire for personal glory and its trappings that often comes at the expense of those less fortunate. Melville concludes that "this cruise made loud fame for Paul. . . . But poor Israel . . . what had he?" (113). "Poor" here serves once more to emphasize the novel's final point, that the results of revolutionary heroism, often built upon the sufferings of the poor common soldier or sailor, has not bettered the impoverished conditions of the lower class—even in the America of Melville's day. Thus not only in its violence, but in its denial of support to those like "poor Israel," America may be "the Paul Jones of nations" (120). A brilliant encapsulation of these traits is Melville's reference to Jones as "the Coriolanus of the sea" (95). Like the Shakespearean character, Jones is a valorous conqueror whose arrogance alienates those common people beneath him. Coriolanus, too, is a bit of a cannibal: he turns on the Romans, his own people, in favor of the Volscians, who ironically end up slaying him.

Melville's portrait of Ethan Allen, considerably more compressed and slightly more positive, nevertheless shows the concern for reputation and the ambivalence that undercuts it that are evident in his Franklin and Jones. For all his seemingly

---

[21]Fanning, *Memoirs*, 106–7.
[22]Ibid., 82–83.

ingenuous venting of rage, Allen's conduct is based on a Franklinesque pragmatism. "By his facetious scorn for scorn," Melville says, "under the extremest sufferings, he finally wrung repentant usage from his foes; and in the end, being liberated from his irons, . . . was carried back to America" (151). His vituperations, threats, and insults, that is to say, are calculated to develop a reputation that will serve Allen well, as it did the historical Allen, who in his *Narrative of the Captivity* directly states that his conduct was designed to help him survive or at least "exhibit a good sample of American fortitude."[23] Yet interestingly, Allen's tactic in the narrative itself is quite the opposite: in order to counter this reputation for wild savagery, he presents—using suitably philosophical terminology—these rationales and almost continually asserts that he is a "gentleman." Melville develops this characteristic in his Allen, who, arrayed in a half-savage costume and generally looking like "some wild beast" (144), "talks like a beau in a parlor" when ladies approach (145). In such chameleonic behavior, Allen shows himself as shifty as Franklin; Allen, too, is "a conjuror by profession" (146).[24]

Melville thus playfully (yet with serious intent as well) retouches the portraits of these three revolutionary heroes, yet through the traits they have in common he also calls attention to issues concerning the Revolution in general, issues prominent in the narratives he uses as sources. In each figure Melville shows a vital violence: Jones's overt savagery, Franklin's philosophic violence evident in his resembling Hobbes (46),[25] and Allen's largely verbal violence. It is as well a violence that bespeaks the primitive side of man, which lurks, like Jones's tattoos, beneath the surface refinement or is revealed, like Franklin's "primitive orientalness" (46) and his "conjuror's robe" (38), only in his private chambers. Melville here reiterates a point made in *Typee* and *Omoo*: that all men are both

[23]Allen, *Narrative*, 13–17.
[24]Sparks, *Ethan Allen*, 128, concludes by describing Allen's ambivalent character; Melville's phrase here is Allen's (*Narrative*, 16).
[25]See the discussion of Hobbes in chap. 3 above.

savage and civilized, and therefore any portrait is skewed that would attempt to gloss over the savagery beneath the civilized surface. This was a significant bone of contention in the revolutionary narratives, each of which attempted to reverse the British depiction of the American revolutionaries as less civilized. For instance, in London Potter hears the Yankees "not unfrequently represented as a set of infuriated beings," while Allen rages against the "prejudiced and depraved minds" of his captors; Sands and Sparks express a similar disgust for British editors and historians who call the Americans barbaric.[26] In their own narratives the Americans consequently attempt to reverse this portrayal: they not only stress their own civility as Allen does—and as Franklin's *Autobiography* does as a whole— but also deplore, in Jones's words, "the barbarous and unmanly practice of the Britons." Melville's portrayal, however, deletes the political propaganda from the issue; although some British "honest rustics seemed to think the Yankees were a sort of wild creatures" (15), neither Israel nor Melville's narrator retaliates at length about British inhumanity. To Melville, neither nation is the more savage (as neither Tommo nor the Typees was); it is rather that revolution or war is the awakening of "the primeval savageness which ever slumbers in human kind, civilized or uncivilized" (63). The attempts by Sands or Sparks or Allen to whitewash the savagery of the Revolutionary heroes are humorously exposed.

This idealization of the national character gains Melville's censure here as in *Redburn* and *White-Jacket*, and all are parts of Melville's anti-idealist convictions, which Milton Stern ably discusses.[27] Moreover, accompanying this idealization—perhaps even its motivation—is a personal pragmatism equally censurable to Melville. That is to say, in his characterizations Melville speculates that patriotic fervor may be largely self-interest. Melville's Allen develops these traits himself, in order to survive; Franklin's pragmatism, however, may be little more than

---

[26][Trumbull], *Life*, 17; Allen, *Narrative*, 34–35; and Sands, *John Paul Jones*, 6–7. Melville includes examples of this prejudice (147 and 150).
[27]Stern, *Steel*.

a habitual acquisitiveness, a corruption of the very rationalism he promotes. His wry statement in the *Autobiography* is revealing: "So convenient a thing it is to be a *reasonable creature*, since it enables one to find or make a *reason* for every thing one has a mind to do."[28] His philosophy allows Franklin to "help himself" to everything from Israel's sugar to his French maid, just as the America of the 1850s, with a similarly rationalized altruism, had helped itself to Texas. "The type and genius of his land" (48), Melville's Franklin is akin to Jacob and Hobbes (46–47): the former acquired his brother's birthright by taking advantage of Esau's extreme hunger (Gen. 25), while the latter developed a philosophy of self-interest that culminated in the totalitarian Leviathan.[29] Jones's self-interest, which Melville stresses in Jones's readiness to accept Franklin's philosophical dictum (61) and in his fascination with his own image in a mirror (62), is likewise frequently linked with his zeal for liberty. As Jones himself says, "The common class of mankind are actuated by no nobler principle than that of self-interest; *this*, and this alone, determines all adventurers in privateers." Jones here attempts a philosophical justification of the controversial practice of privateering, a subject that Cooper raises with some hesitation.[30] Melville is even more skeptical about the results of self-interest, particularly for the poor. Jones's self-interest nets him the benefits of a hero, Israel nothing (113). As in *Redburn*, economics usurps morality and a Machiavellian double standard results: "it is among nations as among individuals: imputed indigence provokes oppression and scorn; but the same indigence being risen to opulence, receives a politic consideration even from its former insulters" (151; cf. Franklin as Machiavelli [46]). Thus in the world's eye the economic end is all-important, the means to that end hypocritically eclipsed.

In the previous quotation Melville is also referring to another aspect of Revolutionary heroism, what might best be

[28]*Works*, 1:46.

[29]Paul's sailing off on the *Leviathan* at the end of *Omoo* is by no means positive; see my analysis in chap. 3.

[30]Sands, *John Paul Jones*, 54; Cooper, "Preface" to *The History of The Navy of the United States of America*, 2 vols. (Philadelphia, 1839).

called the myth of the rise from obscurity. The narratives of Franklin, Jones, and Allen—and their biographies such as Sparks's—all stress the heroes' relatively humble origins in order to heighten their ultimate achievements.[31] To Bancroft, as later to Horatio Alger, this is a peculiarly American revolutionary pattern: "For America, the period abounded in new forms of virtue and greatness. . . . Heroism, greater than that of chivalry, burst into action from lowly men."[32] Melville satirizes this myth not only in the pretensions of Franklin and Allen, the distance they now put between themselves and those like Israel, but also in the novel's plot. By the middle of the book, Israel seems to have risen from his obscure origins to the Olympian heights, a pattern which Melville's audience would surely expect, but one which makes Israel's fall to an even greater obscurity all the more poignant. The myth, Melville indicates, is by no means pervasive or accurate; the very idea of a "revolutionary beggar" runs counter to it but may perhaps be more realistic and typical.

Extending his criticism of this unquestioning validation of success, Melville explodes the tendency to perceive Revolutionary heroes in quasi-monarchical terms. Antimonarchical sentiments are essential to the stated aims of narrators such as Allen, who ridicules "considerable unintelligible and grovelling ideas, a little tinctured with monarchy," and of biographers such as Sands, who attacks "monarchical and English prejudices."[33] Melville adds this trait to his Israel, who "in the Lion's Den" has "dim impulses, such as those to which the regicide Ravaillac yielded" (30; cf. Potter's *Life*, 43–45), but he only denies to George that he has a king (31). Such statements nothwithstanding, Israel is quick to submit to the "venerable" Franklin, "the caressed favorite of the highest born beauties of the Court" (48) who lives in what had been "the hotel of a nobleman" (49); he follows Jones, "a democratic sort of sea-king" (90—a self-professed oxymoron that reaffirms Jones's

---

[31]See the opening pages of each; *Putnam's* January 1854 issue presents a similar biographical sketch of Washington.

[32]*History*, 2:327.

[33]Allen, *Narrative*, 22; Sands, *John Paul Jones*, 6–7.

ambivalent character); and he is in awe of the "knightly" "gentleman" Allen (145–46). Melville here indicates that in America's hero worship grow the seeds of the very monarchism that the heroes fought against, a tendency amply in evidence in the narratives. Both Franklin and Jones spend considerable time at the French court (and others), basking in the beneficence of royalty while pursuing the democratic cause, so that it is little wonder that someone like Fanning would perceive a hypocrisy in such actions. Even Allen voices repeated praise for "His Most Christian Majesty . . . the illustrious potentate . . . of the ancient kingdom of France."[34] More significant is the perception of Franklin and company by their biographers and by the general public in Melville's day, for the veneration that stresses the heroes' nobility and superiority is tantamount to latent monarchism.

This tendency, like the tendency to prioritize "Opulence" (151), is to Melville irrational. Melville heightens the historical Potter's "tendency in some degree to prepossess me in his [George III's] favor,"[35] and concludes his Israel's encounter with the King by saying, "Thus we see what strange and powerful magic resides in a crown, and how subtly that cheap and easy magnanimity, which in private belongs to most kings, may operate on good-natured and unfortunate souls" (32). "Cheap and easy magnanimity" aptly characterizes the appeal of the Franklin clad in astrologer's robes—compare Franklin's proposed religious sect, the Society of the Free and Easy—but the main thrust of Melville's sly criticism here points to those like Sands, who scorns "superstitiously believing in the virtues of a hereditary monarchy" but can say of Jones "that he must have 'borne a charmed life.'"[36] Thus Melville likens them to the missionaries in *Typee* and *Omoo*, who label the natives' religion "superstition" but whose own is no more rational. The "magic" of hereditary superiority is merely another confidence game, which Melville exposes from the first. His dedication "To His Highness the Bunker-Hill Monument" is satiric in several re-

[34]Allen, *Narrative*, 43.
[35][Trumbull], *Life*, 45.
[36]Sands, *John Paul Jones*, 260, 199.

spects. First, this monarch, although ironically called "the Great Biographer," is nothing but a dumb stone, but not much less articulate than Melville's stammering George III (30–31). And yet in the absurd reverence for revolutionary heroism it represents, it does chronicle (as does the book as a whole) an important if irreverent history. Second, the monument, more than the "other" revolutionary heroes, deserves to be addressed as "His Highness," for it is literally, but only literally, high—and a marked contrast to Melville's ending the dedication with "the grave of Israel Potter." To raise any hero to monumental status, Melville is saying, is to ignore the end, not only of leveling death, but the end—poverty, despair, oblivion—of common men like Israel. To raise monuments does nothing for "the anonymous privates of June 17, 1775, who may never have received other requital than the solid reward of your granite" (viii). The historical Potter, who wanted a pension to help ease his poverty, would perceive this "solid reward" as a cold comfort, a stone silence, a purely symbolic "requital."

The general effect of the course of the novel, that is to say, exposes perhaps the most crucial paradox in the concept of revolutionary heroism. The American Revolution, fought largely by anonymous privates like Potter in hope of attaining or perserving the Jeffersonian democratic ideal—Israel leaves his plow for Bunker Hill (13)—engenders a class system that enshrines the Sons of Liberty while leaving the lower classes out in the cold.[37] The historical Potter sees class as a problem endemic to the Old World and sustains himself by dreaming of the better conditions in America.[38] Although Melville reduces the issue of Old World poverty by compressing forty-five years into a single short chapter, he heightens Israel's class consciousness by having Israel bristle at calling a knight "Sir" (24–26), an action not in the original. Yet gaining liberty from this system of nobility does not bring equality, for "poverty and

[37]See Kammen, *Season*, 45, on the class issue; and Karcher, *Shadow*, 103–15, on its relation to slavery. Fanning, *Memoirs*, 139, calls slavery and beggary the major disgraces of a nation; see also "Dwellings and Schools for the Poor," *North American Review* 74 (April 1852): 464–67.
[38][Trumbull], *Life*, 62, 75–77.

liberty, or plenty and a prison," he thinks, "seem to be the two horns of the constant dilemma of my life" (69). Jones, like Franklin, gets "loud fame" and rewards, but such liberty and plenty are only for the heroes.

The poverty and despair of Israel Potter, and of the many Israel Potters, is Melville's broadest criticism of the American Revolution and of the success America trumpeted in the 1850s. Melville, himself struggling to remain above poverty, could see much irony in the statements of Bancroft, whose *History* paints a glossy portrait of American equality and prosperity, the stated results of its glorious Revolution.[39] The "natural equality" that Bancroft says replaced "hereditary privilege" has effected little change, for in keeping "faith with the ashes of its heroes" America has fostered the very problems it sought to alleviate.[40] And perhaps necessarily so, for embedded in the ideology of the American Revolution are conceptions of tradition and heroism that engender their opposite. A tradition of radical egalitarianism produces a conservative class system unresponsive to the poor; a veneration of heroism encourages a self-interested superficiality that further ignores the accomplishments of the common man. In contrast, Melville's "Biography, in its purer form" (vii), is indeed "one given and received in entire disinterestedness," for he exposes the interest of America, its heroes, and its conservative biographers, and he implies an unselfish regard for the oppressed and forgotten.

II

Melville's argument against Revolutionary heroism is thus another dimension of his long-standing opposition to the oppressive tendencies of attempted transcendence. All attempts of an individual to transcend his situation, whether Tommo's primitivism or Redburn's messianic nationalism, ineffectively mask a desire for personal superiority that frequently leads to the op-

[39]See particularly his "Introduction," *History*, 1:1–3.
[40]Ibid., 2:325–26.

pression of those imagined below. Just as Tommo's idea of progress and primitivism places him above the Typee the revolutionaries' belief in their own heroic mission, reinforced and heightened by their biographers, distances them and subordinates those like Israel. Like Tommo's, too, their revolutionary activities, and Israel's as well, are precursed by and perhaps psychologically based upon a revolt against their original families. Each of the protagonists in Melville's narratives of facts engages in the resistence to filiopiety: each attempts to assert his independence, to distance himself from his immediate cultural unit, to claim consciously or not a superior position. Paul's shamanistic wandering and White-Jacket's main-top philosophizing are to Melville dubious attempts to increase status by becoming more of an "isolato."

The historical Potter begins with his growing up "in the full enjoyment of parental affection and indulgence, until [he] arrived at age 18," when his parents forbade his association with a neighbor's daughter. Considering this "unreasonable and oppressive," he lights out for the territories. Melville repeats this scene, adding a statement that makes Israel's revolt emblematic of the American political revolt: "ere, on just principles throwing off the yoke of his king, Israel, on equally excusable grounds, emancipated himself from his sire" (7). Furthering this association, Melville also adds to the historical account two important details concerning the parents' motivation and conduct, that the girl's poverty may contribute to her unsuitability and that his father had "taken secret means to thwart his son" (7). Thus Israel rebels against his father's kingly and conspiratorial authority and for the cause of the poor, as of course America does. In so acting, Israel repeats Tommo's Rousseauvian drive for natural liberty, which also serves as a basis for America's revolutionary actions and as an opposition to the perceived un-naturality of monarchism.[41] But Melville turns Israel's desire for a natural liberty free from familial control back against him, for his eventual marriage deepens his pover-

---

[41]Melville (33) calls attention to this issue by repeating "natural"; see also Zaller, "Melville," 618.

ty and precludes his immediate return home (162), and when he can return forty-five years later, he is sadly liberated from all traces of his family, whose home is now reduced entirely to nature (168–69).

Melville's ironies, in short, raise the question of whether the hero's revolutionary fervor is little more than youthful rebelliousness, more a psychological displacement than a genuine commitment to the cause of liberty.[42] The cases of Franklin and Jones certainly contain the seed for this speculation, as each is involved in a similar, and similarly ironic, revolt against filiopiety. (Allen, who retains "no trace" of the character of his birthplace, evinces little of this displacement of authority.) Melville's additions to Potter's story serve not only to raise the larger question but again to direct it toward the reputation of the revolutionary heroes. As recent critics have noticed, Franklin's description of his own rebellion from his family in the first pages of the *Autobiography* exposes his uneasy relation to the Revolution itself.[43] And indeed, ambivalences abound. Franklin chafes at subordinating himself to his father's wishes and soon leaves his Boston family behind; nevertheless, he frames his narrative as a work supposedly meant to be paternal advice to his own son. This episode might also be considered a fore-shadowing parallel to his later Revolutionary role—as Melville makes Israel's initial revolt—but Franklin repeatedly defers his discussion of the Revolution and generally avoids using that word in the book.[44] For all his revolutionary activities, personal and political, Franklin reveals a more compelling wish to claim his own authority, even to demanding filiopiety from others. As Melville notes, the Doctor repeatedly gives Israel "a paternal detailed lesson" (41) and exercises a fatherly authority by confining Israel to his room.

Jones's filial rebellion is equally ambivalent and perhaps

---

[42]Exploring the issue of filiopietism and the Revolution are Breitwieser, *Mather and Franklin*; Looby, "'Affairs,'" and Jay Fliegelman, *Prodigals and Pilgrims: The American Revolution against Patriarchal Authority, 1750–1800* (Cambridge, Eng., 1982).

[43]See Looby, "'Affairs.'"

[44]Ibid., 82–87.

more closely connected to his revolutionary actions. The narratives Melville read indicate what Sands calls a "vulgar invention" (by Fanning and others) that Jones "ran away to sea against the will of his relations";[45] but his adoption of his mother's surname, Jones, over his father's, Paul, certainly gives evidence of some filial revolt. His raid on the Solway Firth, where he was raised, and his attempt to kidnap the Earl of Selkirk, for whom his father worked, are an explicit conflation of personal and political revolutions, one that produced much criticism of him and much rationalization by and for him.[46] Melville's version of the events (chaps. 16 and 17) emphasizes the "combination of apparent incompatibilities" (99) at the heart of Jones's attitudes. At Whitehaven he spikes the cannons (the interpretation of which is best left to the Freudians) and sets fire to the colliers, but he also takes "paternal care" (104) of the townspeople themselves. At Selkirk, he interrogates the countess in terms "hyperbolical" but "most heedfully deferential" (108); he allows his men to plunder the silver but buys it himself and restores it to the countess.[47] In short, like Franklin he attacks paternal authority even as he usurps it for himself.

Melville's insistent and heightened relation of the private and public spheres here closes a fissure insisted upon by both Sparks and Sands. Sparks's American Biography Series tends to emphasize the public self at the expense of the private, usually by concentrating upon the figure's revolutionary exploits and limiting the discussion of his character to the last few pages. His biography of Allen, for example, devotes little more than two sentences to his parents and his childhood, and he presents instead an extensive history of border disputes involving Vermont that noticeably delays Allen's own story. Yet such dichotomization flies in the face of the American biographical tradition, clearest in Cotton Mather, which typologically unites the private self and the public. Melville's portraiture restores this typology, but to a destructive rather than constructive

[45]Sands, *John Paul Jones*, 15; Fanning, *Memoirs*, 106.
[46]Sands, *John Paul Jones*, 87–88; Cooper, *History of the Navy*, 1:165.
[47]See Bezanson's summary of the event, "Historical Note," *Israel Potter*, 197–98.

effect: his glimpses into the private chambers of Franklin, Jones, and even Allen reveal an often disconcerting though frequently comic motivation, one far more personal than political. That Israel's revolutionary actions may amount to little more than filial discontent is perhaps excusable; but Franklin's and Jones's using their political status to effect personal goals is shameful or even pathetic, and certainly no nobler than the British attempt to degrade Allen's person for his political actions.

If Franklin's and Jones's narratives betray an anxiety about their own filial relationships, they suggest in addition a national ambivalence about America's filial relationship with England. Melville sees in the fight between the *Bon Homme Richard* and the *Serapis* "something singularly indicatory. . . . It may involve at once a type, a parallel, and a prophecy. Sharing the same blood with England, and yet her proved foe in two wars . . . America is, or may yet be, the Paul Jones of nations" (120). America revolts against her father-land, yet it does share the same blood, as Bancroft and many others in the 1850s noted.[48] Indeed, most of the claims to America's special status depended upon establishing a special line of descent back through England's constitutional liberties to the Saxons. While a Revolutionary biographer like Sands repeats Jones's castigations of the British, he also qualifies them by saying, "Yet in the excitement of the moment, he said more than he meant to imply. The blood of England is good enough—there is none better."[49] By the 1850s a twofold irony had thus arisen: while celebrating the revolution against the father-land, America also celebrated its inheritance from it; and in enshrining those who led the filial revolt, it established an antirevolutionary regard for its own fathers.[50]

A major aspect of the usurpation of the father's role, on both levels, is sexual. The historical Potter's quarrel with his father began with the elder's quashing his relationship with the neigh-

[48]See Bancroft's "Introduction," *History*, 1:1–3; see also my analysis of this issue in chap. 5.

[49]Sands, *John Paul Jones*, 348.

[50]See Rogin, *Subversive Genealogy*, on Melville and "the American 1848."

bor's daughter, an event Melville repeats and highlights by
adding details of the "beautiful, but amiable" girl and later by
revealing that Singles had married his Jenny (151). It is thus
clear in Israel that revolutionary action is connected to if not
compensatory for sexual desire, and Melville emphasizes this
connection equally clearly in the three revolutionary heroes.
Franklin shows a sly fondness for Israel's French maid (52–
53); the rakish Jones "throw[s] a passing arm round all the
pretty chambermaids he encounter[s], kissing them resound-
ingly, as if saluting a frigate" (63); and Allen momentarily
mutes his verbal scourging to flirt with the ladies (145–46).
This sexual adventurism is highly acquisitive—God helps them
who help themselves to available women—and is therefore an
aspect of the savage primitivism war brings out. Fighting for
the possession of women, as Allen playfully offers to do (146),
is the handmaid to fighting against other men; and in Jones's
case, sexual gallantry takes precedence over his war efforts
(106–11).[51] Both behaviors further exemplify the Franklinian
self-interest involved in revolutionary actions as well as the
continuing confusion of individual and national spheres of
action.

Here Melville is again developing tendencies found in the
originals, for both Franklin and Jones were notorious for their
sexual exploits. Franklin presented the spectacle of a sep-
tuagenarian indulging himself with the ladies of the French
court but virtually ignoring his marriage in his *Autobiography*.[52]
He appears to have put into healthy practice his wry precept on
"Chastity": "Rarely use venery but for health or offspring, never to dullness, weakness, or the injury of your own or another's
peace or reputation"—the final word showing Franklin's ultimate concern. Jones, too, delighted in the company of the
ladies of France, though both he and Sands try to keep his
practice from harming his reputation.[53] They, like Franklin,

[51]Jones's return of the silver may have been gallant, but his men could
certainly have used the money from the plunder to buy clothing and supplies.
[52]See Sparks's testy comments on this issue in *Works*, 1:374.
[53]Sands, *John Paul Jones*, 247, 260–61, 287–88; cf. Fanning, *Memoirs*, 112–
13.

seem to realize that an all-too-human sexuality might diminish an almost-superhuman heroic status. Such narrative control of sexuality, as Michel Foucault shows, is not so much a puritanical modesty as an exercise of power, which Melville also recognizes in depicting Franklin's final robbery of Israel (of the maid) as his ultimate attempt to control Israel—by controlling his sexual behavior.[54] Israel's own revolutionary activities begin as a reaction to a similar gesture of control by his father, but when he finally can consummate a love affair, his marriage (one of necessity?) saps the money he might have used to get home (162), keeps him in exile for forty-five years, and thus precludes his receiving the benefits of his revolutionary activities. Israel's experiences in England, like Franklin's "paternal" robbery, thus closely link the issues of sexuality and authority. As he does in both *Typee* and *Omoo*, Melville exposes sexuality in order to subvert the established (or establishing) power; he presents "His Highness" the highly phallic Bunker-Hill Monument as an ironic reminder that Sands and Franklin each cover up the hero's sexuality by erecting a desexed narrative monument to him.

To see more clearly how sexuality is related to authority, one might further consult Foucault's *History of Sexuality*. Foucault observes that beginning in the seventeenth century "sex was driven out of hiding and constrained to lead a discursive existence." This move to turn sex into discourse, particularly "true," logical, and scientific discourse, is accompanied in part by an attempt to govern sexuality by the process of definition, as Melville's Franklin does by defining the "vocation" of the chambermaid (53). The effect is, Foucault says, "to bring us almost entirely—our bodies, our minds, our individuality, our history—under the sway of a logic of concupiscence and desire." Thus Foucault sees the ultimate thrust of these historical observations not as exposing a new sexuality but as revealing the exercise of a new sort of power: not juridical power—deriving its force from law—but a power that is a complex set of force relations that demand "true discourses," of which sex-

[54]On the politics of sexual discourse, see Foucault, *History of Sexuality*.

uality is central. More specifically, juridical power, Foucault says, "was the monarchic system's mode of manifestation and the form of its acceptability. . . . [This is] a fundamental trait of Western monarchies: they were constructed as systems of law, they expressed themselves through theories of law, and they made their mechanism of power work in the form of law."[55]

In short, an increasing awareness of sexuality and an attempt to govern it, as we see in the Revolutionary biographers, is a manifestation of the breakdown of monarchy and the erection of a new system of power. Foucault's analysis thus sheds significant light upon the motivations for the concupiscence of Franklin, Jones, and Allen in their revolt against monarchical power. In them and Israel, Melville also provides evidence for Foucault's idea that this new power structure focuses upon the family and familial relations. If power is deployed through sexual inquiry and definition, then it stands to reason that the family unit would become "an obligatory locus" of the process of historical change that Foucault describes.

The rebellion against the fathers in the novel thus gives not only psychological but political insight into Israel and Revolutionary heroism, and it is closely connected to the theme of identity, which many critics discuss.[56] To shrug off parental control and assert one's own sexuality is partly to attempt to create and secure one's own identity, just as embracing the political adventurism of a Jones is partly an attempt to create a national identity. Sands, for example, uses the familial trope in saying he wants to make available the truth of the Selkirk affair for young officers "when arraying in their mind's eye the character of those whose deeds are our country's inheritance, and whose examples they may desire to emulate."[57] Yet, as the verbal attacks on the British indicate, this "inheritance" also includes a paradoxical denial of (British) inheritance; for nei-

[55]Ibid., 33, 78, 87. Norman O. Brown, *Love's Body* (New York, 1966), also provocatively links eighteenth-century politics, sexuality, and religion; Bailyn, *Ideological Origins*, 55–60, stresses the centrality of power politics in the Revolution; and Zaller, "Melville," discusses power and anarchy in Melville's novel.

[56]Seelye, *Melville*, develops this issue most convincingly.

[57]Sands, *John Paul Jones*, 92.

ther lineal nor dialectical descent adequately grounds the emerging national identity, which is thus as confused as Melville's Israel's identity so often proves to be.

In short, Melville shows identity, both personal and national, to be situational and fluxional, a further result of Franklinesque pragmatism. He develops this idea through the clothes trope, which he adopts from the Revolutionary narrators and biographers. Sparks dwells at length on Allen's "Canadian dress," which contributes to what Melville calls his "essentially western . . . spirit" (149); Sands notes of Jones that "it became, of course, necessary for him to adopt the manners of the different courts and circles into which he was introduced"; Cooper, discussing rank in the Revolutionary navy, stresses that it is "the nature of man to pay respect to the instructions of one clothed with an authority superior to his own"; and Franklin ends "The Way to Wealth" by using a coat trope to represent his conservative personal philosophy.[58] Each, that is, upholds the cliché that clothes make the man, but none examines its implications as Melville does. "Seeking here to depict man in his less exalted habitudes," Melville says of his Franklin, "the narrator feels more as if he were playing with one of the sage's worsted hose, than reverentially handling the honored hat which once [i.e., not now] oracularly sat upon his brow" (48). Melville presents in *Israel Potter* what his contemporary, the historian Hildreth, calls "the undress portraits I have presented of our own colonial progenitors, though made up chiefly of traits delineated by themselves."[59] Melville plays with "the sage's worsted hose" for purposes similar to Hildreth's revisionism or to Carlyle's critique of the "clothes philosophy": to indicate the superficiality of such clothed authority and the shiftiness of such identities.

In his Israel, who clothes himself as the situation demands (e.g., chaps. 3 and 13), Melville shows that these practices can

---

[58]Sparks, *Ethan Allen*, 76–77; Sands, *John Paul Jones*, 550; Cooper, *History of the Navy*, 1:xxvii; and Franklin, *Works*, 2:103.

[59]Richard Hildreth, *The History of the United States of America* . . . (New York, 1849), x.

tend even to efface identity, as John Seelye has noted.[60] As "The Shuttle" on a British ship (chap. 20), Israel can find no effective identity and must wander in a Hamletesque madness from station to station. His lack of identity, though initially maddening to the crew, does produce the desired result, for "at length Israel was set at liberty" (141). Liberty is gained, Melville seems to be indicating, not by clothing oneself in an assumed identity but by abandoning such attempts. Yet like Bartleby, Melville's most famous unidentitied person, Israel has as questionable a liberty as an identity, for it brings him an increasing confinement and anonymity just as destructive as what comes to affect the scrivener. Ironically, Israel loses his own identity in helping Franklin, Jones, and Allen create theirs—and America's. But America's is thereby revealed as a superficial and opportunistic identity, as was becoming obvious in the 1850s: a Revolution against imperial control had given way to an imperialistic acquisition of Texas and California; liberty had not yet meant freedom for blacks or the vote for women; and Potter's—the common man's—clothing himself in the garb of Revolutionary heroism gained only poverty and oblivion.[61]

Just as Jefferson based his declaration of independence and natural rights upon a Creator who endows men with those conditions, so the narrators and the Revolution in general ground their identities in Christian terminology. In their narratives and in *Israel Potter* religion is the ultimate justification for revolution; the belief that God is guiding their actions frequently surfaces in the writings of the Revolution, for the heroes and their biographers recognize at least implicitly that claims to a special identity and an extraordinary heroism must rest upon the special relationship with God that Bancroft, for instance, trumpets.[62] To rebel against the British fathers by claiming a particularly close kinship with the heavenly Father, however, may be problematic. As is evident in his quarrels with

[60]Seelye, *Melville*, 116.
[61]See Karcher, *Shadow*, 104; and Rogin, *Subversive Genealogy*, 225.
[62]*History*, 2:319–26; see also Bailyn, *Idealogical Origins*, 160.

the South Seas missionaries, with messianic nationalism, and with millennialism, Melville is keenly aware of this problem; his portrayal of Franklin, Jones, and Allen further problematizes the relationship between Christianity and the Revolution.

All three heroes, both historically and in *Israel Potter*, are most questionable Christians. Though in his *Autobiography* Franklin frequently uses Christian terminology, thanks Providence, and praises the efforts of Whitefield, he cannot resist qualifying Christianity to make it more "useful": he rewrites the Lord's Prayer, equates Socrates and Jesus, implies that Whitefield's importance lies more in his rhetoric than his beliefs, and states that "the most acceptable service of God was doing good to man."[63] In short and as Melville recognized, Franklin's deistic faith is little more than a reductive secularization. His—and Jones's—motto, "God helps them that help themselves," in effect denies the efficacy of God even as it invokes the name of God. Thus the religion Franklin literally clothes himself in is, if anything, a primitive, superstitious mystification calculated to produce a self-serving effect (he has learned at least this from Whitefield). Melville's Franklin himself is no Christian but a lord of the flies (39), a Beelzebub, a failed revolutionary no longer "Clothed with transcendent brightness" (*Paradise Lost*, I, 86; see 2 Kings 1 for Beelzebub as god of failed revolutionaries). Like Franklin, Melville's Jones pays convenient lip service to Christianity, castigating the British, for example, "in the tone of a . . . prophet" (56). But Melville reverses this tactic later (118), when an old lady quotes Psalm 58:10 to censure Jones for the sort of wickedness and violence that the psalm describes. Jones replies, ineffectually, by repeating Poor Richard's motto. More significant, though, is what Jones elsewhere fails to do: given a situation similar to Ishmael's in The Spouter-Inn, Jones does not act with Ishmael's tolerance and sense of brotherhood but resists and deplores the opportunity for charity (61–62). Allen, too, speaks of the British's having "forgotten the Lord their God" (143), of "the Great Jehovah and the Continental Congress" (145), and

---

[63]*Works*, 1:75–79n, 103.

of his study of divinity (146); but his notorious book on *Reason* causes even Sparks to attack his unchristian refusal to accept revelation.[64] His adoption of Christian rhetoric, like his savage pose, is likely little more than another politic tactic gauged to insure his survival.

The heroes' use of Christian language, that is to say, is not a serious proclamation of belief but rather a sort of typological rationalization, characteristic of the Revolution in general, that seeks to secure a privileged individual and national identity. Thus Allen's attack on the British takes on additional force by his viewing them as Satan (and implicitly himself as Christ), and Franklin's analysis of "The Internal State of America" initially privileges it by saying that Americans are "like the children of Israel."[65] Melville invokes the American Puritan tradition of typology by making his Israel a Puritan rather than a Quaker (6)—as the historical Potter was—and by using "type" in the Puritan sense (120). This tradition includes what Sacvan Bercovitch has called a "genetics of salvation," an organic continuity that, adapted and extended, is clearly evident "in the Revolutionary appeal to the example of the Bay planters":

> [The Patriots'] recourse to filiopietism seems well-nigh inevitable. It allowed them . . . to sanctify the basic premises of their culture. . . . The lesson led to the familiar figural imperative: what the fathers began, the sons were bound to complete. Revolution meant improvement, not hiatus; obedience, not riot; not a breach of social order, but the fulfillment of God's plan. As an act of filiopietism, independence was America's long-prepared-for, reverently *ordered* passage into national maturity.[66]

Thus typology allows the revolutionaries to circumvent the uneasy, even paradoxical relationship with the fathers and provides a secure identity for them and a sanction for their actions.

As in *Redburn* and *White-Jacket*, however, in *Israel Potter* Mel-

[64]Sparks, *Ethan Allen*, 124–28.

[65]Allen, *Narrative*, 35; Franklin, *Works*, 2:461.

[66]Bercovitch, *American Jeremiad*, 122–23. Ursula Brumm, *American Thought and Religious Typology*, trans. John Hoaglund (New Brunswick, N.J., 1970), 18–19, notes Melville's use of "type."

ville shows considerable uneasiness about the efficacy and accuracy of typology. Immediately noticeable is the sheer number of typological associations: Israel as Daniel, as Christ, as
Jonah, as the Prodigal Son, as the Wandering Jew, as Lazarus,
as Israel (a fortuitous irony that may have helped attract Melville to the tale), and so on. Like the catalogues of associations
to the epic tradition in *White-Jacket*, the massed biblical allusions in *Israel Potter* betray its narrator's desperation in attempting to give status to his pathetic protagonist, and they reveal
perhaps most clearly Melville's ironic distance from the book's
dominant narrative voice.[67] The ironies are, of course, that
Israel is such a patently unworthy "type" and that those typological associations are highly contradictory—for Israel to be
both Christ and the Wandering Jew is absurd. Most of the
individual allusions exemplify the inapplicability of typology to
the immediate situation and show not a sloppiness in Melville's
writing but a sustained joke on typological Christianity. For
instance, Israel's entombment in Squire Woodcock's chimney—
a "three day's mystery" (73)—and his subsequent "resurrection" (68) may be Christ-like, but Israel rises to become Woodcock's ghost, neither holy nor a spirit; and his death and resurrection save no one but himself, and that barely. Other allusions are similarly nonsignifying: Israel is a Jonah who has
neither attempted to flee his mission nor is regurgitated to
complete it (15); he is a Daniel (in the den of the distinctly
unleonine George III) who can never read the handwriting on
the wall (29–32); he is a Prodigal Son who, like *Redburn*'s Harry
Bolton, returns to no forgiving father and to no fatted calf.
The typology fails, contradicts itself, collapses, for Israel's situation, especially his forty-*five* years in captivity-wilderness (the
typology here absurdly conflated), does not support sanctified
glorification. Melville's typology shows the Revolution illustra-
tive not of a genetics of salvation but of a genetics of oblivion,
like Israel's Puritan parents' ruined homestead, "Type now, as

[67]Dryden, *Melville's Thematics*, 143, shows that for "ironic significance" the
narrator structures the story around a set of biblical analogues; Rampersad,
Melville's "Israel Potter," 74–81, discusses Melville's parody of Bunyan.

it stood there, of for ever arrested intentions, and a long life still rotting in early mishap" (168).

Nor does Melville lend credence to the agent, Providence, by which typology operates. The original *Life* shows Potter's pathetic faith in Providence guiding his affairs, pathetic in that it ironically brings, if anything, considerably more hardship than reward. Indeed, as Potter's hardships in London increase, he continues to cling verbally to that faith, until "by the kind interposition of Providence, I was enabled to obtain a passage to my native country." Although Providence gives him nothing tangible at the end of the passage, Potter ends his narrative with his "thanks to the Almighty" and his vow to continue "devoting myself sincerely to the duties of religion."[68] Potter's narrative differs little from the other Revolutionary heroes' in stating this reliance upon Providence: Franklin acknowledges Providential responsibility for his own life, for the Revolution, and for America; Sands repeatedly claims Jones himself as a Providential gift; and Allen describes a victory of the British army "as though it was ordered by Heaven to shew to the latest posterity, what the British would have done, if they could."[69] Each of these narratives instances what Lester Cohen has shown of Revolutionary writing in general, that "the revolutionary historians do indeed use the language of providence in their histories. . . . [However,] providence was no longer an explanatory concept at all, though it remained a rich and highly charged cultural and ideological metaphor."[70]

The irony of Revolutionary Providentiality, which Melville seems to have recognized, is that it is a purely verbal convenience by which the Revolutionary heroes and biographers can give added status to their actions, just as the classical poets ally their heroes with the gods. But if the faith of Franklin et al. is dubious and superficial, that of Israel is genuine, though it has neither a rational basis nor an effective outcome. Melville's

---

[68]*Life*, 80, 106; see also 3, 78, 84.

[69]Franklin, *Works*, 1:103, 514–16, 2:462; Sands, *John Paul Jones*, 28, 259, 553; and Allen, *Narrative*, 33.

[70]Cohen, *Revolutionary Histories*, 21; Duban, *Melville's Major Fiction*, 82–148, discusses Melville's critique of providential historiography in *Moby-Dick*.

repeated emphasis upon Poor Richard's motto succinctly en-
capsulates these issues, for to say that "God helps them that
help themselves" is in effect to remove the agency of God while
keeping Him verbally associated with the heroic action. In the
end is only the word, which is all that poor Israel (and America)
has.

Nor does Melville entirely credit the latter half of the motto,
for he removes not only divine agency but individual human
efficacy from the Revolutionaries' activities.[71] In *Israel Potter*,
the individual is guided not by Providence or will but by
chance, nature, and other forces beyond his comprehension
and control. Chance, more than divine purpose, directs Israel's
course to an almost absurd degree. He is a sort of shuttlecock,
blown and directed from unlikely event to unlikelier event; his
actions as "The Shuttle" epitomize the madness endemic to
Israel, who seems totally unable to control the smallest part of
his life. The master-of-arms has to "keep leading him about
because he has no final destination" (140). In a world bereft of
divine authority and heroic nobility, the individual is left to
wander aimlessly, exiled by pure chance.

This chaotic turn of life is natural, too, for Melville punctu-
ates the narrative of Israel's "Fifty Years of Exile" with descriptions of nature showing its hostility or indifference to man.
The Berkshire setting, which dominates the initial and final
chapters, certainly develops this theme, as many critics have
shown; yet reading these chapters in relation to a previously
unidentified source, Hawthorne's "Ethan Brand," gives a
heightened sense of Melville's theme.[72] Both the novel and the
tale begin and end with descriptions of the Berkshire area, and
both descriptions are narrated from the perspective of the
"traveler" or "wanderer." To Hawthorne, the region may seem

---

[71]See Seelye, *Melville*, 113–16; and Cohen, *Revolutionary Histories*, 112–17.
[72]See Bezanson, "Historical Note," *Israel Potter*, 186–87, for possible additional sources of the Berkshire passages. "Ethan Brand" was first published in
the May 1851 issue of *The Dollar Magazine*, where Melville says he read it
(*Letters*, 129); it subsequently appeared in *The Snow-Image and Other Twice-Told
Tales* (1851). My references are to *The Snow-Image and Uncollected Tales*, ed. J.
Donald Crowley (Columbus, Ohio, 1974), 83–102.

desolate, but the village nevertheless "looked as if it had rested peacefully in the hollow of the hand of Providence." Nature thus forms a comforting, consoling frame for Bartram and Joe (though both have a superstitious fear of the dark) and a marked contrast to the destructive, ungodly revolt of the title character, whose final prayer is to the earth from which he is estranged. Ethan Brand, a revolutionary and an exile, has lost touch with the spiritualizing and humanizing power of nature and family. Nature to Melville offers no such assurance, especially to Israel, whose situation is similar to Ethan Brand's, though his motivations are dissimilar. The Berkshire scenes in Melville's novel accordingly "present an aspect of singular abandonment. . . . [They] look like countries depopulated by plague and war" (4), as if nature itself has a Paul Jones–like savagery. This abode of "that half-outlaw, the charcoal-burner"—like Ethan Brand—is marked by stones, walls, fog, and snow, all of which serve to distance people from each other, "as if an ocean rolled between man and man" (6). When Israel returns at the end, he finds, as Ethan Brand does, that he has been largely forgotten and that his revolutionary actions have produced no results; the ruined homestead and Ethan Brand's skeleton symbolize the destruction each has ultimately found. Melville last echoes Hawthorne, however, by comparing Israel not to Ethan but to Bartram: Israel and his son rake the rubble as Bartram and Joe do at the end of the tale, but unlike Hawthorne's characters, they find nothing of value, for "Few things remain" (169).

Melville's nature, like Hawthorne's, is also an analogue for the author's perspective, for Melville's own ironic detachment from the revolutionary activities. This is clearest not only at the beginning and end but also in a peculiar and arresting detail, again likely adapted from Hawthorne, that Melville presents during his account of the battle between the *Bon Homme Richard* and the *Serapis*. The passage describes the most famous and stirring event in the novel and is placed at a major climactic point, but as the events are developing Melville shifts the perspective momentarily from the human action to nature: "The Man-in-the-Moon now raised himself still higher to obtain a better view of affairs" (124). In Hawthorne's tale of the Revolution, "My Kinsman, Major Molineux," the Man in the Moon appears at a similar point and to a similar effect, for when the "contagion" is at its most chaotic, "The Man in the Moon heard the far below. 'Oho,' quoth he, 'The old earth is frolicsome tonight!'" Hawthorne's reason for including the outrageously out-of-place Man is the same as Melville's; as Michael J. Colacurcio says of this detail in the tale, it "would be the ultimate insult which the deflationist strategy of 'My Kinsman Major Molineux' offers to the vaunted claims of American typological historiography: so far from being a unique and climactic event in the unfolding of Divine Purpose, the 'majestic' Revolution is no more remarkable, 'structurally,' than any other local resistance to local authority; and no more distinctive, 'psychoanalytically,' than the anxious overflow of Oedipal emotion."[73] Both writers, then, introduce this absurd natural persona as a way of distancing and deflating what they perceive as the absurdly heightened claims of the American Revolution.

III

The distancing—of the narrative from the events and of the characters from nature—suggested by Melville's Man-in-the-Moon is characteristic of the ironic distancing Melville deploys in the novel as a whole. Yet Melville's narrator fights against this distancing, symbolized by the cloud ("instinct with chaotic vitality") which threatens to obscure the battle (124). "To get some idea of the events enacting in that cloud," he says, "it will be necessary to enter it; to go and possess it, as a ghost may rush into a body, or the devils into the swine, which running down the steep place perished in the sea." This attempt to understand and represent the events of the Revolution, which are naturally clouded by time and circumstances, involves

---

[73]Hawthorne, *Snow-Image*, 230; Colacurcio, *Province*, 149. Colacurcio's analysis of the tale's Revolutionary dimensions is completely convincing. On nature and the Man-in-the-Moon in *Israel Potter* see Zaller, "Melville," 615–17.

something demonic, even deadly; Melville, casting out these demons onto his pages, thus usurps the Christly role. His narrator's imaginative grasp, his possession of the events does allow him to portray them vividly, so vividly that readers may fail to notice that he clouds the historical, psychological, and theological foundations of the events, as he does throughout the novel. The chapter describing the battle ends not with a clear vista but with civilization itself a hazy concept (130). The exile that is so prominent a theme in the novel includes an exile of the event from the civilization in which it takes place, and from the ideological context that would give it meaning, a narrative exile of the sign from the signifier.

There seems in the end no return from this exile. Israel first attempts to mitigate his exile imaginatively, by telling his son Benjamin highly romanticized tales of America (165–66). This narrative compensation—likely another sly jibe at Franklin—is shown to be all the more pathetically detached from reality when Israel and his son return "home" to an America that is no fulfillment of their romantic dreams. Again in compensation for this disappointment, Israel "dictated a little book, the record of his fortunes. But long ago it faded out of print—himself out of being—his name out of memory" (169). The narrative, like the tales he tells his son, fails to effect a connection with the intended context, fails to preserve his own being or name. More generally, the other narratives of the Revolution similarly attempt to deny any sort of exile or distancing: they attempt to bring the events of the Revolution temporally closer to their audience; they attempt to make the hero and his actions immediately relevant; and they attempt to construe the events as instances of a unified and continuing American ideology. Yet Melville shows the ultimate effects of the narratives to be more divisive than consolidating, for they foster separations among social classes and idealizations far removed from the actual events.

Melville's narrative structure reinforces this distancing, most basically evident in the "change in the grammatical person" (vii) that eliminates much of the immediate pathos of the original *Life*. Thus Melville presents the events clouded not only by the ideology of his sources but also by his narrator-editor, who deemphasizes Israel's long years of poverty, heightens the adventurous moments, and thereby reveals both a Franklinesque attitude toward the poor and a Paul-Jones-like, amoral love of adventure. The book's tripartite structure further mocks any expectation of closure or synthesis. Although the second part—Israel's Revolutionary activities proper—may initially seem to provide an antithesis to the disappointment, poverty, and obscurity of his home life in the first part, it actually reveals little difference other than a change of scene. And the third part is by no means a synthesis or completion, but merely a further and deeper oblivion. Israel returns to the beginning, as Melville's narrator does; both find that all is past, lost, unattainable, indecipherable. The final sentence attempts to link Israel metaphorically to nature, but the trope is more irony than metaphor, given Melville's description of nature as chaotic and indifferent. Within the three sections, too, the right-angled and cataclysmic changes and shifts accentuate these separations and further parody the secure, integrative system of Providential history and typological meaning. Narrative continuity is repeatedly disrupted, expectations of a developing plot repeatedly denied.

In this final sense, then, Melville's *Israel Potter* is indeed a "Revolutionary narrative." It breaks narrative conventions and frustrates audience expectations, *turns* them against themselves, thus further troping what Lester Cohen has accurately described as the tropic nature of Revolutionary writing. Melville's artistic purposes are revolutionary as well, for the novel evinces a comic yet serious revolt against the tradition of the American Revolution and particularly against those who seek to canonize that tradition. Melville turns his narrative away from the ideology of the Revolution and toward a revolutionary concern—here as in *Redburn* and *White-Jacket*—for the poverty and oppression it has failed to alleviate. The humanity and compassion of Melville's narrative, evident despite the overwhelmingly bleak outcome, mark nonetheless a sort of end to Israel Potter's exile: Melville's final irony surfaces from the novel's final page, for even as he mentions Israel's having "faded out," he brings Israel's narrative back into print, Israel himself back into being, his name back into memory. Melville's *Israel Potter* gives Israel the only resurrection possible and places him comfortably at the only home possible, in the fiction of the American Revolution.

7

Metanarrative Conclusion

Nature, Narrative, and
Billy Budd, Sailor

MELVILLE gives his last, unfinished work the parenthetical subtitle *(An inside narrative)*, indicating that *Billy Budd, Sailor* is vitally concerned with what goes on inside the narrative process and that narrative itself is concerned with the attempt to get inside events, here to find the inner truth about the title character. But the relation between title and subtitle is one of contrast, for all the considerable narrative tactics employed by the novel's characters (who are in a sense narrators along with the book's narrator)—the historical analogues, the biographical memories, the Christian patterns, the nautical legends—all fail to get the inside story of Billy. But for that part of the title that describes his work—"*Sailor*"—Billy remains an enigma, the narrative remains another white lie. The distance between the facts of human experience and the truthful narration of that experience remains unbridgeable. Moreover, as Stanton Garner has convincingly demonstrated, the facts themselves here are more than questionable, they are wrong; and intentionally so.[1] The central issue in *Billy Budd*, that is to say, is

---

[1]Garner, "Fraud as Fact in Herman Melville's *Billy Budd*," *San Jose Studies* 4 (1978): 82–105. Supplementing Garner's solidly historical conclusions is a "tradition" of readings that emphasizes these narrative issues: Stern, *Steel*, 206–39; Kingsley Widmer, "The Perplexed Myths of Melville: *Billy Budd*," *Novel* 2

the inability of narrative to explain natural phenomena, the inapplicability of past historical patterns to account for present occurrences, and the crucial fictionality of "factual" narrative.

Before the narrative itself Melville places a dedication to Jack Chase that further indicates this problematization. To transfer Jack from *White-Jacket*'s fictional *Neversink* to the historical *United States*—in essence inverting the creative process Melville had followed in his narratives—breaks down the distinction between fact and fiction and may also be a sly joke at the expense of those who have read his novels as autobiographies. And to dedicate *Billy Budd* to that ridiculous spinner of ahistorical and self-serving yarns signals an extraordinary level of irony, directed, I believe, back toward his previous narratives of facts.[2] Like Jack, Melville's narratives of facts have been consistently misread as considerably lighter, more positive than they indeed are, an issue of much concern to critics who see *Billy Budd* as Melville's final "testament of faith." Thus Jack Chase signifies that other J. C. whose historicity—like that of Billy, who is frequently identified as a Christ-figure—is so much at issue in the late nineteenth century, and again crucial to the issue is a contrast between historical or natural fact and the faith or confidence one can have in narratives to represent those facts.[3] In *White-Jacket* Jack Chase's station high in the elitist main-top

---

(1968): 25–35; Paul Brodkorb, Jr., "The Definitive *Billy Budd*: 'But aren't it all Sham?'" *PMLA* 82 (1967): 602–12; Barbara Johnson, "Melville's Fist: The Execution of *Billy Budd*," *Studies in Romanticism* 18 (1979): 567–99; William T. Stafford, *Books Speaking to Books: A Contextual Approach to American Fiction* (Chapel Hill, N.C., 1981), 105–14; Thomas J. Scorza, *In the Time of Steamships: Billy Budd, the Limits of Politics, and Modernity* (De Kalb, Ill., 1979); and Walter L. Reed, "The Measured Forms of Captain Vere," *Modern Fiction Studies* 23 (1977): 227–35. All references to the text will be cited parenthetically and will be to *Billy Budd, Sailor (An inside narrative)*, ed. Harrison Hayford and Merton Sealts (Chicago, 1962).

[2]Sealts, "Innocence and Infamy: *Billy Budd, Sailor*," in Bryant, *Companion*, 407, says that the novel "not only sums up the thought and art of Melville's last years but also looks back in setting, characterization, and theme over his writing as a whole."

[3]On the relation of these issues to *Billy Budd*, see Lyon Evans, Jr., "'Too Good to Be True': Subverting Christian Hope in *Billy Budd*," *New England Quarterly* 55 (1982): 323–53.

places him in sharp contrast to Melville's ocean, in which Melville immerses his narrator to little effect and indicates another facet of the facts/narrative opposition. Nature and an understanding of it that is essentially spiritual—albeit dangerous, as Pip's immersion shows—are opposed by a false and essentially politicized faith in narrative. Nature, what is outside man and his institutions, opposes what is inside narrative—its ideology, its tropology, what Hayden White calls *The Content of the Form*.[4] Melville's presentation of these issues in *Billy Budd*, of concern to Melville throughout his earlier narratives of facts and particularly powerful in *Moby-Dick*, shows this final work to be a metanarrative conclusion to his examination of his culture's white lies.

I

Each of Melville's narrators, though he sets out to narrate a voyage of exploration, tenaciously resists recognizing any discovery that might threaten to alter his preconceived ideology. Each clings stubbornly to the "facts"—progress and primitivism, religious elitism, genteel capitalism, millennialism, and Revolutionary heroism—gleaned from the narrative chart he has been following. Those narrators of facts whom Melville's narrators follow also cling to these primarily eighteenth-century ideas by echoing the intellectual voyages of those who formulated them: Rousseau, the philosophes, Adam Smith, the millennial Whigs, and Franklin. Melville's narrators try to carry over into the troubled nineteenth century some of the Enlightenment's confidence in racial, cultural, political, and religious superiority.

Within the Enlightenment itself, however, are forces that will in the nineteenth century become audible as the "melancholy, long, withdrawing roar" of Matthew Arnold's "Sea of Faith." The previous confidence or surety in truth and its representa-

---

[4]White, *The Content of the Form: Narrative Discourse and Historical Representation* (Baltimore, 1987).

tion is connected to a confidence in the logos (or God) and its discernibility in nature, which thus speaks univocally. Puritan typology or Newtonian physics, for example, rests on the conception that natural and historical events follow a coherent set of rules which one can apprehend and which, if followed, can further civilization's progress toward paradise regained—itself perhaps the most basic rule. As George Bancroft worried, "Were it [progress] not so, there would be no great truths inspiring action, no laws regulating human achievements: the movement of the living world would be as the ebb and flow of the ocean; and the mind would no longer be touched by the visible agency of Providence in human affairs."[5] For Bancroft, and more generally, this ideology obviously involves a confidence that "great truths" can be adequately represented in discourse, that narrative can represent history and nature transparently and linearly. In short, the Christian conception of history as progressive, linear, and meaningful is inextricable from the conception that historical narrative is itself linear and truthful.

As explorations and encounters with other cultures bring to light just the sort of problems with these Western cultural assumptions—white lies—that Melville's narratives demonstrate, both the homogeneity of culture and the narrative surety become suspect, become ironically distanced. Nature ceases to speak with one voice, becomes multiplicity, ambiguity, stone silence, or chaos. Then, as Bakhtin stresses, the novel arises out of this "ocean of heteroglossia." Whether on this ocean of discourse, or on the ocean of flux Bancroft feared, or on Melville's ocean, the chaotic decentering of nature and the breakdown of univocal, linear narration are fellow travelers.

Melville's narrators, who demonstrate this natural and narrative entropy, even as they adamantly claim the opposite, fail to gain the benefits Melville says can be attained by "Travelling." In this 1860 lecture Melville extolls the "liberalizing" values of exploration: not only does travel bring pleasure, it also rids one of prejudice and teaches one humility—if one main-

[5]Bancroft, *History*, 2:323.

tains the right frame of mind. Most important, Melville says, "One may perhaps acquire the justest of all views by reading and comparing all writers of travels."[6] Although Melville's narrators of facts likewise read and compare accounts, they by no means enter into their literary explorations with an open, comparative frame of mind. The lesson of judiciousness and humanism Melville teaches is therefore lost to them. Nor can they comfortably retain their own ideologies, for in their experiences and their narratives they must confront Melville's natural world, where the facts encountered threaten their established beliefs. Whether in the Typee valley or in the Berkshires that frame *Israel Potter*, nature exposes a basic discrepancy in their idea of humanity. Melville conceives of people, in his narratives and his lecture, in natural and culturally relative terms: persons differ not essentially but culturally, as in *Typee*. They are neither basically good nor basically evil, but both; they are finite and limited, and their assertions of elitism and transcendence must consequently fail, as they do in *Omoo*. The only "religion" thus possible for Melville's natural person is a humanistic social connectedness which recognizes neither special privileges nor supernatural intervention but demands disinterested cooperation with one's fellow creatures. And yet the desire for superiority lies deep in each person, who, like Darwin's man, must struggle competitively to survive. Problems arise when Melville's protagonists and narrators attempt to mask their essentially conservative politics under self-righteous religiosity, as in *Omoo*, *Redburn*, *White-Jacket*, and *Israel Potter*.

Each of Melville's narrators resists confronting the idea that he, too, is a natural man, and accordingly each ends by fleeing from the natural world, fleeing from the nineteenth-century world back to the eighteenth, in order to preserve his idea of his own privileged status. The last refuge of each is his narrative: if he cannot face the natural world, he must recreate it according to his own ideological convictions. Thus each at-

[6]First reprinted in John Howard Birss, "'Travelling': A New Lecture by Herman Melville," *New England Quarterly* 7 (1934): 725–28; the quotation is from 727.

tempts to reassert the validity of the "facts" he represents by giving them the status of natural events, despite the contradictions between their reports and Melville's nature.

Here again Melville has his narrators follow the practice of those narrators of facts who are the targets of Melville's satire and condemnation. The narrators, completely committed to the ideology of their white culture, confront a world radically alien to their own, radically resistant to the structures their culture provides for understanding and representing the world. This resistance paradoxically generates not uncertainty but an even stronger commitment to assert the factuality of their perceptions. Both White and Foucault have shown, however, that the nineteenth century's "rage for a realistic apprehension of the world" (White's phrase), itself a reaction to the development of ironic historiography in the previous century, contains within itself tropic forms and power matrices that undermine any simplistic conception of factuality.[7] To Melville's sources, such dogged simplicity motivates the seemingly endless catalogues of geographical, sociological, and biographical data, which show an attempt to assert and reaffirm the consistent and unchangeable nature of the world. To them, as to Melville's narrators, exploration means little more than filing their perceptions in the appropriate preexisting pigeonhole. Personality and narrative coherence are avoided, since to examine the effects of the facts of the natural world upon one's self would be to admit the possibility of a necessary ideological change, and to examine the generic prescriptions would be to admit the possibility of their arbitrariness (and hence their un-naturality). For Melville's narrators, as for the white culture more generally, change seems possible only within the system, personal growth possible only according to a preconceived idea of psychic maturity—which to Melville is anything but maturity or change.

Melville, through his narrators, shows that these narrative evasions fail from the same sort of inherent contradictions that

---

[7]Hayden White, *Metahistory: The Historical Imagination in Nineteenth-Century Europe* (Baltimore, 1973), 45–80.

cause their explorations to fail. The facts in Melville's natural world oppose, confuse, and finally render invalid the "facts" his narrators are attempting to present. Placed literally and thematically in the heart of the nineteenth century, Melville's narratives of facts evince the nature and the experimentation that his contemporary, Emile Zola, sets forth. Like Melville, Zola indicates that the experimental novelist must "start, indeed, from the true facts, which are our indestructible basis."[8] The primary fact for Zola is determinism, that all aspects of a character's development must have causes; the experimental method, then, "consists in finding the relations which unite a phenomenon of any kind to its nearest cause, or, in other words, in determining the conditions necessary for the manifestation of the phenomenon." The author's role is that of a controlling observer: he "sets the characters going in a certain story so as to show that the succession of facts will be such as the requirements of the determinism of the phenomena under examination call for." Melville too begins with an intellectual phenomenon—the politicization of myth or the conservatization of revolutionary heroism, in short the determinism of ideology—then proceeds to show the conditions that determine its manifestation. Melville places his ideology-ridden characters in this environment, then directs the effects it has on them. In the end, Melville's position has fully manifested itself in this experiment, thus demonstrating the un-natural and failed ideology of his narrators. "An experimentalist has no reason to conclude," Zola says, "because, in truth, the experiment concludes for him."[9]

II

In *Moby-Dick* Melville's examination of the dynamics of natural facts and narrative representation is perhaps most clearly and

---

[8]Emile Zola, *The Experimental Novel and Other Essays*, trans. Belle Sherman (New York, 1893), 11.
[9]Ibid., 3, 8, 30.

fully developed. Beginning with the fragments Ishmael lee-shores against his ruin, the novel exhibits an almost endless concern with presenting the facts of whaling; *Moby-Dick*'s natural world also resembles that of the narratives, for the powerful, chaotic, living force of nature, which Pip experiences beneath the ocean, is Melville's caution to Ahab's transcendental and self-serving pursuit. Ishmael, however, is unlike all of Melville's narrators of facts in that he can at least approach a cultural, religious, and political relativism: he can embrace the relative truth of Queequeg's paganism at the same time that he recognizes the madly Christian absolutism of Ahab in himself.

His narrative therefore seeks to present the facts with non-judgmental equity. When describing "this equatorial coin," the doubloon, Ishmael first describes in detail what it looks like—the physical facts—then quotes others' statements about what it means. As "some certain significance lurks in all things, else all things are little worth, and the round world itself but an empty cipher,"[10] Ishmael desires to present the significance of the doubloon—and the world, which it more largely symbolizes—but to refrain from referring its signification only to himself or his ideology. His dramatization thus further stresses the relativism of meaning, making the whole passage a model of possible readings of the text of the natural world, from the "monomaniac" solipsism of Ahab to the pious typological moralizing of Starbuck to the pragmatic economic materialism of King-Post. Only the madly sane Pip—whose statement, "I look, you look, he looks; we look, ye look, they look," interprets the interpreters more than the coin—perceives the doubloon relativistically (362). He, from the sort of intoxicating immersion in the natural world that Ishmael attempts in his narrative, has gained the ability to recognize that meaning depends upon perspective and upon the structure of language itself. Ironic narrative distance occupies a space not only between the facts and the representation but also between the representation and the interpretation.

At the foundation of Ishmael's relativism is also a naturalistic

[10]*Moby-Dick*, 358; all subsequent references will be cited parenthetically in the text.

perception of the world. In "The Try-Works" (chap. 96), Ishmael cautions against looking too long into "artificial," daemonic fires, for "To-morrow, in the natural sun, the skies will be bright," and men will not seem to metamorphose into devils. The man who strays from the natural perspective, that is, will, like Tommo or White-Jacket, tend to perceive his fellow man as depraved or diabolic. But this is not to say that Ishmael recognizes a nature exclusively benevolent, for he sees more than a world of Happy Valleys:

> Nevertheless the sun hides not Virginia's dismal swamp, nor Rome's accursed Campagna, nor wide Sahara, nor all the millions of miles of deserts and of griefs beneath the moon. The sun hides not the ocean, which is the dark side of this earth, and which is two thirds of this earth. So, therefore, that mortal man who hath more of joy than of sorrow in him, that mortal man cannot be true—not true, or undeveloped. With books the same. The truest of all men was the Man of Sorrows, and the truest of all books is Solomon's, and Ecclesiastes is the fine hammered steel of woe. "All is vanity." ALL. This wilful world hath not got hold of unchristian Solomon's wisdom yet. (354–55)

Ishmael here urges a balanced view of man; neither good, nor evil, man is natural. It is important to note, too, that this passage stresses that the nature of humanity is molded by the nature of nature; one's own character reflects the character of the world around one.

Unlike Melville's narrators of facts, Ishmael attempts neither to deny nor to escape these natural facts. He embraces all the facets of Melville's world in order to understand and represent the whole, rather than to conform to a preconceived ideology. The result is one of literature's most inclusive, most elusive, and perhaps truest novels. Melville's generic and ideological purposes in chronicling Ishmael's efforts diverge significantly from those of his narratives: rather than exposing and destroying the white myths, he is creating, in *Moby-Dick* as in *Mardi*, his own. This is likely the fundamental difference between the romance and the narrative of facts as Melville conceived them. The confinement he felt while working within the narrative of facts genre most likely reflects the comparatively lesser creativity allowed within the generic prescriptions, since someone who wished to "write the universe" would understandibly feel stifled by retelling—albeit subversively—the stories of those who consistently deny the universe as they tell their own rather limited stories.

Ishmael's acceptance of the facts of the natural world, by no means either superficial or complacent, indicates the depth of Melville's commitment to his romances. In "The Chapel" (chap. 7) Ishmael reads the inscriptions memorializing those sailors whose bodies have been lost at sea and confronts the one fact Melville's narrators most try to avoid, death:

> Oh! ye whose dead lie beneath the green grass; who standing among flowers can say—here, *here* lies my beloved; ye know not the desolation that broods in bosoms like these. What ashes! What despair in those immovable inscriptions! What deadly voids and unbidden infidelities in the lines that seem to gnaw upon all Faith, and refuse resurrections to the beings who have placelessly perished without a grave. (41)

Death in Melville's ocean leaves little room for an easy belief in life after death, for the bodies of the sailors have become part of the natural world, as have those old, green natives in the Typee valley. Though this fact seems "to knaw upon all Faith," Ishmael can still triumphantly assert that "Faith, like a jackal, feeds among the tombs, and even from these dead doubts she gathers her most vital hope." That is to say, Ishmael's acceptance of the natural world is a religious act, yet at the same time not supernatural. His faith comes not in opposition to nature, as Ahab's does, but through it.

The means to this faith is the narrative itself, as Ishmael indicates. Those "deadly voids and unbidden infidelities," which characterize natural death and which threaten a conventional faith, are "in the lines." In *Moby-Dick* Melville seems to recognize what recent critics have seen as a breakdown in logocentrism: language by its nature is marked by a void between sign and signifier, by an unbidden shiftiness of signs that destroys any hope for a transcendental signifier, for absolute meaning. Cruising unchartably in a literal "ocean of heteroglossia," the whale itself shows this trait in the hieroglyphics on his forehead, which seem to mean both everything and nothing, and in his whiteness, in which "lurks an elusive something" that moves Ishmael to muse about the possibility of something simultaneously meaning both one thing and its opposite (164 and 169). Like the whale, and the natural world more largely, narrative must be approached with an attitude of faith, a belief that the reader or narrator can make connections—perhaps only partial and tenuous and temporary—across those deadly voids between word and world, or life would seem little more than a voyage toward imminent death in the whirlpool of nature. The passage on Queequeg's coffin, adorned with the same "hieroglyphic marks" as on his own body (which narrate "a complete theory of the heavens and the earth, and a mystical treatise on the art of attaining truth"), shows him embracing the fact of death and eventually proves a salvific buoy to Ishmael (399); similarly, Ishmael's creation embraces the fact of death and the ungraspable multiplicity of meaning and therefore enables him to survive. He knows, and demonstrates in his narrative, what he rhetorically asks the "demigod" Bulkington:

> Know ye, now, Bulkington? Glimpses do ye seem to see of that mortally intolerable truth; that all deep, earnest thinking is but the intrepid effort of the soul to keep the open independence of her sea; while the wildest winds of heaven and earth conspire to cast her on the treacherous, slavish shore?
>
> But as in landlessness alone resides the highest truth, shoreless, indefinite as God—so, better it is to perish in that howling infinite, than be ingloriously dashed upon the lee, even if that were safety! (97)

The "highest truth," disseminated only in "intolerable" traces, is the "open independence" of the individual from the ideological systems that "conspire" to enslave even as they offer safety.

The problem of faith—and the concurrent problem of historicity in narrative—is perhaps the most crucial to the nineteenth century and an issue closely tied to those narratives of facts Melville read and refuted. The discoveries—in ethnography, sociology, comparative religion, and economics—of the eighteenth century led to a crisis in faith: an apparent disjunction between the Word of Christian tradition and the world of nature thus forms a backdrop to the efforts of Strauss and Renan to ascertain the historicity of the faith-full biblical narratives. To the nineteenth-century person who could not dismiss the newly discovered facts of nature and of a natural, historical Jesus, the Word must indeed seem to harbor "deadly voids and unbidden infidelities." Yet Melville, who was consistently preoccupied with this crisis in faith, is able to assert belief in a way that takes him beyond the nineteenth century and heads him firmly toward the twentieth. While in his narratives of facts Melville denies the validity of the old systems of belief to come to terms with the natural world, in his romances he asserts his faith in creating new symbolic systems and forms to represent the world. This process is at the heart of Melville's criticism of his narrators of facts, whose faith is never more than denial of the facts. Recognizing the centrality of faith, however unconventional, to his friend Melville, Hawthorne, describing their meeting on a desolate shore, says that

> Melville, as he always does, began to reason of Providence and futurity, and of everything that lies beyond human ken, and informed me that he had "pretty much made up his mind to be annihilated;" but still he does not seem to rest in that anticipation; and, I think, will never rest until he gets hold of a definite belief. It is strange how he persists—and has persisted ever since I knew him, and probably long before—in wandering to and fro over these deserts, as dismal and monotonous as the sand hills amid which we were sitting. He can neither believe, nor be comfortable in his unbelief; and he is too honest and courageous not to try to do one or the other. If he were a religious man, he would be one of the most truly religious and reverential; he has a very high and noble nature, and better worth immortality than most of us.[11]

But this is not to say that Melville's concern with faith is less serious in his narratives of facts than in his romances. Harvey Cox discusses "the theology of the future" in terms that shed much light upon Melville:

> I would like . . . to suggest the possibility that what theologians should be doing in the future can most easily be understood as

[11]Leyda, *Melville Log*, 2:529.

itself a form of play. I mean play in three senses of the word: play as "making fun of," play as "making believe" and play as "useless" or nonproductive activity.

As "making fun of," theology is a satirizing activity which debunks destructive myths. . . . The theologian's job is to be a persistent muckraker of spurious mystiques. He is the "demy-thologizer," the exposer of fraudulent meanings and pasted-on values.[12]

Cox's first sense describes precisely the theological dimension of Melville's narratives of facts: his destructive re-presentation of the white myths is a serious, faith-full act. This form of theology, though, differs from the theology of the romances, which include much "making fun of" but more fundamentally involve Cox's second sense of play, "making believe." Cox explains that "theologians should be transmuting old symbols, exploring alternative metaphors, juxtaposing unlikely concepts, playing with new and improbable images of man and woman, God and world, earth and sky."[13] In *Mardi, Moby-Dick, Pierre,* and *The Confidence-Man,* Melville uses these techniques to make believe, to create belief in new, constructive symbolic forms and narrative techniques. Each of these novels attempts to break beyond simple factuality, a major aspect of each, to generate new and improbable images of the nineteenth-century world. Cox's third form of theological play, "'useless' or nonproductive activity," might well apply to the third stage of Melville's career; his poetry, written with little hope of appealing to a commercial or even critical audience, shows Melville writing for the sake of writing, playing—but with the highest seriousness—with words and ideas.

III

At the end of his career, and near the end of the nineteenth century—but reflecting back over his career and set near the end of the eighteenth century—is Melville's final narrative of

[12]Harvey Cox, *The Seduction of the Spirit* (New York, 1973), 319.
[13]Ibid., 320–21.

facts, *Billy Budd, Sailor.* The novel is composed of a number of short narratives—from several points of view and concerning everyone from Billy to Admiral Nelson—inside the central narrative. Each attempts to get inside Billy's story, yet none, upon close analysis, sheds more than "lateral light" upon the story of Billy. Virtually every detail is qualified with a "might have been" or a "seemed to be"; Melville fills the short text with further qualifications, circumlocutions, and inapplicable historical parallels and allusions. The sheer number of narratives inside *Billy Budd* and the strenuousness with which the various narrators—Claggart, Vere, the narrator himself—attempt to tell their stories expose the power of the desire to secure and narrate the facts.

In this desire the narrators of *Billy Budd* resemble Ishmael; but in projecting their own hopes and beliefs upon the events, they are closer to those earlier narrators of facts. After Billy's death, for example, the sailors "recalled the fresh young image of the Handsome Sailor, that facts never deformed by a sneer or subtler vile freak of the heart within. This impression was doubtless deepened by the fact that he was gone, and in a measure mysteriously gone" (131). The sailors, faced with "the fact" of death and with only a "mysterious" idea of what may be beyond, translate their "image" of Billy into a poetic (if ridiculously hackneyed) narrative. Narrative, here again, is an attempt not just to understand the facts but through that understanding to resurrect what has naturally passed away. Like Ishmael's world of "deadly voids," Billy's contains "the deadly space between" not only Claggart and "a normal nature" (74) but between all people, between the narrator and the facts. In a world where transcendence is at best uncertain, connection between the individual and the nature around him becomes the only way to avoid falling into that "deadly space" at the edge of mortal existence. As the means of asserting that connection, narration—"best done by indirection"—is thus among the strongest, most religious of desires in Melville's world and, as with the sailors, among the most open to politicization.

Billy Budd, seen consistently in religious terms, is himself the "text" of the narrative, the subject each tries to understand and re-present. Billy is Melville's natural man, "a sound human creature," whom Melville's civilized narrator again and again describes as an animal or a barbarian standing "nearer to unadulterate Nature." As a natural man Billy exists in a prenarrative state: from an "organic hesitancy" he tells no stories either of himself or of historical events but, like the Typees, lives completely in the present moment. But when he encounters the afterguardsman he must try, always unsuccessfully, to tell his story. Like a natural child (in both senses of the term), he knows little of his origin, merely born of indefinite parents, and cares little of his end. It is precisely because he is a natural man and does not seek to place himself in history that Billy is such a mystery to those around him. Therefore, the others describe Billy in mythic or legendary terms: he is compared to Apollo, the Handsome Sailor, Christ, and so on.

Claggart, a man of little faith, is the most naive reader of the text of Billy and the most pragmatic of his critics. He reads Billy exclusively from his own viewpoint and egoistically assumes that Billy has the same invidious motives that he himself does. Accordingly, he thinks that Billy will react as he would to himself and his clandestine plans—with malicious irony and avaricious cunning. Claggart seeks not to understand Billy but to confirm in him Claggart's own existence and values. The reading of Billy he presents to Vere, then, is grounded in some factual perception of the text, but must postulate a warped idea of what lies beneath the surface, a process that destroys the text.

Vere's moral reading of Billy is more sophisticated yet no more successful. In something of a sardonic self-parody, Melville presents Vere as a habitual reader of narratives of facts ("books treating of actual men and events no matter of what era—history, biography and unconventional writers like Montaigne") who "in illustrating of any point touching the stirring personages and events of the time . . . would be as apt to cite some historic character or incident of antiquity as he would be to cite from the moderns" (63). When Vere hears Claggart's narrative, he considers it in the light of the other stories he has heard of Billy as the Handsome Sailor, "and the more he weighed [Claggart's account] the less reliance he felt in the informer's good faith" (95). Narrative "faith" here, as in *Moby-Dick*, is important: Vere's religious preconceptions lead him to consider Billy a prelapsarian Adam (94), a Christlike "fated boy" (99), and "an angel of God" (101). Yet in reality Vere has no more reason to perceive Billy as Goodness Incarnate than to perceive Claggart as that. He knows nothing of the motivations of either, for neither reveals his inner thoughts. Billy is merely lauded by the crew while Claggart, their superior, is generally disliked. And yet they are quite similar: both have obscure origins, both are exemplary sailors, both have striking appearances. Vere, that is to say, has no good reason to believe either Claggart or Billy, other than their appearance, hearsay, and his own Christian framework of beliefs, which precludes considering them natural men.

When, therefore, Billy's fist intrudes upon Claggart's narration, Vere, like Melville's earlier narrators of facts, has trouble fitting the act into the picture of Billy his faith has generated. In this violent act, Billy shows himself neither an Adam nor a Christ. Vere may call it "the divine judgment on Ananias" and label Billy an angel, but neither of these statements will adequately explain the violence of the attack. Even as he perceives Billy from this Christian perspective, Vere is forced to perceive Billy's actions from a military perspective as well. Thus Vere presents a dichotomy familiar to readers of the earlier narratives of facts: a dubious faith opposed and undermined by an inveterate politics. Vere, as his name might suggest, is a man of the seventeenth century (like Marvell) who can still believe these two spheres compatible, despite living in a century that explodes them. Like Melville's earlier narrators, Vere is caught in this dissociation of sensibility and must act as if "unhinged"; he chooses to place Billy's inner self within the Christian context but his outer within the political. Little wonder the surgeon suspects insanity, for such a schizophrenic determination cannot but warp Vere's perspective, create turmoil for himself, and distance him even further from reality. Indeed, the problem of Billy haunts him until his dying day.

Melville replays these conflicts in his narrator, a contextual critic who amplifies the biases, motivations, and mistakes of Vere. Further testifying to the spiritual desire behind narration, the narrator, like Vere, consistently describes Billy in mythic and Christian terms. And yet, as he tries to approach Billy through the "indirection" and "lateral light" of personal and historical precedents—and incompetently so, as Garner's study indicates—the narrator goes further than Vere. To name a few: he tells of Nelson, the Somers mutiny, the Nore case; he refers to Marvell, the Bible, Thomas Paine; he reminisces about his past and makes the events into a tragedy; he employs inappropriate metaphors, inapplicable allusions, selective detailing, imaginative reconstruction. But all to no avail: he can only "suggest" what Billy "might be like."

Like Vere's, the narrator's biases are exposed by Billy's fist. The facts of the event show Billy not like the Handsome Sailor the narrator remembers, not like a Saint Bernard, not like Christ;[14] nevertheless, the narrator tries all the more strenuously to present Billy as a heroic Christ-figure. His motives in doing so are more self-interested than religious; for—like each of the other narrators of facts—he is using the story of Billy to justify his own conservative politics. By stressing the tragic and otherworldly aspects of Billy's story, he diverts it away from revolution and toward an acceptance of the status quo, just as Claggart uses Billy to cement his own position in the ship's hierarchy and in the captain's eyes, just as Vere uses his narrative of the story to keep order on board and to keep order in his perception of the starry system of the universe. These politicizations are no less ridiculous than the final two stories of Billy, one concocted to justify naval policies, the other to satisfy the sailors' romanticism, but both to keep "the people" firmly in their place. Again Melville criticizes the usurpation, for the

[14]Veblen, *Theory*, 103, states: "The dog has advantages in the way of uselessness. . . . He is often spoken of, in an eminent sense, as the friend of man, and his intelligence and fidelity are praised. The meaning of this is that the dog is man's servant and that he has the gift of an unquestioning subservience and a slave's quickness in guessing his master's mood. . . . He is the filthiest of the domestic animals and the nastiest in his habits. For this he makes up in a servile, fawning attitude towards his master, and a readiness to inflict damage and discomfort on all else."

purposes of political superiority, of the essentially religious desire to understand and narrate the world.

Within the narrator's story Melville places yet another narrative: the surgeon's, as much a comment on the narrator as upon Vere. The surgeon, whose character Melville was developing at the time of his death, is the only person to call into question Vere's judgment by raising the possibility of insanity.[15] He thereby also calls into question the narrator's response to Billy: the surgeon is by no means willing to label Billy either heroic or Christlike. Billy's end, like his whole story, is "phenomenal" only "in the sense that it was an appearance the cause of which is not immediately to be assigned" (125). Unlike Vere, the surgeon is more a man of Melville's late nineteenth century, a scientific naturalist willing only to have faith in facts objectively verifiable. He distrusts terms "imaginative and metaphysical," which would only obscure the facts. Consequently, he refuses his narrative role, refuses to give his version of what goes on inside either Vere (chap. 20) or Billy (chap. 8). Yet the surgeon, like so many of Melville's medicine men, is a rather cold, perhaps heartless scientist who tends to view a person as "a case" (125).[16] In such an attitude are the seeds of an Ahablike arrogance, the dangers of which Melville noted in a monologue originally titled "The Scientist."[17] He retitled the poem "The New Zealot to the Sun" to emphasize his ironic distance from the speaker, who claims that "Science" will ultimately displace religion and "An effluence ampler shall beget, / And power beyond your [the sun's] play." Melville is as skeptical about claims to scientific objectivity—here motivated by a desire for "power" and thus capable of becoming monomaniac—as he is about those claims to cultural superiority voiced in his narratives of facts. Both deny humanity, both threaten the individual.

[15]See Hayford's and Sealts's "Editors' Introduction" to the Chicago edition.
[16]I am grateful to Gail Coffler for sharing her as yet unpublished work "Melville's Medicine Men."
[17]Collected Poems of Herman Melville, ed. Howard P. Vincent (Chicago, 1947), 226.

In Melville's late nineteenth century, more generally, science had to a degree displaced Christianity as the basic nexus of values, the basic story, upon which Western culture "progressed." In addition to the higher criticism and literary naturalism, Freudian psychology, Marxist social thought, and Darwinian science all attempted to rewrite the white, Western, progressive narrative that Melville's eighteenth- and nineteenth-century sources so strenuously defined and defended. Melville, however strongly opposed to the ideology of these sources, cannot accept in its place a scientific objectivity or a systematic explanation that refuses to recognize the essential indeterminacy and chaos of nature, of the universe, or that prioritizes a collective ideology at the expense of an individual's humanity.

If it is clear what stories Melville is un-writing, what, finally, *is* the story that Melville is narrating? I believe that if one is to place Melville, it must be with another movement of the late nineteenth century, with such anarchistic figures as Bakunin, Tucker, Veblen, Bergson, Nietzsche. In his 1851 letters to Hawthorne—perhaps his truest, shiftiest writing—Melville describes his "ruthless democracy" as well as his contempt for those who "*managed* the truth with a view to popular conservatism" and those who "will insist upon the universal application of a temporary feeling or opinion."[18] In opposition, Melville believes that "divine magnanimities are spontaneous and instantaneous" and that "truth is ever incoherent." Therefore, the most admirable course of action is what he ascribes to Hawthorne (though the shift in person is significant):

> By visible truth, we mean the apprehension of the absolute condition of present things as they strike the eye of the man who fears them not, though they do their worst to him,—the man who, like Russia or the British Empire, declares himself a sovereign nature (in himself) amid the powers of heaven, hell, and earth. He may perish; but so long as he exists he insists upon treating with all Powers upon an equal basis. If any of those

[18]See *Letters*, 118–44.

other Powers choose to withhold certain secrets, let them; that does not impair my sovereignty in myself; that does not make me tributary. And perhaps, after all, there is *no* secret.[19]

This insistence on the "sovereignty" of the individual led Melville to dismantle the forms and contents of the "Powers" of his day in those uncompromisingly individualistic novels for which he is known in ours.

As in his narratives of facts as a whole, at the end of the one Melville novel perhaps most vitally of our time, Melville "extinguish[ed] this lamp" of Western ideology, but something did follow of Melville's ideological and narrative masquerade: fabulation, metafiction, postmodernism, deconstruction.[20]

[19]Ibid., 124–25.
[20]*The Confidence-Man: His Masquerade*, ed. Harrison Hayford, Hershel Parker, and G. Thomas Tanselle (Evanston and Chicago, 1984), 251.

Works Cited

Abrams, M. H. *Natural Supernaturalism: Tradition and Revolution in Romantic Literature*. New York: W. W. Norton, 1971.

Abrams, Robert. "*Typee* and *Omoo*: Herman Melville and the Ungraspable Phantom of Identity." *Arizona Quarterly* 31 (1975): 33–50.

Adams, Percy G. *Travel Literature and the Evolution of the Novel*. Lexington: Univ. of Kentucky Press, 1983.

Adler, Joyce Sparer. *War in Melville's Imagination*. New York: New York University Press, 1981.

Albrecht, Robert. "White-Jacket's Intentional Fall." *Studies in the Novel* 4 (1972): 17–26.

Allen, Ethan. *A Narrative of Colonel Ethan Allen's Captivity* . . . Philadelphia: Robert Bell, 1779.

American Review: A Whig Journal of Politics, Literature, Art and Science 5–9 (1847–1849).

Ames, Nathaniel. *A Mariner's Sketches*. Providence, R.I.: Cory, Marshall & Hammond, 1830.

Anderson, Charles R. *Melville in the South Seas*. New York: Columbia University Press, 1939.

———, ed. *Journal of a Cruise to the Pacific*. Durham, N.C.: Duke University Press, 1937.

Arvin, Newton. *Herman Melville*. New York: William Sloane, 1950.

Babin, James. "Melville and the Deformation of Being: From *Typee* to Leviathan." *Southern Review* 7 (1971): 89–114.

Bailyn, Bernard. *The Ideological Origins of the American Revolution*. Cambridge: Harvard University Press, 1967.

Baird, James. *Ishmael*. Baltimore: Johns Hopkins University Press, 1956.

Bakhtin, M. M. *The Dialogic Imagination: Four Essays*. ed. Michael Holquist.

Trans. Caryl Emerson and Michael Holquist. Austin: University of Texas Press, 1981.

——. *Speech Genres and Other Late Essays*. Ed. Caryl Emerson and Michael Holquist. Trans. Vern W. McGee. Austin: University of Texas Press, 1986.

Bancroft, George. *History of the United States, from the Discovery of the Continent*. Rev. ed. 6 vols. New York: D. Appleton, 1876, 1883–1885.

Bayle, Pierre. *A Historical and Critical Dictionary*. 2 vols. London: C. Harper et al., 1710.

Beauchamp, Gorman. "Montaigne, Melville, and the Cannibals." *Arizona Quarterly* 37 (1981): 292–309.

Beaver, Harold. "Herman Melville: Prophetic Mariner." In *American Fictions: New Readings*, ed. Richard Gray. London and Totowa, N. J.: Vision Press/Barnes & Noble, 1983.

Beechey, F. W. *Narrative of a Voyage to the Pacific and Beering's Strait*. 2 vols. 1831; rpt. Amsterdam and New York: N. Israel/Da Capo Press, 1968.

Bell, Michael D. "Melville's *Redburn*: Initiation and Authority." *New England Quarterly* 46 (1973): 558–72.

Bennet, George, and Daniel Tyerman. *Journal of Voyages and Travels*. 2 vols. Ed. James Montgomery. Boston: Crocker & Brewster, 1832.

Bercaw, Mary K. *Melville's Sources*. Evanston, Ill.: Northwestern University Press, 1987.

Bercovitch, Sacvan. *The American Jeremiad*. Madison: University of Wisconsin Press, 1978.

——. *The Puritan Origins of the American Self*. New Haven: Yale University Press, 1975.

Bernstein, John. *Pacifism and Rebellion in the Writings of Herman Melville*. The Hague: Mouton, 1964.

Berthold, Dennis. "Factual Errors and Fictional Aims in *White-Jacket*." *Studies in American Fiction* 11 (1983): 233–39.

Bird, Christine M. "*Redburn* and *Afloat and Ashore*." *Nassau Review* 3 (1979): 5–16.

Birss, John Howard. "'Travelling': A New Lecture by Herman Melville." *New England Quarterly* 7 (1934): 725–28.

Bougainville, Louis de. *A Voyage Round the World*. 1772; rpt. Amsterdam and New York: N. Israel/Da Capo Press, 1967.

Bowen, Merlin. *Redburn* and the Angle of Vision." *Modern Philology* 52 (1954): 100–109.

Bredahl, Axel Carl. *Melville's Angles of Vision*. Gainesville: University of Florida Press, 1972.

Breitwieser, Mitchell. *Cotton Mather and Benjamin Franklin: The Price of Representative Personality*. Cambridge: Cambridge University Press, 1984.

——. "False Sympathy in Melville's *Typee*." *American Quarterly* 34 (1982): 396–417.

Briggs, Charles Frederick. *The Adventures of Harry Franco*. 2 vols. New York: F. Saunders, 1839.

——. *Bankrupt Stories (The Haunted Merchant)*. New York: John Allen, 1843.

——. *The Trippings of Tom Pepper; or, The Results of Romancing*. New York: Burgess, Stringer, et al., 1847.

——. *Working a Passage; or, Life in a Liner*. New York: John Allen, 1844.

Brock, William R. *Parties and Political Conscience*. Millwood, N.Y.: KTO Press, 1979.

Brodkorb, Paul, Jr. "The Definitive *Billy Budd*: 'But aren't it all Sham?'" *PMLA* 82 (1967): 602–12.

Brown, Norman O. *Love's Body*. New York: Random House, 1966.

Browne, J. Ross. *Etchings of a Whaling Cruise*. New York: Harper, 1846.

Brumm, Ursula. *American Thought and Religious Typology*. Trans. John Hoaglund. 1963; rpt. New Brunswick, N.J.: Rutgers University Press, 1970.

Bryant, John, ed. *A Companion to Melville Studies*. Westport, Conn.: Greenwood Press, 1986.

——. "Melville, 'Little Henry,' and the Process of Composition: A Peep at the *Typee* Fragment." *Melville Society Extracts*, no. 67 (1986), 1–4.

Buschmann, Jean Charles. *Aperçu de la langue des Isles Marquises et de la langue taïtienne*. Berlin: C. G. Luderitz, 1843.

Bush, George. *The Life of Mohammed*. New York: J. & J. Harper, 1831.

Butterfield, Herbert. *The Whig Interpretation of History*. London: G. Bell, 1931.

Butterfield, Herbie. "'New World All Over': Melville's *Typee*." In *Herman Melville: Reassessments*, ed. A. Robert Lee, 14–27. London: Vision Press, 1984.

Chambers, Robert. *Vestiges of the Natural History of Creation*, 2d ed. New York: Wiley & Putnam, 1845.

Chase, Richard. *Quest for Myth*. Baton Rouge: Louisiana State University Press, 1949.

Clark, Michael. "Melville's *Typee*: Fact, Fiction, and Esthetics." *Arizona Quarterly* 34 (1978): 350–70.

Cohen, Lester H. *The Revolutionary Histories: Contemporary Narratives of the American Revolution*. Ithaca: Cornell University Press, 1980.

Cohen, Ralph. "History and Genre." *New Literary History* 17 (1986): 203–18.

Colacurcio, Michael J. *The Province of Piety: Moral History in Hawthorne's Early Tales*. Cambridge: Harvard University Press, 1984.

Cooper, James Fenimore. *Afloat and Ashore*. 1844; rpt. New York: D. Appleton, 1883.

——. *The History of the Navy of the United States of America*. 2 vols. Philadelphia: Lea & Blanchard, 1839.

Cox, Harvey. *The Seduction of the Spirit*. New York: Simon & Schuster, 1973.

Creeger, George. "The Symbolism of Whiteness in Melville's Prose Fiction." *Jahrbuch für Amerikastudien* 5 (1960): 147–63.

Dana, Richard Henry, Jr. *Two Years before the Mast*. 1840; rpt. New York: Harper & Row, 1965.

Darwin, Charles. *The Voyage of the Beagle*. 1845; rpt. New York: P. F. Collier, 1909.

Davis, Lennard J. *Factual Fictions: The Origins of the English Novel*. New York: Columbia University Press, 1983.

——. *Resisting Novels: Ideology and Fiction*. New York: Methuen, 1987.

DeLeon, David. *The American as Anarchist: Reflections on Indigenous Radicalism*. Baltimore: Johns Hopkins University Press, 1978.

Derrida, Jacques. "The Law of Genre." In *On Narrative,* ed. W. J. T. Mitchell, 51–77. Chicago: University of Chicago Press, 1981.

——. *Of Grammatology*. Trans. Gayatri C. Spivak. 1967; rpt. Baltimore: Johns Hopkins University Press, 1976.

Dillingham, William B. *An Artist in the Rigging: The Early Work of Herman Melville*. Athens: University of Georgia Press, 1972.

——. *Melville's Later Novels*. Athens: University of Georgia Press, 1986.

Dimock, Wai-Chee. *"Typee*: Melville's Critique of Community." *ESQ: A Journal of the American Renaissance* 30 (1984): 27–39.

——. *"White-Jacket*: Authors and Audiences." *Nineteenth-Century Fiction* 36 (1981): 296–317.

Dodge, Ernest. "Early American Contacts in Polynesia and Fiji." *Proceedings of the American Philosophical Society* 107 (1963): 102–6.

Dryden, Edgar A. *Melville's Thematics of Form: The Great Art of Telling the Truth*. Baltimore: Johns Hopkins University Press, 1968.

Duban, James. *Melville's Major Fiction: Politics, Theology, and Imagination*. De Kalb: Northern Illinois University Press, 1983.

——. "'A Pantomime of Action': Starbuck and American Whig Providence." *New England Quarterly* 44 (1982): 432–39.

Dwight, Timothy. *The Major Poems of Timothy Dwight*. Ed. William McTaggart and William Bottorff. Gainesville, Fla.: Scholars' Facsimiles and Reprints, 1969.

Eigner, Edwin. "The Romantic Unity of Melville's *Omoo*." *Philological Quarterly* 46 (1967): 95–108.

Eliade, Mircea. *Shamanism*. Trans. Willard Trask. 1951; rpt. Princeton: Princeton University Press, 1964.

Ellis, William. *Polynesian Researches*. 4 vols. New York: J. & J. Harper, 1833.

Evans, Lyon, Jr. "'Too Good to Be True': Subverting Christian Hope in *Billy Budd*." *New England Quarterly* 55 (1982): 323–53.

Fanning, Edmund. *Voyages Round the World . . .* New York: Collins & Hannay, 1833.

Fanning, Nathaniel. *Memoirs of the Life of Captain Nathaniel Fanning . . .* New York: Tracy W. McGregor, 1808.

Feidelson, Charles, Jr. *Symbolism and American Literature*. Chicago: University of Chicago Press, 1953.

Feldman, Burton, and Robert Richardson, eds. *The Rise of Modern Mythology, 1680–1860*. Bloomington: Indiana University Press, 1972.

Finkelstein, Dorothee M. *Melville's Orienda*. New Haven: Yale University Press, 1961.

Fish, Stanley. "Consequences." In *Against Theory: Literary Studies and the New Pragmatism*, ed. W. J. T. Mitchell, 106–31. Chicago: University of Chicago Press, 1985.

Fletcher, Richard M. "Melville's Use of Marquesan." *American Speech* 39 (1964): 135–38.

Fliegelman, Jay. *Prodigals and Pilgrims: The American Revolution against Patriarchal Authority, 1750–1800*. Cambridge: Cambridge University Press, 1982.

Foucault, Michel. *The History of Sexuality*. Vol. 1: *An Introduction*. 1976. Trans. Robert Hurley, New York: Vintage Books, 1980.

———. *Power/Knowledge: Selected Interviews and Other Writings, 1972–1977*. Ed. Colin Gordon. Trans. Colin Gordon, Leo Marshall, John Mepham, and Kate Soper. New York: Pantheon, 1980.

Franklin, Benjamin. *The Works of Benjamin Franklin*. 10 vols. Ed. Jared Sparks. Boston: Hilliard, Gray, 1836–1840.

Franklin, H. Bruce. "Redburn's Wicked End." *Nineteenth-Century Fiction* 20 (1965): 190–94.

———. *The Wake of the Gods*. Stanford: Stanford University Press, 1963.

Frederick, John T. "Symbol and Theme in Melville's *Israel Potter*." *Modern Fiction Studies* 8 (1962): 265–75.

Furtwangler, Albert. *American Silhouettes: Rhetorical Identities of the Founders*. New Haven: Yale University Press, 1987.

Garner, Stanton. "Fraud as Fact in Herman Melville's *Billy Budd*." *San Jose Studies* 4 (1978): 82–105.

Gasché, Rodolphe. "The Scene of Writing: A Deferred Quest." *Glyph* 1 (1977): 150–71.

Gay, Peter. *The Rise of Modern Paganism*. New York: Knopf, 1967.

Gerlach, John. "Messianic Nationalism in the Early Works of Herman Melville: Against Perry Miller." *Arizona Quarterly* 28 (1972): 5–26.

Gibbon, Edward. *The History of the Decline and Fall of the Roman Empire*. Vol. 6. 1788. Paris: Baudry's European Library, 1840.

Gilman, William. *Melville's Early Life and "Redburn."* New York: New York University Press, 1951.

Giltrow, Janet. "Structure in Herman Melville's Early Narratives." *American Literature* 52 (1980): 18–32.

Grejda, Edward S. *The Common Continent of Men*. Port Washington, N.Y.: Kennikat Press, 1974.

Gross, John. "The Rehearsal of Ishmael: Melville's 'Redburn.'" *Virginia Quarterly Review* 27 (1951): 581–600.

Gunson, Neil. *Messengers of Grace: Evangelical Missions in the South Seas, 1797–1860.* Oxford: Oxford University Press, 1978.

Hawthorne, Nathaniel. *The Snow-Image and Uncollected Tales.* 1851. Ed. J. Donald Crowley. Columbus: Ohio State University Press, 1974.

Hayford, Harrison and Walter Blair. "Introduction" and "Explanatory Notes." In *Omoo: A Narrative of Adventures in the South Seas,* xvii–lii and 341–438. New York: Hendricks House, 1969.

Herbert, T. Walter, Jr. "The Force of Prejudice: Melville's Attack on the Missions in *Typee.*" *Border States* (1973): 5–18.

———. *Marquesan Encounters: Melville and the Meaning of Civilization.* Cambridge: Harvard University Press, 1980.

———. *"Moby-Dick" and Calvinism: A World Dismantled.* New Brunswick, N.J.: Rutgers University Press, 1977.

Hildreth, Richard. *The History of the United States of America . . .* New York: Harper, 1849.

Hirsch, E. D. *The Aims of Interpretation.* Chicago: University of Chicago Press, 1976.

An Historical Account of the Circumnavigation of the Globe . . . Edinburgh: Oliver & Boyd, 1836.

Howe, Daniel W., ed. *The American Whigs.* New York: Wiley, 1973.

Irving, Washington. *The Sketch Book.* 1820; rpt. New York: New American Library, 1961.

Jaffé, David. "The Captain Who Sat for the Portrait of Ahab." *Boston University Studies in English* 4 (1960): 1–22.

Johnson, Barbara. "Melville's Fist: The Execution of *Billy Budd.*" *Studies in Romanticism* 18 (1979): 567–99.

Jones, Howard Mumford. *O Strange New World: American Culture: The Formative Years.* 1952; rpt. New York: Viking, 1964.

Joswick, Thomas P. *"Typee:* The Quest for Origin." *Criticism* 17 (1975): 335–54.

Kahler, Erich. "The Persistence of Myth." *Chimera* 4 (1946): 2–11.

Kammen, Michael. *People of Paradox: An Inquiry Concerning the Origins of American Civilization.* 1972; rpt. New York: Vintage Books, 1973.

———. *A Season of Youth: The American Revolution and the Historical Imagination.* New York: Knopf, 1978.

Karcher, Carolyn. *Shadow over the Promised Land: Slavery, Race, and Violence in Melville's America.* Baton Rouge: Louisiana State University Press, 1980.

Kaul, A. N. *The American Vision: Actual and Ideal Society in Nineteenth-Century Fiction.* New Haven: Yale University Press, 1963.

Ketterer, David. "Censorship and Symbolism in *Typee* Revisited: The New Manuscript Evidence." *Melville Society Extracts,* no. 69 (1987), 6–8.

Keyssar, Alexander. *Melville's "Israel Potter": Reflections on the American Dream.* Cambridge: Harvard University Press, 1969.

Kotzebue, Otto von. *A New Voyage Round the World in the Years 1823–1826.* 2 vols. 1830; rpt. Amsterdam and New York: N. Israel/Da Capo Press, 1967.

Langsdorff, George von. *Voyages and Travels in Various Parts of the World.* 2 vols. 1813; rpt. Amsterdam and New York: N. Israel/Da Capo Press, 1968.

Lawrence, D. H. *Studies in Classic American Literature.* 1923; rpt. New York: Viking, 1964.

Leary, Lewis. "Introduction." In *His Fifty Years of Exile (Israel Potter)*, vii–xii. New York: Sagamore Press, 1957.

Ledyard, John. *A Journal of Captain Cook's Last Voyage.* 1783; rpt. Chicago: Quadrangle, 1963.

Leech, Samuel. *Thirty Years from Home.* Boston: Charles Tappan, 1844.

Lenox Library Short-Title Lists. Nos. 8 and 12. New York: New York Public Library, 1887, 1890.

Lish, Terence. "Melville's *Redburn*: A Study in Dualism." *English Language Notes* 5 (1967): 113–20.

Looby, Christopher. "'The Affairs of the Revolution Occasion'd the Interruption': Writing, Revolution, Deferral and Conciliation in Franklin's *Autobiography*." *American Quarterly* 38 (1986): 72–96.

Lovejoy, A. O., George Boas, et al., eds. *A Documentary History of Primitivism and Related Ideas*, Vol. 1. Baltimore: Johns Hopkins University Press, 1935.

Lucas, Thomas. "Herman Melville: The Purpose of the Novel." *Texas Studies in Language and Literature* 13 (1972): 641–61.

Lucid, Robert. "The Influence of *Two Years before the Mast* on Herman Melville." *American Literature* 31 (1959): 243–56.

McCarthy, Harold. "Melville's *Redburn* and the City." *Midwest Quarterly* 12 (1971): 395–410.

McCarthy, Paul. "Elements of Anatomy in Melville's Fiction." *Studies in the Novel* 6 (1974): 38–61.

——. "Symbolic Elements in *White-Jacket*." *Midwest Quarterly* 7 (1961): 309–25.

McNally, William. *Evils and Abuses in the Naval and Merchant Service Exposed.* Boston: Cassady & March, 1839.

McWilliams, John P., Jr. *Hawthorne, Melville, and the American Character: A Looking-Glass Business.* Cambridge: Cambridge University Press, 1984.

Manuel, Frank. *The Eighteenth Century Confronts the Gods.* Cambridge: Harvard University Press, 1959.

Marryat, Frederick. *Peter Simple.* Leipzig: Bernhard Tauchnitz, 1842.

Melville, Herman. *Billy Budd, Sailor (An inside narrative).* Harrison Hayford and Merton M. Sealts, Jr., eds. Chicago: University of Chicago Press, 1962.

———. *Collected Poems of Herman Melville.* Ed. Howard P. Vincent. Chicago: Packard/Hendricks House, 1947.

———. *The Confidence-Man: His Masquerade.* 1857. Ed. Harrison Hayford, Hershel Parker, and G. Thomas Tanselle. Evanston and Chicago: Northwestern University Press/Newberry Library, 1984.

———. *Israel Potter: His Fifty Years of Exile.* 1855. Ed. Harrison Hayford, Hershel Parker, and G. Thomas Tanselle. Evanston and Chicago: Northwestern University Press/Newberry Library, 1982.

———. *The Letters of Herman Melville.* Ed. Merrell Davis and William Gilman. New Haven: Yale University Press, 1960.

———. *Mardi; and a Voyage Thither.* 1849. Ed. Harrison Hayford, Hershel Parker, and G. Thomas Tanselle. Evanston and Chicago: Northwestern University Press/Newberry Library, 1970.

———. *The Melville Log.* Ed. Jay Leyda. 1951; rpt. New York: Gordian Press, 1969.

———. *Moby-Dick.* 1851. Ed. Harrison Hayford and Hershel Parker. New York: W. W. Norton, 1967.

———. *Omoo: A Narrative of Adventures in the South Seas.* 1847. Ed. Harrison Hayford, Hershel Parker, and G. Thomas Tanselle. Evanston and Chicago: Northwestern University Press/Newberry Library, 1968.

———. *Pierre; or, The Ambiguities.* 1852. Ed. Harrison Hayford, Hershel Parker, and G. Thomas Tanselle. Evanston and Chicago: Northwestern University Press/Newberry Library, 1971.

———. *Redburn: His First Voyage . . .* 1849, Ed. Harrison Hayford, Hershel Parker, and G. Thomas Tanselle. Evanston and Chicago: Northwestern University Press/Newberry Library, 1969.

———. "The South Seas." In *Melville as Lecturer,* ed. Merton M. Sealts, Jr., 155–80. Cambridge: Harvard University Press, 1969.

———. *Typee: A Peep at Polynesian Life.* 1846. Ed. Harrison Hayford, Hershel Parker, and G. Thomas Tanselle. Evanston and Chicago: Northwestern University Press/Newberry Library, 1968.

———. *White-Jacket; or, The World in a Man-of-War.* 1850. Ed. Harrison Hayford, Hershel Parker, and G. Thomas Tanselle. Evanston and Chicago: Northwestern University Press/Newberry Library, 1970.

———. Untitled review in *Literary World* 1 (1847): 105–6.

Mercier, Henry. *Life in a Man-of-War.* 1841; rpt. Boston: Houghton Mifflin, 1927.

Midwinter, Eric. *Old Liverpool.* Newton Abbot: David & Charles, 1971.

Miller, Edwin H. *Melville.* New York: George Braziller, 1975.

Miller, James E., Jr. "*Redburn* and *White-Jacket*: Initiation and Baptism." *Nineteenth-Century Fiction* 13 (1959): 273–93.

Miller, Perry. *The Raven and the Whale: The War of Words and Wits in the Era of Poe and Melville.* New York: Harcourt, Brace, 1956.

Mitchell, Lee Clark. *Witness to a Vanishing America: The Nineteenth-Century Response*. Princeton: Princeton University Press, 1981.

Mosblech, Boniface. *Vocabulaire océanien-français et français-océanien*. Paris: Jules Renouard, 1843.

North American Review 65–74 (1847–1852).

Nye, Russel B. *Society and Culture in America, 1830–1860*. New York: Harper & Row, 1974.

O'Gorman, Edmundo. *The Invention of America*. Bloomington: Indiana University Press, 1961.

Olmsted, Francis Allyn. *Incidents of a Whaling Voyage*. 1841; rpt. Rutland, Vt.: Charles E. Tuttle, 1969.

Page, Evelyn. *American Genesis: Pre-Colonial Writing in the North*. Boston: Gambit, 1973.

Parker, Hershel. "Evidences for 'Late Insertions' in Melville's Works." *Studies in the Novel* 7 (1975): 407–24.

——. *Flawed Texts and Verbal Icons: Literary Authority in American Fiction*. Evanston, Ill.: Northwestern University Press, 1984.

——. "The 'New Scholarship': Textual Evidence and Its Implications for Criticism, Literary Theory, and Aesthetics." *Studies in American Fiction* 9 (1981): 181–97.

Paul, Stephen de. "The Documentary Fiction of Melville's *Omoo*: The Crossed Grammars of Acculturation." *Criticism* 28 (1986): 51–72.

Petrullo, Helen B. "The Neurotic Hero of *Typee*." *American Imago* 12 (1955): 317–23.

Picture of Liverpool, The. Liverpool: Towes & Wright, 1808.

Pirsig, Robert M. *Zen and the Art of Motorcycle Maintenance*. New York: Bantam, 1974.

Pops, Martin. *The Melville Archetype*. Kent, Ohio: Kent State University Press, 1970.

Porter, David. *Journal of a Cruise Made to the Pacific Ocean*, 2d ed. 2 vols. New York: Wiley & Halsted, 1822.

Pullin, Faith. "Melville's *Typee*: The Failure of Eden." In *New Perspectives on Melville*, 1–28. Kent, Ohio: Kent State University Press, 1978.

Radin, Paul. *The Trickster*. London: Routledge & Kegan Paul, 1956.

Rampersad, Arnold. *Melville's "Israel Potter": A Pilgrimage and Progress*. Bowling Green, Ohio: Bowling Green University Popular Press, 1969.

Reed, Walter L. "The Measured Forms of Captain Vere." *Modern Fiction Studies* 23 (1977): 227–35.

Reynolds, Larry J. "Antidemocratic Emphasis in *White-Jacket*." *American Literature* 48 (1976): 13–28.

Robbins, Caroline. *The Eighteenth-Century Commonwealthman*. Cambridge: Harvard University Press, 1959.

Rogin, Michael Paul. *Subversive Genealogy: The Politics and Art of Herman Melville*. Berkeley and Los Angeles: University of California Press, 1985.

Rosenberry, Edward H. *Melville and the Comic Spirit*. Cambridge: Harvard University Press, 1955.

Rousseau, Jean-Jacques. *The Social Contract and Discourses*. 1762. Trans. G. D. H. Cole. New York: E. P. Dutton, 1950.

Rowland, Beryl. "Sitting Up with a Corpse: Malthus according to Melville in 'Poor Man's Pudding and Rich Man's Crumbs.'" *Journal of American Studies* 6 (1972): 69–83.

Ruland, Richard. "Melville and the Fortunate Fall: Typee as Eden." *Nineteenth-Century Fiction* 23 (1968): 312–23.

Ruschenberger, W. S. *Narrative of a Voyage Round the World*. 2 vols. London: Richard Bentley, 1838.

Russell, Michael. *Polynesia*. Edinburgh: Oliver & Boyd, 1842.

Sands, Robert C. *Life and Correspondence of John Paul Jones*. New York: D. Fanshaw, 1830.

Schlesinger, Arthur, Jr. *The Age of Jackson*. Boston: Little, Brown, 1945.

Schroeter, James. "Redburn and the Failure of Mythic Criticism." *American Literature* 39 (1967): 279–97.

Scorza, Thomas J. *In the Time of Steamships: Billy Budd, the Limits of Politics, and Modernity*. De Kalb: Northern Illinois University Press, 1979.

Sealts, Merton M., Jr. *Melville's Reading*. Rev. ed. Columbia: University of South Carolina Press, 1988.

Seelye, John. *Melville: The Ironic Diagram*. Evanston, Ill.: Northwestern University Press, 1970.

——. *Prophetic Waters: The River in Early American Life and Literature*. New York: Oxford University Press, 1977.

Slotkin, Richard. *Regeneration through Violence: The Mythology of the American Frontier, 1600–1860*. Middletown, Conn.: Wesleyan University Press, 1973.

Smith, Adam. *An Inquiry into the Nature and Causes of the Wealth of Nations*. 1776; rpt. Chicago: University of Chicago Press, 1976.

Somkin, Fred. *Unquiet Eagle*. Ithaca: Cornell University Press, 1967.

Sparks, Jared. *Ethan Allen*. 1848; rpt. New York: Harper, 1902.

Spengemann, William. *The Adventurous Muse: The Poetics of American Fiction, 1789–1900*. New Haven: Yale University Press, 1977.

Stafford, William T. *Books Speaking to Books: A Contextual Approach to American Fiction*. Chapel Hill: University of North Carolina Press, 1981.

Stern, Milton R. *The Fine Hammered Steel of Herman Melville*. Urbana: University of Illinois Press, 1957.

Stewart, Charles S. *Journal of a Residence in the Sandwich Islands*. 1830; rpt. Honolulu: University of Hawaii Press, 1970.

——. *A Visit to the South Seas . . .* 2 vols. New York: John P. Haven, 1831.

Strauss, W. Patrick. *Americans in Polynesia, 1783–1842*. East Lansing: Michigan State University Press, 1963.

Strout, Cushing. *The American Image of the Old World*. New York: Harper, 1963.

Sweeney, Gerard. "Melville's Smoky Humor: Fire-lighting in *Typee*." *Arizona Quarterly* 34 (1978): 371–76.

Taylor, Bayard. *Views A-Foot*. New York: Wiley & Putnam, 1848.

Thomas, Russell. "Yarn for Melville's *Typee*." *Philological Quarterly* 15 (1936): 16–29.

Thompson, Lawrance. *Melville's Quarrel with God*. Princeton: Princeton University Press, 1952.

Thorpe, Willard. "Redburn's Prosy Old Guidebook." *PMLA* 53 (1938): 1146–56.

[Trumbull, Henry]. *Life and Remarkable Adventures of Israel R. Potter* . . . Providence, R.I.: Henry Trumbull, 1824.

Tuveson, Ernest L. *Millennium and Utopia*. Berkeley and Los Angeles: University of California Press, 1949.

———. *Redeemer Nation*. Chicago: University of Chicago Press, 1968.

Tyler, Alice F. *Freedom's Ferment*. 1944; rpt. New York: Harper & Row, 1962.

United States and Democratic Review 20–24 (1847–1849).

Vancouver, George. *A Voyage of Discovery to the North Pacific Ocean*. 3 vols. 1798; rpt. Amsterdam and New York: N. Israel/Da Capo Press, 1967.

Van Deusen, Glyndon. *The Jacksonian Era, 1828–1848*. New York: Harper & Row, 1959.

Veblen, Thorstein. *The Theory of the Leisure Class*. 1899; rpt. New York: New American Library, 1953.

Vincent, Howard P. *The Tailoring of Melville's "White-Jacket."* Evanston, Ill.: Northwestern University Press, 1970.

Wenke, John. "Melville's *Typee*: A Tale of Two Worlds." In *Critical Essays on Herman Melville's "Typee,"* ed. Milton R. Stern, 250–58. Boston: G. K. Hall, 1982.

White, Hayden. *The Content of the Form: Narrative Discourse and Historical Representation*. Baltimore: Johns Hopkins University Press, 1987.

———. *Metahistory: The Historical Imagination in Nineteenth-Century Europe*. Baltimore: Johns Hopkins University Press, 1973.

———. *The Tropics of Discourse: Essays in Cultural Criticism*. Baltimore: Johns Hopkins University Press, 1978.

Whitney, Lois. *Primitivism and the Idea of Progress*. Baltimore: Johns Hopkins University Press, 1934.

Widmer, Kingsley. "The Perplexed Myths of Melville: *Billy Budd*." *Novel* 2 (1968): 25–35.

Williams, David. "Peeping Tommo: *Typee* as Satire." *Canadian Review of American Studies* 6 (1975): 36–49.

Williams, John. *A Narrative of Missionary Enterprises to the South Sea Islands*. London: John Snow, 1842.

Wilson, James. *A Missionary Voyage to the Southern Pacific Ocean*. 1799; rpt. Graz, Austria: Akademische Druck- u. Verlagsanstalt, 1966.

Witherington, Paul. "The Art of Melville's *Typee*." *Arizona Quarterly* 26 (1970): 136–50.

Wright, Louis B., and Mary Isabel Fry. *Puritans in the South Seas*. New York: Henry Holt, 1936.

Zaller, Robert. "Melville and the Myth of Revolution." *Studies in Romanticism* 15 (1976): 607–22.

Ziff, Larzer. *Literary Democracy: The Declaration of Cultural Independence in America*. New York: Viking, 1981.

Zirker, Priscilla Allen. "Evidence of the Slavery Dilemma in *White-Jacket*." *American Quarterly* 18 (1966): 477–92.

——. "The Major and Minor Themes of Melville's *White-Jacket*." Ph.D. diss. Cornell University, 1966.

Zola, Emile. *The Experimental Novel and Other Essays*. 1880. Trans. Belle Sherman. New York: Cassell, 1893.

Index

Library of Congress Cataloging-in-Publication Data

Samson, John, 1953–
    White lies.

    Includes Index.
      1. Melville, Herman 1819–1891—Criticism and inter-
pretation. 2. Narration (Rhetoric) I. Title.
PS2387.S19   1989   813'.3   88-43324
ISBN 0-8014-2280-9 (alk. paper)